NEW MEDIA POLITICS
Comparative Perspectives in Western Europe

edited for the Euromedia Research Group by
Denis McQuail and Karen Siune

SAGE Communications in Society Series
Series editor: Jeremy Tunstall
SAGE Publications · London · Beverly Hills · New Delhi

First published 1986
Reprinted 1987, 1988

SAGE Publications Ltd
28 Banner Street
London EC1Y 8QE

SAGE Publications Inc
275 South Beverly Drive
Beverly Hills, California 90212

SAGE Publications India Pvt Ltd
C-236 Defence Colony
New Delhi 110 024

British Library Cataloguing in Publication Data

New media politics: comparative
perspectives in Western Europe.
1. Mass media — Political aspects —
Europe
I. Euromedia Research Group II. McQuail, Denis
III. Siune, Karen
320.94 P 95.82.E/

ISBN 0-8039-8000-0
ISBN 0-8039-8001-9

Printed in Great Britain by J. W. Arrowsmith Ltd., Bristol

Contents

Notes on contributors

Marit Bakke is Associate Professor at the Institute of Political Science, University of Arhus. Her book, *Fritid som Velfaerd* (Leisure as Welfare) was published in 1981.

Kees Brants is a lecturer in the Sub-faculty of Political Science at the University of Amsterdam. He has published books on journalism, media in elections and fascism in the Netherlands as well as articles in international journals.

Marjan Flick is a research associate in mass communication at the University of Bergen, Norway, whose major fields of research are feminist approaches to consumer behaviour, and the scope and usage of visual symbols in mass communication.

Karl Erik Gustafsson is Associate Professor of business administration at the University of Gothenburg. He is Principal Secretary of the Fifth Commission of Inquiry on the Press and attached as an expert to the Commission of Inquiry on Mass Media.

Mario Hirsch is a journalist, teacher and researcher on economic and policy aspects of mass media. Since 1977, he has been economic editor of *d'Letzeburger Land*, Luxembourg.

Hans J. Kleinsteuber is Professor at the Institute for Political Science, University of Hamburg, specializing in comparative government and journalism. He has published books on German broadcasting policy and on American television.

Denis McQuail is Director of the Netherlands Press Foundation and Professor of Mass Communication at the University of Amsterdam. He is the author of *Mass Communication Theory*.

Helena Mäkinen is a researcher at the Finnish Academy of Science, Helsinki. She has carried out research and published on aspects of media economics and technology.

Gianpietro Mazzoleni is a senior researcher in the Department of Sociology, University of Milan. He has published a book and articles on aspects of political communication.

Michael Palmer lectures at the University of Nantes. His main field of research and publication have been: press history, international news agencies and media policy.

Vibeke G. Petersen is research secretary for the Committee on Local Radio and Television of the Ministry for Cultural Affairs, Copenhagen, and has done extensive research on matters to do with mass media.

Asle Rolland is head of media research, the Norwegian Broadcasting Corporation (NRK). He was secretary to the governmental commission on media policy, 1979–81.

Karen Siune is Associate Professor at the Institute of Political Science, University of Ärhus. She has carried out research and published widely on election campaigns and has been a member of the Danish governmental commission on media policy.

Claude Sorbets is Chargé de Recherche, Centre Nationale de la Recherche (CNRS), University of Bordeaux, with research and publications in the field of public policy and administration, with particular reference to media and telecommunications.

Jeremy Tunstall is Professor of Sociology at the City University, London. He has published extensively on, *inter alia*, journalists, mass media, international communication, communications policy. His most recent book is *The Media in Britain*, 1983.

Olav Vaagland is Associate Professor of Sociology, University of Bergen, Norway. His main fields of research are mass communication and consumer behaviour.

Helge Østbye is Senior Lecturer in mass communication, University of Bergen, Norway and has written articles on media politics, as well as books on Norwegian mass media and the press reporting of social affairs.

Bernt Stubbe Østergaard is a researcher on technology assessment for the Danish PTT, having graduated in political science at the University of Ärhus.

Corresponding members: Hans Fabris, University of Salzburg, Austria; Panyote Dimitras, EURODIM, Athens, Greece; Mary Kelly, University College, Dublin, Ireland; Rosario de Mateo, University of Barcelona, Spain; Miguel de Moragas í Spa, University of Barcelona, Spain; Emilio Prado, University of Barcelona, Spain; Ulrich Saxer, University of Zurich, Switzerland.

Foreword

This book constitutes the first results of an attempt by a group of European social scientists and professionals in the field of mass media to reach an understanding of current developments in relation to policy for new communications media in their public uses and to do so on a comparative basis. The project originated as a Workgroup of the European Consortium for Political Research (ECPR), meeting at the University of Ärhus in March 1982, under the convenorship of Karen Siune. She has continued to provide the central organization for the project which has subsequently been adopted as an official Research Project of the ECPR. There have been some additions to the original group, especially to draw in information from a wider range of countries, but the nucleus of close collaborators, represented in the main by the authors of chapters in this book, has remained intact.

Our manner of work has been to prepare and circulate detailed information about each country, either according to agreed common schedules, or in reply to individually formulated lists of questions. Most important has been a series of working conferences, held in Britain, Denmark, France, Federal Republic of Germany and the Netherlands, between June 1983 and July 1985, at which ideas and information were exchanged and the framework for this book and the chapter drafts were worked out and discussed. The research has received no central funding and has relied entirely on the resources of individual participants and their employing institutions. We are, however, very grateful for assistance received in the form of hospitality for our meetings from: the University of Ärhus; the University of Hamburg; the University of Bordeaux; RAI, Italy; the City University, London.

The area in which we have been working obviously overlaps with terrain which has been extensively surveyed and reported on by a number of commercial and other intelligence-gathering agencies, mainly because of its potential importance to investors. However, our aim has been quite different. We have been trying to uncover underlying dynamics of policy making and disclose long term patterns, rather than provide an up-to-date report on matters of ever-changing detail. Unlike most other work in this area, we have also sought to develop a comparative framework and to provide an integrated, rather than country-by-country, assessment of what is happening in Europe in the mid-1980s. Since the situation changes in each country from week to week, we cannot expect to be entirely accurate at the time of publication. However details should be correct, unless otherwise indicated, as of July 1985.

In order to achieve an integrated result, we have tried to work as closely as possible as a team and, to this end, we adopted the identity of the Euromedia Research Group. While the division of responsibility for different parts of the work is reflected in the authorship indicated for each chapter, this does not always adequately represent the relative contribution of all participants. Quite a few early drafts and chapters have been changed, discarded or submerged in others and there is much hidden work by members of the groups. The final editing was carried out by Denis McQuail and Karen Siune. Although not separately identified as chapter authors, Michael Palmer and Helena Mäkinen were active participants and draft contributors at one or other stage of the work. We are particularly grateful for detailed information received from Mary Kelly in Ireland, Panayote Dimitras in Greece and Rosario de Mateo and Miguel de Moragas from Spain.

The book ends with a number of conclusions based on discussions within the group as a whole. While there was a wide measure of agreement on our findings, the views expressed in the final chapter cannot be taken to have been endorsed by all participants. Finally, we would like to express our appreciation to our Sage editor, Farrell Burnett, for encouragement and practical advice in the task of turning ideas and drafts into a completed manuscript.

The Euromedia Research Group,
Europe, October 1985

Chapter 1

Media policy in transition*

All European countries have some elements of policy for their mass media — press, television, radio, cinema and newer additions — to varying degrees and in varying forms. This is despite a general and deeply-rooted tendency for governments to keep their distance from the means of free expression in matters of opinion, information and culture. Moreover, at a point in time — the mid 1980s — when the spirit in which many policy areas are approached can be summed up by the term 'deregulation', imported to Europe from the USA, it is paradoxically more common now to refer to questions of media policy than it was, for instance, twenty years ago. This might be explained by the fact that in order to implement deregulation, one has to have a policy, or consciously worked out plan to remove old, or avoid new, restrictions. There is some substance in this, but there are other explanations deriving mainly from the fact that recent and current developments of a public policy character have been triggered less by social and political circumstances, as is the case in other areas of government such as education, health and welfare, than by technological changes which either put existing policies under pressure or seek implementation, as it were, in new organizational and commercial forms.

It happens that the changes in question, mainly in ways of processing and distributing the traditional content of mass media, have most immediate implications for that sector of media which was everywhere most regulated — broadcasting — and tend also to call into question the boundary between publicly regulated broadcasting and the telecommunication sector which nearly everywhere in Europe was considered to belong almost entirely under government control. Several forces have thus been released more or less concurrently and to a certain extent coincidentally: a strong wish by national governments to expand the area of information technology, especially by private business initiative, whether from choice or perceived necessity; pressure to incorporate new distribution possibilities within the regime of public broadcasting or to draw boundaries more clearly, or establish a completely new framework; a need or demand to recognize and do something about the consequences for other sectors of the media, especially the

* Written by Karen Siune and Denis McQuail.

newspaper press, of any policy decisions formulated to deal with new media.

While press media are generally regarded in Europe as properly free from direct regulation by governments and are minimally governed by any laws, a situation jealously guarded by the press themselves, the same press interests are also inclined to claim protection from any government action which might effect them economically and are also, in consequence, drawn into the arena of policy-making. This situation which is, in varying degrees, true of virtually all West European countries, has been compounded by the decreasing national autonomy for media systems and the creeping internationalization in many aspects of media operation. Again it is the electronic media which are more vulnerable to these tendencies, mainly because of their reliance on music and pictures, and again there is pressure on governments, already in the business of regulation, to respond or to justify non-response.

The rise of media policy

The history of media policy in a recognizably modern form goes no further back than radio in the 1920s, although the printed press before that had been the object of many forms of state action designed to control ownership, content and, indirectly, distribution. When broadcasting started as a means of communication to large masses after 1920, many in power felt the need for some regulation, since broadcasting by wireless radio was perceived as a potentially dangerous instrument in the hands of those who did not adhere to established political systems.

Although, in many European countries, broadcasting started as a private initiative, the state or the parliament in all European countries very soon took over. In the beginning of the 1920s, private radio initiatives flourished, but already by the second half of the decade radio broadcasting was, in most of the European countries, regulated in one way or another by the state. In most countries, broadcasting regulation took the form of a state permission to an institution, which was given monopoly to broadcast to the whole nation. This happened in Scandinavia, in Great Britain and in Italy. In the Netherlands several voluntary political and religious groups were licensed to broadcast. Where post and telegraph had been in the hands of a state monopoly, this monopoly was often extended to radio broadcasting as well.

The pattern established in the 1920s for radio proved to be a strong guideline to how the new medium of television would be handled when it entered the European arena around 1950. In a few countries television experiments took place as private initiatives, but almost everywhere the new electronic medium, which was expected to have even greater power than that attached to radio was regulated from the very beginning. In the majority of European countries, television was placed under the same organization that had managed radio since the 1920s. In some countries, the Second World War gave rise to special situations for the post-war organization of broadcasting. In Germany, the allied occupying forces demanded a totally new model for broadcasting after the war, adopting principles of regionalism and impartiality as a reaction to the state centralism and propagandist use of the 1930s and the war period. In Greece, the state monopoly after the war was violated by the armed forces, who wanted to use radio and television for their own special purposes.

But in most of the European countries television was regulated and controlled by the state as a public institution with the same responsibilities and duties as radio. The legitimation for this political control was the limited number of air waves, which made very few channels available for national broadcasting. Formally, public regulation was accepted for technical reasons. But behind most of the regulation was a belief in the power of the electronic mass media and the fear of this power if used for purposes contrary to the establishment. The established political system wanted to keep the control of these media. And in Europe they were able to do so for quite a number of years. The challenge to monopolies and political control came gradually, but it was not really taken seriously until the end of the 1970s, when the notion of 'communication revolution' began to gain currency.

Cheap instruments for radio communication made it possible to establish local senders, and this happened in a number of European countries as a private initiative without waiting for the state or the parliament to make new laws for the electronic media. The broadcasting 'pirates' were successful for years, as many still are. These private initiatives managed to provoke the established interests who were unwilling to abolish or change public regulation. The result has been a history of prosecution and attempts at suppression, which is not yet over.

Until very recently, television was too expensive a medium for effective private initiatives which remained on a very limited scale. Broadcasting of pictures was left to those economically powerful organizations which had held a monopoly for many years. But due to the great interest in, and the believed power of television, pressure for breaking or modifying the reigning monopolies has become very strong. Both liberalizing and commercial interests have combined in an effort to break these monopolies. In some countries this happened in a relatively peaceful and in a well-organized way. Great Britain is an example of a country which managed at an early time to break the monopoly given to the BBC and to do it in a way which has lasted for thirty years and become a model as a solution to conflicting public and private (commercial) interests.

In other countries, the issue of breaking the monopoly is still on the agenda. This is especially the case in the Scandinavian countries, but breaking the monopoly has nowadays a much wider implication than it had in earlier days. The many private initiatives which have grown up all over Europe have led to a forest of local radio experiments. In some countries these experiments with local media were planned and regulated by the state. In other places the political system is still struggling with the regulation of private initiatives. Italy is one example of this and the Netherlands is another.

New communications created new possibilities for transmission. Electronic mass communication was no longer carried out only over the air. Cable gained in significance and became one of the technological innovations which has produced a new era in electronic mass communication. Cabling the local society or parts of it, or cabling the whole nation, became new communication possibilities for a country short of airways and channels. Cabling with coaxial cables as a local phenomenon for the purpose of better transmission of signals from public national or foreign channels is now established all over Europe. Chapter 5 describes in detail the situation and the issues in the cable sector of electronic mass communication. Optical fibres able to transmit not only radio and television, but also, at the same time on the same cable network, telephone and other point-to-point communication, has made this form of cabling one of the hot issues on the European agenda for mass media policy. It is not so much the consumer wanting better or more transmission of broadcasting, but the electronics industry which came to play an active part in media policy-making. The media infrastructure is not only a technical and social network for communication, but it has also to be considered as a goal for industrial production, especially a goal for new products. To have them tested on the national ground gives the industry a show piece to refer to in arguments with potential buyers from other countries. And a production for the home market may eventually provide the basis for production able to compete internationally.

Cabling only gradually developed into a political and policy issue, unlike satellites which were suddenly in the air somewhat to the surprise of those people concerned with mass communication. This despite the fact that since the 1960s everybody had been looking to the skies either to admire, or be alarmed at, the sputniks and all the other satellites put up there for purposes other than mass communication. In a way, satellites were introduced rather incidentally as an elegant means of mass communication when the whole world wanted to follow the Olympic Games in Mexico. Transmissions were made from these games to the whole world using satellite technology.

Communication satellites were initially used for telephone traffic, but plans for direct broadcasting satellites developed gradually. The satellites were not perceived by traditional actors in media policy as a threat to the established pattern of electronic communication before the public announcement of German and French plans for DBS satellites to bring television to other European countries as a kind of overspill from national satellite coverage. For technical reasons most Europeans had been able to follow radio and television programmes from neighbouring countries only to a limited degree, but the announcement of satellites designed to cover one nation but with a great overspill to other nations, made politicians aware of a need to deal with satellite technology as an aspect of mass media policy. Some perceived a new threat to national broadcasting and to national culture. Many politicians and others traditionally interested in regulating or liberating mass communication suddenly saw a vision of a new world of communication. The potential impact of communication via satellites and cables was a challenge to the established order of radio and television communication and possibly to national autonomy and cultural integrity. And the introduction of new electronic data management via telephone and television in the form of videotex and teletext was gradually perceived as another challenge that had also to be seen in relation to the traditional elements in the communication system. Even traditional print media were threatened. The public heard that we were on the way to an 'age of information', or an 'age of communication'. How was the coming of this new era to be handled?

This question brings us back to the points made at the outset about the new-found significance of media policy in the 1980s and sets the stage for the substance of this book. What merits special emphasis in the light of this discussion is the degree to which pressures have grown for a *coherent* policy for media, certainly at national level and possibly also at international level. As to the first, it is clear that it is both difficult and unsatisfactory to treat each medium on its own, especially where different media may serve the same function, for society as well as for audiences, and yet belong within quite different regulatory frameworks, as might be the case, for instance, with television and video, or broadcast television and cabled television. It has already become an uncomfortable anomaly that broadcast television serves as much the public and political information function in democratic processes as does the press, yet has much less legal freedom.

As to the second, there has always been some international regulation of telecommunication and there is no public policy reason or pressure to extend the scope of this, but there are several reasons why policy may be called for at the European level, of a more conscious and prescriptive kind, despite the general wish to promote expansion rather than hold it back and the wish to avoid undue interference in the international flow of information and culture. One reason, affecting a large part of Western Europe, stems from EEC developments and associated efforts towards at least harmonization and at most some form of political integration. Another is the somewhat contrary wish to respect and preserve national identity for cultural and linguistic reasons and, in particular, to protect the smaller and less economically powerful countries. Naturally, there are many economic and commercial interests inextricably tied in with, sometimes concealed behind, the political, cultural and social arguments. Thirdly, there is the fairly widespread wish either to defend common European economic and cultural media interests against American 'imperialism' or to compete with America in the rest of the world as a media producer and exporter of hardware and software, deploying the cultural and linguistic, and possibly also political, advantages of Europe. While the development of a European media policy as such is not a primary theme of this study it is an item, albeit with the status of 'any other business', on the policy agendas within Western Europe and has some potential to stimulate particular bilateral or multilateral arrangements.

Scope and aims of the comparative research

This Group of political and media scientists, brought together as described in the Foreword, has concentrated attention on the electronic media, for reasons which have already been explained. The printed press has not been excluded from the scope of the project, where its concerns interact with those of electronic media or where its interests have tried to influence the development of the latter. All kinds of 'actors' — bodies and organized interests which take relevant economic and political decisions — have also been attended to in the work of the Group, but some actors have received more attention than others. In particular, we have focused mainly on the political system, with government, parliament and the political parties as principal players, together with other grass roots and organizational interests. In the case of mass media, perhaps more than in any other policy field, a great variety and number of interests feel 'called' to act, since virtually all areas of social life are affected by media as are the fortunes of any participant in the arena of public life. Thus actors were from the start a central focus in our study. We have asked: Who were acting and within what logic? What goals did they pursue? And to what degree was their activity to be explained by reference to political ideology or more pragmatic goals? From the answers to such questions we learned about the issues involved and the process at work.

As described earlier in this chapter, broadcasting was the very first electronic mass medium and the first to be institutionalized in the public sector. Consequently, an expectation at the beginning of the project was that broadcasting would provide the frame for reactions to new communication technology, a frame that could give a pattern for general predictions about the reactions in Europe to the new communication technology in the form of cables, satellites, telematics and video. Another expectation was that the constellation of interacting actors would be much the same in all European countries. If such a pattern was found to exist, we could eventually ask whether, in certain countries, actors with a prima facie interest in media policy were concealing their activities behind those of other, more open, participants in the policy debate.

In Chapter 2, theoretical expectations are presented about national, transnational and local actors and in the same chapter the logic expected from such actors is described. The empirical evidence presented in the analytical chapters will later show whether the expectations were confirmed. A general pattern of actors has indeed been found, but significant national deviations raise the need for specific explanations. Not all of the European countries follow the same pattern, but generally the logic described in Chapter 2 has relevance across Europe.

European researchers usually perceive Europe, by contrast to the United States (and often by contrast to American researchers), as a conglomerate of countries with quite different histories and political systems, although usually grouped in some categories of political type. In the same manner European communication scholars usually group European countries according to their degree of development, by reference to the number of radio and television channels, the general scope of their electronic media system, the balance between public and private sectors, the degree of centralization, etc. But with changes currently under way in communication, especially in connection with satellites, a new and more relevant kind of grouping will have to be devised, based on the availability or not of DBS satellite reception possibilities and the extent and capacity of cable networks.

Since 1980 almost every self-respecting European country has proposed plans for satellite television. The Nordic countries were the only ones who — at the time of distribution of channels at the WARC conference in 1977 — decided that they were not going to have a satellite each and, for that reason requested a joint position in the stable zone 36,000 km above the Equator. All other countries received a national position for their satellite transmissions, although several nations later decided to start with joint satellites. Plans and realities for European satellites are described in Chapter 6.

Satellites became an issue at the same time as cable became an issue when the possibility of a two-way integrated services digital network was introduced as a concept with much promise for participation. Video was another medium discussed in Europe at the beginning of the 1980s and its history and rise is described in Chapter 7. Although video can only with some modifications be defined as a mass medium, it is usually treated as such in the policy debate, mainly because of its technical outlet via television, and its similarity of content with other media. The incidence of violence and sexual perversion in many of the video films for rent were on the policy agenda in Scandinavia and Britain although it has not grown to be a big issue in southern Europe. Finally, one of the expectations behind the comparative project was that some issues would become common to all European countries as a result of the challenge from the communication technology. This expectation was confirmed at an early stage in our work and the nature of these common issues attracted much of our attention and is dealt with extensively in Chapters 9 to 12 of the book.

Common issues of media policy in Europe

While there are few signs as yet of a European media policy there is at least a convergence on very much the same themes of discussion, and the same issues have emerged in the policy debate in many countries, albeit with varying salience according to national traditions and circumstances. These are briefly outlined here.

First of all, there is a theme concerned with the broadcasting monopoly, in those countries where elements of a legal monopoly still remain. At the core of discussion is the extent to which new technologies should belong within or outside the monopoly. The struggle against monopoly is waged most openly by commercial interests seeking profitable new outlets but there are also liberal or alternative political forces seeking more openness, choice or access for themselves or on behalf of consumers or citizens. Ideological and pragmatic interests are often both opposed and intermingled. Established broadcasting authorities have sometimes made enemies in quarters where they need political support and there is much inter-media rivalry over the exploitation of new possibilities. Even where no true monopoly remains, public broadcasters want to lay claim to as much of their former jurisdiction as possible. The issue is thus not necessarily over the principle of breaking the monopoly, although it often is, but also over the division of new territory amongst existing institutions, or between the public and the private spheres.

A second matter around which policy debate turns is the amount and kind of commercial exploitation which should be associated with new media. This issue is closely tied to the monopoly question, since the main alternative to extending current monopoly rights is to allow entry for private operators. As with the case of monopoly itself, there are ideological and pragmatic arguments lined up for and against an extension of the so far rather limited scope of commercially operated electronic media in Europe. While the discussion is shaped by traditions of public service broadcasting, the present context is also strongly influenced by the circumstance that few if any governments are able or willing to provide or sanction any extra public expenditure for extending television and radio services. These are widely expected to be self-financing, but there are complications in the shape of the claims of existing commercial media, the cultural and moral objections to more 'commercialization' and the financial uncertainties of many of the potential new ventures.

The cultural dimensions of the debate are not exhausted by the question of the possible commercialization of broadcasting, since there are other relevant hopes and fears associated with the new media, and this is the third theme. Amongst these is the concern for national and cultural identity in the face of increased cross-border television flow and the internalization of media fare. It is not only commercialization which is feared, but creeping neglect of smaller language communities and of other social and cultural minorities. There are positive expectations as well — especially for increased provision at local and regional level and for a measure of decentralization in media structures which national television has tended to hold back or work against. Media abundance holds out a promise of cultural diversity as well as a threat of 'massification' of culture. More broadly, there is an effort in all countries, by certain actors at least, to preserve and extend some of the social and cultural benefits which public broadcasting has been thought to bring. Here culture has to be understood in the widest sense to include the sphere of thought, letters and political expression as well as the creative arts and entertainment.

Fourthly, there is the matter of the believed coming of the informational economy, a relatively new addition to the spectrum of media-related policy issues. The widely-diffused concept of the 'information society', the real and rapid growth in the information technology sector of the economy, the wish to maximize participation in, and profit from, the application of new technologies, have all helped to extend the concern of industrial policy to the sphere of mass media. The driving forces behind most of the fragmentary elements of 'media policy' in most European countries in the past were mainly political or cultural, concerned, overtly at least, with the 'spiritual' rather than the material aspects of communication. This order seems to have been reversed and actors in the policy arena are more openly concerned with practical questions of how to gain a stake in this sector, with divisions mainly according to the means to achieve economic advance — whether by public investment and promotion or on the back of market forces.

This summary foreshadows the main question to be tackled and some of the answers which have emerged. It appears, as noted above, that certain recurrent preoccupations of past media policy have become less salient, especially those which have to do with *content* and with the functions of mass communication in society. European policy used to focus on the role of media in democracy, on threats to diversity of opinion and information, on preventing moral or social disorder, on preserving and making available the cultural heritage, on maintaining social cohesion. These concerns have not gone away, but they seem temporarily in abeyance, as if put on one side until matters of economy and structure are dealt with. Previously, media-policy-makers tampered with structures as little as possible and at their peril, once foundation decisions had been taken. Now this is central to what is going on. It is partly for this reason that we have adopted as our title the expression 'New Media Politics'. Not only are we concerned with the *politics* of new media, but also with a relatively *new* kind of media politics.

Manner of work: a footnote

The original plan of work called for a series of comparable interviews with relevant policy-makers in each country. In some countries such interviews were carried out at an early stage, but in others, and more generally, it was found possible and necessary to draw on public statements on behalf of the many actors and interests, on published plans and proposals of governments and political parties, on views put forward in advocacy of, or in opposition to, particular policies, on background documents and reports, especially those from official committees and commissions which have been held in several of the countries under study. The volume of relevant material is enormous and the flow unceasing, even now.

We chose eventually a modified procedure to facilitate cross-national and comparative analysis. For each country, a report was written as a first stage and kept up-to-date, describing broadcasting history, legal and financial arrangements for electronic media, the state of play in the introduction of new media and the policy positions of the main actors. With the help of this material, members of the Group have tried to keep informed of developments in all European countries and to integrate their analysis.

The main weakness, which will be obvious to anyone familiar with this field, is that we can never be fully up-to-date or remain so and any detailed description and assessment of the situation is subject to rapid obsolescence. We have tried, therefore, to extract and sketch broad lines and directions of change and to project them into the immediate future. While the durability of our conclusions is unpredictable, there is some security to be derived from our focus on the Europe-wide scene. The broad picture we try to convey of European developments will change less quickly than any one national case, where an act of policy, change of circumstance or of government can radically alter the situation and the prospects for the future. This is bound to affect the location of a given country within the total 'property-space' of the media policy scene in Europe, without necessarily adding to or taking away from the main features of this space. Our aim is thus to generalize about the policy options available and the probabilities associated with given options.

Despite this striving for generalization, the foundations of our work are the empirical data about media structures, policy, politics and actual events and both concerns are apparent in the structure of the book. We deal in sequence with processes of policy-making, with the main new media (or means of electronic media distribution) and with the issues as outlined above.

Chapter 2

A framework for comparative analysis of European media policy-making*

Policy-making for European electronic mass media

During the last decade, technological development has presented a series of challenges to the existing mass media structure. Satellite technology and the evolution of optical fibres are one source of challenge. In many European countries, the structures of national broadcasting based on monopoly institutions for radio and television are threatened and this situation is part of the background to an increased awareness of a need for a coherent public policy for the electronic mass media.

The traditional broadcasting form of electronic mass communication falls within the sphere of influence of a limited number of actors — mostly public authorities — sharing control over issues like access, finance, transmission networks and content. At the time of the first major innovation — television — the institutionalized power structure for radio proved stable enough to incorporate it without much difficulty. But television is an expensive medium and the parallel development of FM radio, although much less spectacular, soon resulted in local radio and pirate activities, because the means were much more accessible to private initiatives.

We must assume that the stability of the old broadcasting structure depends on the significant actors (those sharing control) being reasonably satisfied with its ability to serve their interest. Technological change may alter this. Actors may pursue inconsistent goals, where support for the established broadcasting system is an 'internal' compromise between conflicting interests. With the advent of new technology, these interests must be reconsidered.

An example of such a case could be that of political parties pursuing both cultural and economic goals. As long as electronic mass communication is limited to an earthbound network with capacity to carry only a few nation-wide radio and television channels, their (secondary) cultural interests may be well served even by a public broadcasting monopoly. But when technological change potentially opens the way for transnational (satellite) and local broadcasting, cabled information and entertainment services, a market for video distribution, etc., these goals may be dropped in favour of their (major) economic interests.

* Written by Karen Siune, Claude Sorbets and Asle Rolland.

Examples of actors seeing the public broadcasting monopoly as the best of all possible solutions, could be political parties with little support in the press. This situation arises in Britain, Denmark and Norway. Having no adequate information system of their own, they may be reasonably satisfied with their share of control over the public broadcasting system. If new technology is incorporated into the same system, it will increase their total share of control over the mass communication processes. If competitive services are set up, this will divert audience interests from the system they control — and increase the power of those actors who are able to control the new enterprises.

If we look at the new media, we see that only teletext has been fairly easily incorporated into the traditional broadcasting system. Both nationally and internationally (European Broadcasting Union) the broadcasting institutions have argued that teletext is only a textual supplement to the sound and picture services already under their control. Although other actors have taken part in the teletext experiments in some countries, there seem to be few objections to this argument. In one sense this illustrates the capacity of broadcasting institutions to control issues concerning themselves. On the other hand, it is not an illustration of broadcasting companies being powerful enterprises, because the value of controlling teletext seems to be very low. A few other actors — for instance people from the printed press in Germany — have shown interest in the medium, but none of them has employed any significant amount of its resources in order to secure a favourable outcome. But, for these, teletext was perceived as a potential means of admission to broadcasting in general.

Within most of the traditional broadcasting systems in Europe, there is a rough division of control between the broadcasting organizations themselves controlling content, the national postal and telecommunications authority (PTT) controlling the transmission network, and political authorities controlling issues concerning organization (including access) and finances. In one sense, then, the PTT is the most powerful institution, since all the other actors depend on the PTT's capacity to keep the system running. However, the traditional role of the PTT has been to carry out service functions for the other actors; as long as the system is stable, the 'technical' actor rarely interferes in issues concerning communication.

Unlike teletext, where it seems that the broadcasting companies have taken command, satellites, cables and, possibly, videotex (although the value of controlling videotex seems to be very low) are open for transactions between actors and a subsequent redistribution of power and control. One obvious goal must be to break the broadcasting monopoly where such a regulation of the market exists, and this opens the way for coalitions with actors wanting to break the monopoly for other reasons — its centralized structure, unsatisfactory content, or position as an impediment against commercial exploitation of broadcasting. The governments are then faced with the classical problem of aggregating interests and developing a new structure for the implementation of public control, and for this purpose they will use whatever means they have at their disposal (legal amendments, reorganization of the administrative apparatus, taxation and subsidies, etc.).

Compared to other forms of technology the electronic mass media present themselves as a direct challenge to the stability of the political system, a challenge that can be transformed into a support for the political system if the system takes decisions to mould these media in a proper way. For this reason, the new media do represent input to the political system in the form of demands and supports forcing the political system to take decisions in favour of the new media.

Analysing the policy-making process

What has roughly been described here is the distribution of initial control over the different forms of electronic mass communication at the time when new technology is introduced. It appears that no actor is really completely in control; they all share control over issues affecting their interests, and therefore depend on support in order to fulfil their wishes. Any public policy can be considered as an intermediate moment between two successive states of the field that institutional structure has to regulate. This goes for media policy as well as for any other publicly regulated policy area. What has been the situation in the different European countries with respect to the electronic mass media and what are we heading for in these countries regarding these media? What are the conditions of adaptation to the new situation?

The appearance of new technology has destabilized the old broadcasting pattern of control and created uncertainty. Actors lack information about the opportunities offered by new technology, the intentions of other actors, the consequences of solving issues in specific ways, etc. Those actors who are able to reduce uncertainty — the producers of knowledge — are therefore potentially very powerful. Uncertainty can also be reduced by way of rules for new media established as an extension of rules for the established media. If the logic dominating a media policy can be said to follow the administrative regulation known so far, we can talk about a 'logic of administration'.

Policy-making can be seen as a reaction to a challenge, a reaction that is intended to find a reasonable balance between 'forces of change' and 'forces of preservation'. In the current process of adaptation to technological progress public action strategies in most European countries may seem to be a reaction to the risk of disintegration, especially in cultural matters, in the broadest sense.

A description of the situation in each of the European countries and an explanation of the principles and traditions in national media policy can bring us a long way in our understanding of European electronic media policy, but describing and explaining national patterns in media policy are not sufficient for a comparative analysis of policy-making. The analysis of the policy-making process as such is not our chief purpose, at least not directly. However, behind every specific aspect of the present study is the fundamental question of whether or not it is possible to specify a *European* media policy. A pattern across Europe or a pattern covering leading Western European countries can be labelled 'European media policy', if such a pattern exists in the form of traditions and policies of the same kind regarding different mass media and the media structure as a totality. In the analysis we have had to assume and accept the complexity of national social systems with many different actors intervening directly or indirectly in media policy. The purpose of analysing policy-making is not to reduce differences to the smallest common denominator, but to find a scheme that makes it possible to understand the phenomena found in different European countries. How much alike are the patterns we find in broadcasting and how much alike are the patterns we find in the policy initiatives that we can observe all over Europe? In what respect are the policy initiatives different? Can the differences be explained with reference to differences in regulatory traditions?

Mass media have their own traditions and history in all countries and, since new media policy is not being formed in a vacuum, traditions of a political as well as an administrative kind have to be included in the analysis. The question is whether policy initiatives can be better explained by reference to traditions, or by references to ideologies — making allowance for specific goals. The alternative would be to turn to a general power analysis to explain what is going on. A conceptual framework from the study of power does provide us with basic parameters associated with: actors; issues; interests and control. And the guiding rationale for the actor is expected to be control to maximize power.

Actors in general and actors in media policy-making are thought of as being intentional in their behaviour; they have a specific set of goals and purposes they want to fulfil. What are the goals and purposes an actor can have in relation to the electronic mass media? Given the belief in the power of the electronic mass media in relation to its viewers and listeners it is natural for an actor to seek control of the media as much as possible. Mass media are seen as instruments of power because of their potential influence on masses. And when an issue, defined as any matter or event having two or more possible outcomes of different desirability for the actors, is on the agenda, it is of relevance to look at the actor's interest in what is on the agenda. What interests do prominent actors have in relation to the new communication possibilities?

An actor's interest in an issue can be said to be equal to the consequences of different outcomes for the fulfilment of expressed wishes. If the potential actors do not care about what the media structure is going to be, they can be said to have no interest in media policy. Wishes, goals and the associated interests are thus elements in what can be termed the 'logic' of an actor. Logic is the perception of the situation and the structure of goals and means as it is perceived by an observer in a given situation. Different actors are expected to have a different logic guiding their behaviour and their initiatives in relation to mass media.

Mass media in general and electronic mass media in particular attract a great number of actors, who are specifically interested in the issues raised in relation to changes in the media structure. Potential changes in power and control over the established electronic media — either as a result of new media or as a result of changes in the world surrounding the media — do lead to initiatives in favour of keeping the old pattern as well as to initiatives in favour of new patterns of power and control. Forces of preservation are pitted against forces of change. Challenges from new technology reach the political system which evaluates them in the light of goals in general as well as in the light of goals eventually formulated especially for the media. The evaluation is influenced by the ongoing policy-making covering other policy areas as well as media policy.

The chief actors and their logics

In principle we can expect a large number of interested actors. We describe below those which we consider to be the most significant, with a short indication of the logic which can be expected to guide their behaviour. We also give some attention to the position of government ministries, which are not themselves actors but rather administrative instruments for political actors. In some cases, however, the logic that dominates initiatives within media policy, or the lack of such initiatives from political actors, results in a policy of a sort that can be called 'administrative logic'. An administrative logic can be perceived as a counter-pole to an innovative logic guided by new visions or new goals which can be obtained by means of the new media. Non-decision-making from political actors often results in regulations created according to an administrative prolongation of existing rules for established media. Lack of a coherent media policy can lead to passivity among decision-makers in public bodies and such a passivity can create great chances for policy-makers outside the traditional political system.

Public opinion can — as far as it is known to different potential actors — influence their activity and guide their behaviour, but the public very often only reacts to limited aspects of the whole body of media political problems.

Media industry

Industry, independently of whether the new media and their technology are wholly or partly produced by domestically-based concerns, is generally interested in the development of new technology. This applies equally to hardware and software. A major argument is the need to expand national know-how in the field of information technology. But industry acts not only with the goal of developing technological innovations and know-how. New media industries are industries wrapped up in the same logic as other business organizations. Economic benefit is a major part of their rationale, and for most industries it is essential for survival. For instance, the unit of production cannot survive without capital input and, in this connection, input from sales is the most important and highly valued input. And this rationale goes for producers of software in the form of films, television programmes, etc., as well as producers of hardware.

The logic of industry is at a level where the survival of the industrial unit as such is the major goal. Because of this, industry puts pressure on the political system for decisions to be taken in its own interest. In some European countries the national media electronics industry is fortunate and finds a political system which favours an economic argument and matches its own logic accordingly. This is the situation in France where the government has decided to invest 140 billion francs over five years to develop new markets. Here, to a large extent, industry and government share a joint logic.

In all other Western European countries, industry will have to argue at another level as well, referring to the needs of the society as such, and not just to the needs of the industrial unit. If the argument refers to a national industry wider than just one place of production or one company, then the logic of argument is already at a level where it can interact with that of national political bodies, such as government and ministries. In some countries, the producers of software for the mass media refer to the external challenge to the national culture, and this type of argument is reinforced by the expectation of overflow from foreign channels.

The national political system: state, parliament, government

When technology challenges the national political system then the system can be perceived as being in a situation of uncertainty. Sometimes new technology is a result of state political initiatives, and as such not expected to result in the same state of uncertainty as new technology which is not politically planned. But every new technological element which opens up new patterns of communication can, in principle, be a challenge to the existing power structure. The parliamentary system and the state are not necessarily in a political crisis but, since the new technology opens new lines of communication, it leaves the political system in a more or less manifest crisis. It has usually to take some action in order to maintain the established balance. Governments more than any other part of the political system are expected to take such initiatives and form a policy for new means of communication — uncertainty will continue as long as no decisions are taken. Some will argue that uncertainty does not manifest itself until a decision without the necessary consent has been taken, but the uncertainty can be said to be in the system already when the challenge to the system is presented. To the question of how to react, one response can be not to react, not to take up the challenge! But since technology presents a potential support for the system as well as a threat, then a reaction or some form of adaptation is most likely. To take no decision would, after all, also be a kind of political reaction, a political decision.

The support potentially offered by the new technology is of two kinds. One is support to the economic system in the form of an expected positive impact on the balance of trade or economic growth in general. In some countries the employment potential associated with the new industry is also an 'offer' brought to the political system by industry. This kind of logic in arguments from industry to government has been very outspoken in France, Britain, Italy, Germany, Holland, Sweden and Denmark.

A second, narrower, logic presented by business organizations is the possible development and system acceptance of business communication. But since this logic is of a narrower and more single-minded type it will not be accepted as a general argument at national level, although some political parties and, for the same reason, some governments will be more willing than others to accept and follow it.

Ministries

Ministries and permanent ministerial commissions or offices can be considered as institutions in themselves but can also be perceived as part of the government. Depending on whether or not a change in government leads to a change in cabinet secretaries and ministers, we can argue for one or the other. In European countries the relevant office is usually one of the following: minister of communication; minister of culture; minister of industry; minister of public affairs (where such a label is used); minister of finance; or minister of commerce. In some countries the minister of education and/or labour may also be concerned in one way or another.

Sometimes there are conflicting interests as between the different ministries even where all are led by members of the same government. The most commonly involved are the ministries of culture, industry and the ministry with responsibility for the technical side (PTT). But different logics often prevail in the ministry of culture and that of industry, to take one obvious example of potential differentiation. Examples of such different logics show up in most European countries, but in some cases one ministry has a monopoly of power in relation to the media compared to other ministries. The French ministry for communication technology has dominance on matters of structure and a certain influence on broadcasting content. But the minister of industry has control over industrial aspects of broadcasting and these two ministries sometimes disagree in their argumentation and, fundamentally, in their logic.

An evident disagreement between the rationale used by the minister of commerce and that used by the minister of culture can be expected, since they formally have different interests to protect. However, this expected difference in logic does not necessarily have practical implications where the minister of culture is willing to sell commercials on television channels to business interests. In principle, actors focusing on media content differ from actors focusing on the transmission technology.

The administrative apparatus will tend, independently of the minister, to have a logic that is a bureaucratic prolongation of already established rules and regulations. This administrative logic, which stands against an orientation guided by specific goals, is more likely to keep the media structure like the established form than is a logic centred on the new communication technology. Administrative regulations are often to be found in countries where so-called 'framework laws' are to be found instead of laws with specified rules.

Interdepartmental institutions

In France, interdepartmental institutions have been created to solve a wide range of communication problems:

> 'La mission interministérielle' shall coordinate interests and considerations such as distribution, culture, industry, social and technological aspects of decentralization, creativity, social requests and liberty in relation to the state.[1]

Other European countries do not all have such a developed structure of institutions related to the communication structure. But in several countries the need for a stronger coordination among ministries in order to reach and carry out a coherent media policy has received political attention and, for this purpose, cross-ministerial organs will have to be set up. Denmark provides an example of this. Common for all European countries is the existence of a PTT or similar telecommunication institution and one or a number of public broadcasting institutions. Some aspects of their logic have already been mentioned.

In all European countries we find a number of ad hoc committees or commissions functioning almost as a kind of interdepartmental activity although not as permanent institutions. Within the past five years, most European countries have formed national or governmental commissions to work on media policy. Earlier, the practice was to have committees looking at single media such as the printed press or broadcasting, but with the increasing interchange between the new media and the old media and the impact of one on the other it has become much more common to have general policy commissions looking at all media at the same time. This is, or has been, the situation in Norway, Denmark, the Netherlands and Switzerland. But, despite this purpose, they often end up with media-specific recommendations.

These committees are often set up in order to find a rational solution appealing to quite a lot of different interests, and it is therefore obvious that we cannot talk about any one logic pertaining to all members of such commissions. Members of broad commissions will have to be treated differently according to their individual background and logic.

Political parties

When we come to look at political parties we have to consider the different ideologies that guide their logic with respect to the issue of new electronic mass media. The ideology of some parties will naturally correspond to the logic employed by industry. Parties traditionally representing business life will naturally be more inclined to include business logic in their own, while parties traditionally representing workers' interests will be much more inclined to follow a logic based on references to employment. Cultural policy will also influence parties to the right and left in the political system, although cultural policy does not necessarily indicate such specific goals and means as are to be found in relation to industrial policy and employment policy. An important factor influencing political parties is their relative access to communication channels to reach their own supporters or the general public. Parties without an own party press are much more dependent on access via public broadcasting.

Organizations specifically related to mass media

At a level above that of specific national industrial companies we find institutional or organizational interests built within or across media. Those institutions which have a form of monopoly in respect of transmission will generally favour a continuation of their monopoly status. It is very seldom that an institution or an organization will want to give up a power position. National telecommunication institutions and broadcasting organizations will have their own interests to pursue in any struggle over the new media. Their logic can be purely based on their wish to continue their monopoly basis or central position, but it can also be based on broader elements. If they themselves have some part in the technological development, then they might argue with reference to the stimulating effect of technological innovation per se. Very often, as we see in some of the Nordic countries, they run into internal conflicts or latent competition about which of them is going to administer the new media. The alternative solutions to the question about who is going to run the videotex system are an indication of this problem. Telephone companies, either as parts of a national PTT or as private companies with concessions, are examples of actors interested in this new medium.

Transmission of satellite communication is another issue that has been and will be for some time a matter of debate between the communication institutions. In general, we find that these and other actors can use the same logic to argue for different solutions when their main goal is to retain or expand their own position in the new communication systems.

Breaking the broadcasting monopolies is very often a major goal behind activities and policy initiatives from the printed press.

Associations of publishers, advertisers or news agencies often refer to responsibility for public service and so do broadcasters in their fight for continuation of their institutions. Commercialization is a logic predominantly associated with advertisers, but because of their traditional market orientation, it is also often used by publishers. Publishers have two main aims: to gain a position in any possible new market opportunities and to be able to supply software (media content).

Labour unions

A logic in which employment plays a great role will also tend to dominate labour organizations and, for this reason, the latter can agree with industry on grounds of the number of jobs which new media technology and applications may stimulate. At the same time the new technology is expected to reduce the manpower per given unit of production. In those industries and other kinds of employment, such as services, where such expectations are openly discussed, a change of logic occurs. The argument for new technology as an end in itself tends to replace that for increased employment. Keeping people employed, even where not technologically necessary for a given production process, can also become a goal. The agreements between publishers and printers are examples of this logic. Concern for the social environment, and especially the further training of employees at the expense of employers, may also be an element in the logic of labour unions. A further aspect of this is the demand for a reduction in the number of working hours. The 'society of leisure' has also been discussed by labour unions, and the question is whether the labour organizations 'logically' differentiate sharply between working technology and leisure-time or take the latter only as a residual of the former. Labour unions will often in their actions be guided by conflicting goals.

Transnational actors

UNESCO can be taken as an example of a transnational actor wanting to influence media policy as well as communication policy. In Table 1, other examples of organized transnational actors such as the EEC and Council of Europe are given, but they may also be large industries producing hardware or software instead of institutions with political integration, economic growth or European culture as the basis for their logic.

The software industry, traditionally very strong in the US, but also in Britain, has increased its influence on European communication during the last ten years. Transnational publishers have expanded their sphere of interest to include new media, for instance from print to electronic media as in Germany, where a group of publishers in 1985 opened a nation-wide television programme based on cabling. Geographically, the sphere of interest of software producers has expanded and they have turned into transnational actors (see Chapter 3 below).

TABLE 1
Different types of actors and their logics with examples from transnational, national and local levels

Level of activity	Type of actor	Examples of actors found in Europe	Logic expected to be behind policy
All levels	Media industry	Software as well as hardware	Economy, profit/survival; development of know-how
Transnational	Political system	EEC	Economic growth employment; European integration
	Institution	UNESCO	International education and culture
		Council of Europe	European culture
	Broadcasting	EBU	Professional cooperation
	Technological/ technical	European Space Agency	Technology development
		ITU/CEPT	Technical standardization
National	Political system	State/parliament/ governments	Economic growth/export, employment, culture
		Ministries	Administrative logic
		Political parties	Power/political ideology
	Institution	Churches	Ideological influence
	Broadcasting	PTT	Continuation of monopoly
		Radio & TV	Defence of public service
	Organization	Newspaper publishers' associations	Breaking monopolies
		Advertisers	Commercialization
		News agencies	Public service
		Labour unions	Employment
Local/regional	Political system	Administrative boards	Administrative logic; local integrity
	Broadcasting	Radio/TV stations	Decentralization
	Organization	Grass roots	Local democratization

The European Broadcasting Union (EBU), established with the aim of exchange between European broadcasting organizations, is predominantly professional in its logic. Others, such as the European Space Agency, have development of a special technology as their basic aim, and the technical standardization of PTT is the basic logic behind the work of CEPT (Conférence Européenne des administrations des Postes et des Telecommunications).

Local and regional actors

On the local or regional level we find different bodies mainly interested in the decentralized aspect of media policy. Often these boards are very administrative in their logic, concerned with protecting the local integrity, if such exists. The increasing number of local radio and television stations is a significant element in the national picture in Europe and, the independence of national broadcasting often being their main characteristic, they form the basis for a logic centred on decentralization and local democratization. Local radios such as neighbourhood radios are often supported or organized by grass roots fighting for decentralization in media structure and access to the electronic media.

Decision-making processes

Many different actors want to participate in policy-making and influence decision-making about the new electronic media. Because of their formal positions, some of these are decision-makers, others are in the neighbourhood of decision-making, while some are at such a distance from decision-making authorities that they hardly or seldom can communicate or try to influence the policy-making in any way.

In a certain way, technological developments put themselves on the agenda, putting pressure on those authorities with power to make decisions to do so in favour of the technology. Industrial actors are seldom at the table where the politically authoritative decisions are taken, but they can be very close behind or very active in the lobbies.

Political decisions are formally, and sometimes really, taken in parliaments and other bodies of an institutional character. But very many decisions will long before have been taken at tables where industry and finance are those with the power to make decisions. These processes are hard to study since the results are seldom published as anything more than decisions, if they are published at all. By contrast, decisions taken in parliaments are easier to follow as they are in principle public and are immediately public in reality thanks to the mass media, which are very keen on following what is going on within their own world, that world of their own which influences all of us.

Mass participation in decision-making is in no way direct, and only very indirectly do the public, the mass, have any kind of influence on decisions about the new media. Some is possible through their elected representatives and, more specifically, through opinion polls that sometimes guide party politicians in their decision-making.

It is possible, with the help of examples, to map a picture of the processes of policy- and decision-making and to indicate the position of actors in the policy arena in different national settings. The comparison of these maps and actor studies will be helpful for the mapping of a European scene in general. The main question remains: Who has the power to influence the decisions about the structure and content of media for the future? Guided by such general maps, we can ask other questions: Are all actors acting in public, or are some hidden behind others although acting according to the same logic? Are some actors inactive in a given national arena and if so for what reason? Is it due to lack of initiative, lack of power or lack of money? Or is it a result of different perceptions of what will be the media of the future?

Independently of what the answers will be, the questions are relevant to a better understanding of the media for the future and to future policy-making.

Summary

Reactions to new situations in media structure can, according to the theories mentioned above, be explained either with reference to traditions in legislation and regulatory practice or with reference to specific goals, of which power can be considered a particular case as well as a means of political action. Other forms of logic are presented in Table 1. Policy, implemented in decisions taken about new media and new communication situations, is the main topic of the following chapters. What is the situation of the specific media and what are the issues that attract attention all over Western Europe? Issues do mirror the divergent attitudes towards changes in the media structure and have to be understood within the frame of the different logics employed by different actors. As the area of media policy attracts increasing attention, it is necessary to stress the dynamic of a growing involvement of new actors in the process of conception and implementation of policies. Amongst the issues, that of breaking the monopoly is one central aspect of power and control over mass media. Commercialization is another aspect which is very often related to the question of power and control.

Who will lose and who will eventually gain power over mass media as a result of increases in commercialization? Cultural integration is often presented in Western Europe as a specific national or European goal independent of questions of power and control, despite the fact that cultural dominance could be a means to achieve control at both the national as well as the European level. Cultural integrity is also a form of defence against external cultural, and possibly political, dominance (for instance from the USA, or larger European neighbours).

Finally economic growth as a goal, and the belief that it can be achieved with the help of new communication technology, is widely shared in the Western world and one of our hypotheses is that an economic logic prevails in much Western European media policy-making. The question is whether the initiatives taken in European media policy can be explained as following one pattern or several. In any case we will have to raise the question of whether power, in general, or in the form of special goals following political ideologies pursued by powerful actors, is the explanation behind the pattern. If the pattern we find looks more than anything else like a prolongation of patterns known in advance from traditional broadcasting, we will probably have to conclude that the administrative logic has been the dominant logic in media policy. The systematic comparative study of Europe should give us the possibility to conclude whether European media policy is specifically national, transnational, European or global.

Note

1. 'La Bataille du Câble, Telecable, 83', *Correspondance Municipale*, 238, mai 1983: 20.

Chapter 3

The transnational context*

The coming of cable and satellite television has intensified the pressure or demand for certain kinds of regulation or coordination of the flow of programme content across national borders in Europe. There has always been a certain degree of overspill from national television senders using terrestrial broadcasting transmitters, but the scale of the phenomenon was too small, with one or two exceptions, for it to be regarded as very significant or problematic. The widespread relay by cable of foreign transmissions in, for instance, the Benelux countries has gradually attracted attention to the issue and it now appears that this once marginal feature of European television foreshadows the pattern of the future, or an important part of it. It can at least no longer be disregarded by national government and television authorities and a number of existing international bodies have been drawn into the sphere of debate and proposal, since there is a good deal of uncertainty about the norms which should apply and how they should be translated into specific rules or guidelines. There is also much that is missing in the way of instruments and procedures.

Until recently at least it was assumed that each national state could operate its broadcasting entirely as it wished according to widely varying cultural and political norms. There is nothing novel about the export marketing of cultural goods or about transnational media operations in general, but the 'gates' of national television systems and markets were formerly controlled by a small number of institutionalized actors able to sort out problems of access, egress and any associated property rights of owners, writers and performers. There are now hundreds of actors and many holes in the fence as well as the main gates. Moreover there are powerful private media groups probing the system in search of new and possibly profitable fields of operation, and governments have in some cases woken up to the potential national economic benefits which may accrue from increased international television flow. The changed situation is thus much more than a matter of technological innovation.

There are too many issues and too many bodies to deal with in detail, but in this chapter we concentrate mainly on the EEC as the main relevant public transnational actor and also describe the

---

* Written by Vibeke G. Petersen, Mario Hirsch and Denis McQuail.

activities of some of the key transnational business groups seeking to exploit satellite broadcasting. Amongst the issues, we concentrate on two with the most economic significance for new media expansion — questions of copyright and of international advertising. We also employ a distinction between actors in the sphere of content, legal frameworks and economic matters on the one hand and those which are most concerned with the regulation of existing communication technology. The main relevant 'non-technological' bodies are as follows: the EEC Commission; the Council of Europe (COE); the United Nations (especially UNESCO); the World Intellectual Property Organization (WIPO); the European Broadcasting Union (EBU). The important 'technological' actors are: the International Telecommunications Union (ITU) with its European branch, CEPT; INTELSAT; EUTELSAT; the European Space Agency (ESA). These last four bodies are briefly described below, but more will be said of their activities in Chapter 6, which deals with satellites.

The scope of international regulation

When considering the role of international organizations in the formation of mass media policy in Europe, it is important to bear in mind that international agreements generally function only to the extent that individual states ratify them and incorporate them into their own laws and regulations. Solutions to problems arising from the international nature of the new media must, therefore, ultimately be found in national regulations. International efforts at reaching uniform rules in the area of exchange of programmes via satellite and cable thus emphasize the creation of guidelines for national regulations and — in the field of copyright — the interpretation of existing conventions in the area.

Before embarking on an account of the international actors and issues it may be relevant to note that national policies on issues such as infrastructure for cable and broadcasting, must-carry rules in connection with cable development, and broadcasting monopoly are far more important to the introduction of new media in Europe than international agreements on legal and programming issues.

It is further worth noting that the level at which international solutions are most likely to succeed is the European or other regional level (as opposed to global). This is firstly because Europe is *the* arena for problems of copyright, overspill, and cable-distribution of television programmes across borders, and secondly, because the substance of agreements and the efficacy of the instruments of regulation increase with the geographical and cultural proximity of the parties involved.

European-level actors in the cultural, legal and economic spheres

In considering the nature of Europe as an arena of policy-making, influence and lobbying, it should be recalled that it is a relatively small and densely-populated continent, with a disproportionate number of national states, parliaments, parties, politicians, civil servants, technical experts and internationally organized professional and business interest groups. The theme of European cooperation, harmonization and even integration is ever more prominent in more contexts, even while some countries, such as Germany and France, ostensibly pursue policies of decentralization and regionalization. For simplicity we call attention mainly to the three most active and relevant bodies which are likely to set the policy agenda and shape the debate: the Council of Europe; the Commission of the EEC; and the European Broadcasting Union. The first represents the wider Europe of twenty-one member states and has been active for longer in relation to mass media than has the EEC. The EEC Commission is the main executive body for the ten member states (soon to be twelve) of the European Community, the signatories of the Treaty of Rome. The EEC is mainly active in economic matters, the Council of Europe more in relation to cultural, social and legal affairs. According to critics there is something of a turf-war between the two bodies and it is evidently extremely difficult to keep the two sets of issues separated, especially in relation to mass communication.

The EEC

In March 1982, the European Parliament asked the EEC Commission in a 'resolution on radio and television in the Community' to deliver a report on legal problems in the broadcasting area, especially on issues related to the establishment of a European television programme. The Commission finished its report (Realities and Tendencies in European Television) in May 1983. Its main recommendation is support for the EBU plans for a European programme series. The Commission has also published (June 1984) a *Green Paper*, *Television without Frontiers*, on a common market for television, with special regard to the free supply of services within the Community and free access to television programmes across borders. The *Green Paper* states (p.4):

> The subject of this Green Paper is the opening up of intra-Community frontiers for national television programmes (freedom to provide services). This entails the step-by-step establishment of a common market for broadcasters and audiences and hence moves to secure the free flow of information, ideas, opinions, and cultural activities within the Community.

The Commission aims at the suppression of all discriminatory laws and other restrictions on broadcasts from other member states not in accordance with the directly applicable rules of the Community Treaty — in particular article 59 on the free movement of services, and article 62 on the prohibition of new restrictions on the free exchange of services. Furthermore, it has suggested Community measures, in the form of directives, concerning 1) advertising on radio and television, 2) protection of children and young persons in broadcasting regulations, and 3) limited coordination in the copyright laws (the introduction of non-voluntary licences).

The *Green Paper* is meant to form a basis for a broad public debate on the issues. In 1985 the new Commission should have presented its proposals for the necessary directives. Before that, however, the member states will have to agree on the measures suggested in the *Green Paper*. Considering the wide variety of inconsistencies in relevant national laws, the process of reaching agreement is likely to be long-winded and complex. Some resistance to the idea of the Common Market becoming involved in broadcasting policies can probably also be expected, especially since the tendency will be towards deregulation and thus threatening to national public control as now exercised.

The EEC has also been active in encouraging technological development in its member states on the basis of information technology. In three long strides, it has attempted to launch a European concept in the information field in the form of three programmes known by their acronyms as FAST, ESPRIT and RACE. The first of these stands for Forecasting and Assessment in the field of Science and Technology and the programme was launched in 1978 with the aim of identifying long-term priorities for joint research and development and also to examine possible effects on society and the economy. Its second phase (FAST) concentrates more specifically on the information field and has operated since 1982 with a budget of 8.5 million écus for the period until 1987. A major concern of the EEC is the international competitiveness of European firms in information technology both within the European market and worldwide. The main aim of the ESPRIT programme (European Strategic Programme for Research and development in Information Technology) is to strengthen the concept of a large homogeneous home market for European firms. Twelve large European firms are cooperating with the EEC in this venture. The latest EEC venture, RACE (Research in Advanced Communication technology in Europe) was dreamed up by the same firms and has as its objective the establishment of a

European-wide integrated broadband communication system consisting of the network and the broadband services to go with it, something which is not on the agenda of the regional and international telecommunication organizations, CEPT and CCITT. The primary aim is to give European industry a market and market experience to answer the US and Japanese challenge.

The EBU

The European Broadcasting Union was set up in 1950 as a cooperative body by mainly Western European broadcasting organizations. It has forty members from thirty-one states and performs long-established daily Eurovision news exchanges, carries out joint negotiations and provides production teams for the coverage of major international events. In 1982 an experimental series of European television programmes, under the title 'Eurikon', were started by the EBU. The programmes were transmitted via the OTS (Orbital Test Satellite) to broadcasting institutions in fifteen countries. In the Spring of 1985, the European Space Agency and EBU made an agreement according to which a consortium consisting of the Dutch NOS, the Irish RTE, the West German ARD and the Italian RAI start broadcasting a European pro-gramme via the European Communication Satellite in the autumn of 1985. The programme, which is to be broadcast to the public, will later be transferred to the Olympus satellite.

The Council of Europe (COE)

As noted above, the Council of Europe represents the wider Europe and operates in relation to cultural, social and legal matters. Its mass media policy committee, itself a successor of earlier committees, was established by the Council of Ministers in 1976 to propose solutions to the media problems of a free and democratic society. The foundation stone or initial premise of the actions of the COE in the media field is Article 10 of the European Convention of Human Rights (1948), which states:

> 1 Everyone has the right to freedom of expression. This right shall include freedom to hold opinions and to receive and impart information and ideas without interference by public authority and regardless of frontiers. This article shall not prevent states from requiring the licensing of broadcasting, television and cinema enterprises.
>
> 2 The exercise of these freedoms, since it carries with it duties and responsibilities, may be subject to such formalities, conditions, restrictions or penalties as are prescribed by law and are necessary in a democratic society in the interests of national security, territorial integrity or public safety, for the prevention of disorder or crime, for the protection of health or morals, for the protection of the reputation or

rights of others, for preventing the disclosure of information received in confidence, or for maintaining the authority and impartiality of the judiciary.

This mass media steering committee, the Parliamentary Assembly and the Council of Ministers have debated, researched and issued declarations on issues as varied as: advertising in radio and television broadcasting (1982); legislative control and self-regulation of the press (1982); economic and financial aspects of the mass media (1982); the interdependency of mass media (1983); intellectual property rights and cable distribution rights of television programmes (1983); principles and criteria governing television programme content (1983).

International organizations in the field of technology

The ITU

The International Telecommunications Union was established in 1865 and has 157 member countries. Its purpose is to maintain and extend international cooperation in all fields of telecommunications. The ITU Convention (as revised in 1982) encompasses a set of regulations for telegraphy, telephony and radio. Among the tasks of the ITU are the allocation of the frequencies of the radio spectrum and support of the development of new communication systems such as satellite services. National PTTs generally follow the recommendations of the ITU when setting up specifications and deciding on technical standards. The ITU thus functions as a forum where the teleadministrations of the world can reach agreement on common policies. The European regional division of ITU is known as CEPT, standing for Conférence Européenne des Administrations des Postes et des Télécommunications.

INTELSAT

The International Telecommunications Satellite Consortium (INTELSAT) was set up in Washington in 1964 by the USA and thirteen other countries, mainly Western European. It manages the communication satellite systems at a global level and has, according to its statutes, a monopoly in this field. The establishment of any new organization in the area must be approved by INTELSAT.

EUTELSAT

In 1982 the PTTs of twenty-six European countries established EUTELSAT to provide for special satellite services in Europe. INTELSAT has permitted this regional organization to operate until 1988. EUTELSAT allocates available transponders of the European communication satellites. Because of its policy of 'first-come-first-served' EUTELSAT has been instrumental in speeding up the use of these statellites for commercial television.

The ESA

The European Space Agency dates from 1972. It is a cooperative effort on the part of eleven Western European countries to build up an independent European capacity in the field of satellites and launchers. ESA produces the Ariane launcher system and the European Communication Satellites (ECS) and Olympus satellites.

The main issues of cross-border television

General

The Committee of Legal Experts in the Media Field, appointed as a sub-committee of the Council of Europe, was charged with preparing recommendations on policy in a number of areas, including the question of satellite-to-cable services, television advertising by satellite, protection of individual rights, cooperation between broadcasting organizations and the leasing of satellite channels. In 1983 the Committee produced a draft survey of problems and possible solutions.

On the question of how to regulate programmes from communication satellites, it recommended that they should *not* be considered broadcasting until they are redistributed by a cable operator (either PTT or private), the point being that cable operators can be regulated within national law. If a programme from a communication satellite were to be regarded as broadcasting it would be very difficult for a state to forbid reception even if it might be harmful to the state's own broadcasting system and to domestic advertising revenue. The dangers would include: the draining of advertising resources; exclusion of national broadcasters from transmission of important sports events to the detriment of the national audience which is not connected to a cable system.

Another, perhaps more obvious, reason for not considering programmes from communication satellites to be broadcasting until they are redistributed, is that these satellites mostly carry point-to-point signals, not meant for the public, but for specified, individual receivers. According to international regulations, such signals are covered by a right to secrecy, to be guaranteed by national teleadministration bodies. The main legal problems concerning communication satellite programmes thus lie in national broadcasting monopolies prohibiting such programme services, and in international telecommunications regulations.

Advertising

As noted already, the EEC *Green Paper* (1984) contains proposals which, if adopted, would make it more difficult for member states to exclude foreign television advertising and thus bring pressure to bear to allow advertising in countries where it is still excluded. In the interests of economic development, homogenization of the European market and of freer flow, it recommends a relaxation and harmonization of existing national restrictions on advertising. The *Green Paper* wants to rule out any general ban on advertising in radio and television. Only Denmark and Belgium would be affected by such a directive, since broadcast advertising is allowed in the other member states. As regards specific regulations on advertising, the *Green Paper* suggests: a maximum advertising time of 20 percent of the total daily broadcasting time; no advertising for cigarettes and other tobacco products; special restrictions applying to alcoholic drinks. Other provisions to be included in the directive would constitute the basic regulatory framework with which all broadcasting carrying advertising would have to comply. Each member state would have to establish an authority to ensure that the advertising rules were complied with.

A guide to the kind of Europe-wide regulation which might be adopted can be found in the Council of Europe's recommendations, completed in 1983 and adopted by the Committee of Ministers of the COE in 1984. Originally, the advertising recommendation was meant to apply to programmes on direct broadcast satellites (DBS) only. But in April 1983, the subject was redefined (by the Ministers' deputies) as 'satellite broadcasting' to include point-to-point satellite services. The principles of television advertising correspond broadly to those decided upon by the EBU for DBS advertising (July 1983). The principles are, as can be expected in a compromise between many national interests, rather vague and with few prohibitory elements. Experts from several countries have wished that the recommendations would aim more clearly at a real prohibition of advertising of tobacco and alcohol. The principles governing advertising, especially when carried by satellite are as follows:

— All advertisements should be fair, honest, truthful and decent.
— They should comply with the law in the country of transmission and, depending on the proportion of the audience which is in another country, should take the due account of the law of that country.
— Utmost attention should be given to the possible harmful consequences that might result from advertisements concerning tobacco, pharmaceutical products and medical treatments and to

the possibility of limiting or even prohibiting advertisements in these fields.
— Advertisements should avoid harming the interests of children.
— They should always be clearly identifiable.
— They should be clearly separated from programmes.
— They should not influence programme content in any way.
— They should not detract from the function of television as a medium of information, education, social and cultural developments and entertainment.
— No subliminal advertisements should be permitted.

The *Green Paper* recommendations have not been received with unmixed enthusiasm. They are said to be over-reliant on evidence compiled by a self-interested party — the European Advertising Agencies Tripartite (loosely speaking a subdivision of the International Association of Advertising Associations (IAA). Objections have been voiced by, amongst others, the European Consumers' Union (BEUC) who want strict control of advertising messages. The CAEJ (Communauté des Associations d'Editeurs de Journaux de la CEE) has strongly expressed the point of view of publishers of national and regional newspapers, largely following a statement of the German newspaper publishers' association (BDZV — the political weekly press). The main fear on the part of these actors is the risk of loss of advertising revenue for print media. The European Association of publishers of periodicals (FAEP) has also reacted defensively to the *Green Paper* and, like other bodies, has argued that broadcasting is not strictly or mainly an economic activity, in the sense of the Treaty of Rome. Reactions to the *Green Paper* are thus often couched in arguments of principle, as is the document itself, when the central points of conflict are mainly to do with economic or other self-interest. This is not to suggest that there are not essential matters of principle at stake.

Copyright

From the point of view of copyright, satellite distribution of programmes does not by itself pose particular problems. DBS-transmitted programmes are protected in the same way as other broadcasts, and so are communication satellite programmes from the point of distribution by cable. Normally, copyrights will be cleared by the programme company or institution before the satellite transmission takes place. The copyright issue becomes important in relation to cable distribution of broadcasts across borders. What is at stake here is essentially the well-established exclusive right of the copyright-holders — artists, performers, etc. — to decide over the exploitation of their work. Against this exclusive right stands the desirability of a free flow of programmes made possible by the cable technology.

The Berne Convention of 1886, the World Convention of 1952 and the Rome Convention of 1961 are the most important conventions in the area of copyright and related rights. They are administered by WIPO, UNESCO and ILO respectively. Since the late 1970s subcommittees from WIPO, UNESCO and ILO have been working on copyright issues in connection with cable distribution. By the end of 1983, the subcommittees agreed that they could not reach an agreement and published instead *Annotated principles of protection of authors, performers, producers of phonograms and broadcasting organizations in connection with the distribution of programmes by cable* as a set of useful guidelines for national legislations.

The European Television Convention of 1960 regulates the right of broadcasting institutions regarding the retransmission of their programmes. Under this convention broadcasters are protected also where no copyrights are affected, and they can forbid retransmission of their broadcasts. For this reason, the EEC Commission considers the convention 'the only major barrier in international law to the liberalization of broadcasting exchange' (*Green Paper*, p.322) and foresees that the member states may have to denounce it.

The Brussels Convention (the so-called satellite convention) from 1974 is the convention relating to the distribution of programme-carrying signals transmitted by satellite. It imposes on states the obligation of preventing the distribution of communication satellite signals to persons to whom they are not intended — in other words, it protects against theft of programmes. This convention has so far only been signed by Austria, West Germany and Italy.

The European Convention for the Protection of Human Rights of Fundamental Freedoms from 1950 says in article 10(1):

> Everyone has the right to freedom of expression. This right shall include the right to hold opinions and to receive and impart information and ideas without interference by public authority and regardless of frontiers. This article shall not prevent States from requiring the licensing of broadcasting, television or cinema enterprises.

This convention, which is signed by all Western European states, is widely quoted in international proposals for facilitating the progression of the satellite and cable media.

In order to make payment by the new audiences feasible it is necessary to ensure that all relevant rights are included in an agreement. It is probably not possible in practice to clear all these rights in a system based on exclusive rights — that is by contract — because not all copyright-holders are members of organizations with which agreements can be reached. If the rights are not fully cleared, the cable operators redistributing the programmes are operating illegally — several European court cases over the past few years have proved this to be an unacceptable position, not least for the PTTs.

As long as foreign programmes are only re-received — be it over the air or by cable — in the 'natural' reception zones (the border regions), most European broadcasting institutions have so far not pressed very hard for payment in foreign countries. But the situation changes when a whole country — or large parts of it — is included in the reception zone, because that zone is substantially extended by cable systems. In that cast the initial copyright clearance cannot by considered sufficient. The Council of Europe lists a number of solutions to the copyright problem in a draft survey on television by satellite and cable, but makes no recommendation as to which should be preferred.

The Nordic Council, in a report (May 1984) on cable television across Nordic borders, considers unsatisfactory the purely contractual solution, based on the upholding of exclusive rights. The reason is that it cannot give a comprehensive coverage of all the rights involved. The Council points to two types of suitable solutions. One consists of provisions of the so-called 'extended collective agreement effect', i.e. provisions in the legislation whereby the terms of collective agreements are also made applicable to right-holders outside the contracting organizations. In order to secure the proper operation of such a licence scheme, it could be supplemented by provisions on arbitration in cases where no agreement has been concluded within a reasonable period of time.

The other type of solution is a non-voluntary licence. This system directly permits transmission of broadcasts, regardless of authorization by right-holders, but with a provision for remuneration. The size of the remuneration should be agreed on between the copyright organizations and the users (cable distributors) in the country where the retransmission takes place. Both the payment and the sharing of it should be decided by a court of arbitration if agreement is not reached. Non-voluntary licences are not favoured by right-holders because such licences disregard the traditional exclusive rights and thereby deprive the right-holders of the possibility to withhold permission. Right-holders' organizations are thus likely to resist the introduction of non-voluntary licences.

In its *Green Paper*, the EEC Commission views statutory licences as the most effective means of achieving liberalization. This is a non-voluntary licence that permits cable transmission through legislation, changing the property-owners' right of prohibition into a right of remuneration. In the absence of an international agreement, different European countries have opted for various solutions to the problems of copyright.

In Switzerland a federal regulation from 1982 states that copyright questions in relation to cable-transmitted programmes from other countries have to be handled by Swiss organizations under state regulation. Three such organizations have been authorized to agree on tariffs and to make agreements with foreign right-holders.

In Belgium an association of Belgian cable companies made (in 1983) contractual agreements with the copyright-holders' organizations — mostly broadcasting organizations — which provide the country with fourteen foreign and four national television programmes. The agreements attempt to overcome the complex problems involved in securing all rights. But there is considerable doubt as to whether such a solution could function on a European scale.

In Austria, non-voluntary licences were introduced by law in 1982. In spite of the fact that many legal experts and legislators throughout Europe consider non-voluntary licences necessary for the assured free flow of programmes across borders, the Austrian model has drawn some international criticism because of the low remuneration to right-holders. In Denmark also, a law introducing non-voluntary licences was passed in May 1985.

Multimedia groups as national and international actors

The slowly developing free market in television in Europe, encouraged by the advertising industry, multimedia groups and the Commission of the EEC, will modify radically the existing landscape characterized by the scarcity of resources and outlets, which goes hand-in-hand with existing but increasingly threatened broadcasting monopolies. Considerable growth perspectives are the driving force behind initiatives to diversity media markets. CSP International estimates the turnover of 'Pay-television' channels in the eight leading European markets at 1.8 billion dollars by 1990. The *Green Paper* published by the Commission of the EEC in 1984 advances the realistic hypothesis that if Community countries would authorize television advertising under the fairly liberal conditions already prevalent in Italy and the UK, television advertising revenues could easily double and even triple to over 7 billion dollars.

Attractive commercial prospects of this kind contain the seeds of an attack on, and potential substitute for, the television status quo. The actors most likely to contribute to the recasting of the traditional pattern of broadcasting are those who combine the prerequisites of success, typically the groups referred to as multimedia groups. They have both the will and the financial means to move into commercial television on a national or an international network scale. Most of these groups are complementary in both the motion picture and television sector, having built up over the years substantial stocks of motion picture and television programme rights, besides being active in production and pursuing their traditional publishing activities which contain by themselves numerous ingredients for audiovisual programming. The entry price will be high and many candidates would seem to be lightweights. Because of this, many joint-venture operations are expected to evolve, as is evidenced already by developments in the UK, France and Germany. In these countries typical candidates for operating a network are obliged to link up within their countries, across European borders and even across the Atlantic.

This need to team up derives partly from the fact that there are not enough available frequencies (for over-the-air-television) and that satellite operations are costly in view of the intrinsic complication of the pan-European market and its small size. Because of this, viability may be years away, hence the need to spread starting costs. This situation explains also why, in most cases, US partners have proved to be indispensible. American involvement in Europe has been paced by two main groups. First is Premiere International which comprises Columbia, Fox, Warners, HBO, Showtime/TMC and the British multimedia group Thorn-EMI. Then there is UIP Pay-TV which represents Paramount, Universal and MGM/UA. The Viacom group is also active in Europe under its own banner offering its programming expertise.

The strategy consists in finding local partners in any marketplace that is likely to develop pay-television. The frontal participation of a native company is supposed to ward off political animosity, even though some of these joint ventures face cartel action. The American involvement, while real, seems to be exaggerated in some quarters as far as its impact is concerned. In early March 1985 the three most senior executives of the three US groupings active in European media developments were called back to the USA and London offices scaled down. *Variety* (13 March 1985) made the following observation:

> Industry sources seem convinced the mini-exodus marks an end to the early euphoria over cable and satellite prospects, but beyond that the picture remains clouded and forecasts mixed. Part of the brief all three executives had was to get their respective companies in on the cable-satellite ground floor in Europe, an objective that so far has led to various supplier partnerships, but precious little in the way of a marketplace.

Among the European companies which jockey for position, the most effective would seem to be Thorn-EMI, the British electronics, music and software conglomerate. Thorn-EMI is not only a hi-tech, consumer electronic, lighting, music and screen entertainment group. It is also a 46 percent shareholder in Thames-TV, operator of the biggest film-theatre circuit in Britain, the country's leading film bankroller, largest music combine and biggest videocassette distributor. Besides, Thorn-EMI is a cable operator in its own right and the leading non-broadcasting member of the twenty-one-member consortium originally set up to develop programming and marketing for Britain's ill-fated DBS endeavour, involving the BBC and ITV. The company controls three out of the twelve existing or planned pan-European satellite programme channels (Music Box, Premiere, Children's Channel). The company sees itself as a credible alternative to big American outfits with foreign operations and it is styling itself as neither a film company nor a video company but as a marketing organization that causes films to be made and takes them to a buyer or an audience, whatever the medium. The key to its success is quite clearly a multimedia policy: 'If it fails in one it might work in another.'

On the Continent, Thorn-EMI finds no serious competitor, except maybe the German publishing group, Bertelsmann. This is the second largest publishing group in the world after Time Inc. and even though most of its activities still relate to that field, it has big ambitions in pay-television or commercial television in whatever form, keen as it is to multiply outlets for its resources in publishing and the movie business (UFA Film). Bertelsmann has been involved, since early 1984, with Compagnie Luxembourgeoise de Télédiffusion (CLT) in transmitting the first German-language private television channel, RTL-plus, to be carried with a pan-European coverage on a Eutelsat satellite by mid-1985. In early 1985, Bertelsmann created a big surprise by joining the publishing group Springer Verlag, Beta-Taurus (this group holds the most extensive library of German-dubbed films and series) and Premiere International in a pay-television company to be marketed as Teleclub. Despite its considerable clout, Bertelsmann is playing its entry on the new media scene carefully, wanting to limit risks and its exposure, as is evidenced by its partnership with CLT and the pay-television consortium (Bertelsmann had had earlier plans for a pay-television service of its own, involving a deal with UIP Pay-TV).

Another German example of multimedia policy is the satellite-delivered cable programme service consortium, SAT I, involving extensive publishers' interests: Frankfurter Allgemeine Zeitung,

Burda, Bauer, Springer, Holtzbrinck and APF (Aktuell Presse-Fernsehen), which is itself a consortium of 165 German newspapers. The German situation is especially telling in so far as the reasons for the publishers committing themselves to new media initiatives would seem to apply elsewhere as well. A key issue is certainly the potential erosion of hard copy product. But as recent statements from the publishers' professional organization BDZV indicate, the impact of new media on the advertising market is seen as very critical. Print publishers have traditionally benefited from the severe restrictions on European television advertising. In the past, publishers have not suffered much overall impact from television advertising because total advertising has grown. The situation is bound to change, particularly when cable advertising will reach more distinct demographic and geographic target audiences with low cost and high frequency advertisements. This inevitably convinces publishers that they should try to be among the primary players in cable television as well as satellite television or commercial television over the air. In most European countries publishers are positioning themselves to protect revenue sources and exploit new market opportunities.

Since the biggest threat seems to come from developments on the local and regional level, it is no surprise to notice a very active strategy at precisely this level. The cooperation agreement reached between publishers from French-speaking Belgium and RTL-Télévision in April 1985 is a typical example on how to pre-empt loss of advertising revenues. RTL has similar arrangements for its German programme RTL-plus, involving regional newspapers in the coverage zone. Typically cable developments in many European countries have strong publisher participation. In the UK, ten of the thirty-seven applications submitted for interim cable franchises involved publishers. Four of these received licences. Robert Maxwell's Pergamon/BPCC diversified publishing empire's purchase of all of Rediffusions' cable networks at the end of 1984 is a much bolder move. This goes well beyond the prevalent attempt to 'get one's foot in the door'. Comparable moves can be observed also in Scandinavia where a number of new cable licences have also gone to press interests. Pan-European cable and satellite programme services have also substantial publisher involvement, as evidenced by the following associations: Rupert Murdoch/Sky Channel; Robert Maxwell/TEN-The Movie Channel; Goldcrest-Pearson Group/Premiere; WH Smith/The Games Network; VNU/Abonnee Televisie Nederland; Hersant Group/TVE; Havas/CLT; Hachette/CLT; Grupo 16/Spanish private television, etc.

These moves on the international level are matched by a

considerable activity on the local and regional level. Thus in France most newspapers have now their 'radio libre', some of them (notably the Parisien-Libéré Group and the Ouest-France Group) have important stakes in telematics and quite a few (*Le Seuil, Le Monde*, Télé-Libération, Télé-Hachette, Europe I, Editions Mondiales) have become active in audiovisual production, applying well-developed skills in information gathering, advertising sales, marketing and sensitivity to local and specialized markets to the emerging new media. The key players like, for instance, the Luxembourg broadcasting Compagnie Luxembourgeoise de Télédiffusion have long come to realize that owning film rights amounts to disposing of a capital that the new networks will make profitable sooner or later. CLT has diversified considerably its interests in publishing, production and the movie industry. Havas, the French state-controlled advertising agency (which is one of the largest shareholders in CLT) exemplifies, perhaps best, what a multimedia group is. Havas has stakes in several markets of the leisure and information industry, making the best use of synergies between these different activities. This is to say that a typical multimedia group is not just engaging in financial operations in a promising market. It intends to be an active operator, playing with the complementarities between its different activities. Distribution tends to become even more important than the product itself, so a successful multimedia publisher will try to have access to a variety of means of distribution in order to be able to select the most promising for a particular product. As evidenced by Thorn-EMI, the multimedia publisher sets up a viable distribution structure geared to exploiting features through various delivery systems. This implies of course that he tries to take a strategic foothold in all aspects of cable and satellite operations and programming.

Concluding note

This sketch of actors and interest operating in and shaping the environment in which national policy decisions are being made (and these are still the most significant moments and events in the immediate and short term) should have conveyed some idea, not necessarily of chaos and confusion, but at least of the enormous complexity and uncertainty of the situation. There are a very large number of actors, with varying status and power, often with conflicting interests and sometimes with ambiguous and even internally inconsistent motives and objectives. The uncertainty and inconsistency derive not only from the normal competitiveness of politics and the rapid pace of technological change. Even the business actors are caught up in the same ambiguity. Some want to defend and advance at the same time, though in different sectors and with different strategies for different countries, since potential markets are still often national markets. The emerging transnational multimedia actors are especially exposed to contradictory requirements from their component media enterprises.

References

Commission of the EEC (1983) *Realities and Tendencies in European Television: (The Kahn Report)*. Brussels.

Commission of the EEC (1984) *Television without Frontiers: (The Green Paper)*. Brussels.

Chapter 4

Broadcasting, point of departure*

Following the theoretical considerations presented in Chapter 1, we expect that the history of European broadcasting regulations and the actual situation provide a relevant frame of reference for dealing with reactions to the challenge of new communication technology. New media will be evaluated within the frame of the traditional media and that of their impact on society. For this reason, this chapter offers a short description of broadcasting in Europe, with special reference to those aspects that can, potentially, give explanations or predictions of the political reactions towards new media throughout Europe. We will look at the main actors in current broadcasting policy and their logic. In particular, we raise the question: can the issues on the agenda in relation to new media and the related policy be explained or predicted from the traditions in European broadcasting, or are there new visions that guide emerging media policy? The rapid introduction of satellite and cable is expected to provide the greatest test which public service broadcasting in Europe has faced since its beginnings (Milne, 1984). A central question is whether the idea of public service broadcasting — in its various arrangements — will survive.

Public service is a significant concept attached to European broadcasting. Usually it is based on the following four elements (Kuhn, 1985a):

— There should be a commitment to balanced scheduling across the different programme genres.
— Broadcasting institutions are public bodies with, in principle, financial independence from governmental and commercial sources.
— The service is provided to all in return for a basic payment usually in the form of a licence fee.
— Political content is obliged to be balanced and impartial.

The structure of public broadcasting systems

In most European countries national radio and television channels are organized within the same institution. This is the situation in the Nordic countries with the Norwegian NRK, the Finnish YLE, and the Danish DR being the national broadcasting institutions. The British BBC, the Italian RAI, RTL in Luxembourg, ERT in Greece

* Written by Karen Siune.

and ORF in Austria are other European examples of organizations which include both radio and television channels.[1] Recently the Swedish broadcasting institution, SR, has established separate divisions for television, national radio, local radio and educational radio. In France, radio and television are divided into separate organizations and only the third television channel (Fr 3) is connected with radio. In France the third channel is regionalized, but like TF1 and A2 it is managed by state broadcasting companies, while the new fourth channel (Canal Plus) is a private pay-television channel. In Germany broadcasting is attached to the different Länder, and nine Länder corporations normally offer three radio programmes for their respective regions and furnish productions for the first and third television channel. The second channel (ZDF) was from the beginning a joint channel.[2] In the Netherlands, production is divided amongst several independent organizations under the umbrella of one coordinating body, the NOS, but the principle of joint control of national radio and television remains. Numbers of channels on national radio and television in different European countries are given in Table 2.

Legal regulations and political control

In almost all European countries there are legal regulations governing the activity of radio and television. And in quite a number there is a close relationship between the political system and broadcasting, although in some countries, like Sweden and Britain, broadcasting is, according to the law, independent of political influence. Up till 1985 there was no specific legal framework for broadcasting in Switzerland, but for fifty years the Société Suisse de Radiodiffusion et Television (SSR), an association under private law, had a de facto monopoly due to the state prerogative of the PTT. The framework to come is of a public service character, as in the description above (Roslau, 1984).

A close relationship between broadcasting and the political system of the kind established in Eastern Europe and the Soviet Union is unknown in Western Europe but the closest relationships are likely to be found in Spain, France, Italy and Greece. In Italy the government controlled radio and television up to 1975, but from that time the parliament has elected a committee, with forty representatives from all political parties, which now controls public broadcasting. According to Law No. 103 from 1975, broadcasting (and cable) is an 'essential public service which is reserved to the state'. The Italian state does not run the public service directly, but contracts it to RAI (which is a public-owned company) by means of a special convention, renewed every six years. RAI runs three

TABLE 2
Public broadcasting: number of national channels on radio and television and sources of revenue

Country	Oganiza-tion	No. of TV chan-nels	No. of radio chan-nels	Licence in Swiss francs, 1984	Licence	Adver-tise-ments	Other[1]	No. of hours on TV, 1982
		1984			in per cent of total, 1982			
Austria	ORF	2	4	224	56	35	9	6,973
Belgium	BRT	2	3		95[4]	2	3	3,990
	RTBF	2	3	164	83[4]	0	17	4,429
	BRF	0	1		100	0	0	0
Denmark	DR	1	3	257*	91	0	9	2,636
Finland	YLE	2	2	228*	75	22	3	4,461
France	TF1	1			34	61	5	4,192
	A2	1	1	136*	42	53	5	
	FR3	1			94	2	4	2,067
Germany[2]	ARD1	1						
	ZDF	1	3	162	55	40	5	4,314
	Div.	1						
Great	BBC	2	4	143*	99	0	1	9,662
Britain	IBA/ITV	2	1	0	0	100	0	5,400
Greece	ERT	2	4	8-63[5]	48	47	5	5,500
Ireland	RTE	2	2	132*	40	50	10	5,576
Italy	RAI	3	3	103*	58	30	12	17,816
Luxem-bourg	RTL	2/3	6	0	0	100	0	2,600
The Nether-lands	NOS	2	5	116	69	26	5	4,771
Norway	NRK	1	2	219*	81	0	19	2,443
Spain	RTVE	2	3	0	0	79	21	6,182
Sweden	SR	2	3	198*	96	0	4	4,722
Switzer-land	SBC (SSR)	3	8[3]	174*	75	22	3	10,751

Source: EBU statistics.

* For colour TV, private households (no licence for radio). If no star the licence is for both TV and sound.

1 Taxes on equipment (NRK) or income from sale of records, video, etc. (BBC, RAI).

2 Under the ARD coordination only a few programmes are fed in centrally, like national news, weather, sports. The rest of the time is given to the different Länder like the third television channel which is organized by the Länder.

3 Each region in the Federal State of Switzerland is served by two and in some cases three full radio programmes.

4 Public funds comparable to licence fees.

5 Paid via electricity bills for all households according to the consumption of electricity.

television channels, and three radio networks, plus a series of services for linguistic minorities. All channels have been an object for party political struggle.[3]

In France radio and television were for years controlled by the government. The political dominance has been reduced by the Socialist government in the Law of July 1982, according to which 'La Haute Autorité de la Communication Audiovisuelle' was established. The Haute Autorité shall serve as a buffer between state and broadcasting. In that capacity it is entitled to appoint the head of the national and regional French broadcasting agencies and to grant broadcasting rights to local radio stations and cable television. The members of the Haute Autorité are appointed for nine years according to a procedure similar to the appointment of members of the Conseil Constitutionnel. The board running French radio and television has one-third of its members appointed by the government, and another third from parties represented in parliament. The final third is left to pressure groups. In France, channel 1 (TF1) has traditionally been supportive of government.[4]

In Greece the constitution of 1975 includes an article on the electronic media. That article provides for state control of radio and television, as well as for objective and fair information and news broadcasting. Greek Radio and Television (ERT) is a 'Public Entity of Private Law' with the form of a joint-stock company, the only stockholder being the Greek state. The governing board of seven members are chosen by the government.

In Spain, control of RTVE is directly political, in the form of an administrative board with members chosen from congress or senate according to their representation in parliament. In none of the other Western European countries, with the possible exception of Italy, are there today such overt political affiliations or dominance. But political influence does exist. In Ireland, RTE is organized by the state and the board and the director general are all appointed by the minister of post and telegraph.

In Scandinavia, political control functions exclusively via the appointments to the different organs. In Finland the Parliament appoints all members of the administrative organ (Forvaltningsrådet). In Norway the minister of culture and science affairs (responsible for radio and television) appoints the board and parliament, together with the ministry, appoints the broadcasting council. Both the Norwegian and the Finnish institutions are labelled state institutions. The Danish DR is formally an independent public institution. Its independence is basically shown in the fact that broadcasting is not on the state budget, but has an independent economy. In Denmark the minister of culture appoints two members to the broadcasting council, the minister of public affairs appoints one, twelve members are appointed by the parliament as representatives of listeners and viewers and all parties represented in the parliamentary financial committee nominate one member each.

It is not only in Scandinavia where this type of political appointment is to be found, since, in Great Britain, the government appoints the ruling organ of the BBC (Board of Governors) and the Home Secretary appoints both the chairman and the eleven members of the Independent Broadcasting Authority (to govern commercial television). Formally the British government can veto BBC activities, but the power is seldom used. For instance, Prime Minister Margaret Thatcher attacked the BBC coverage of the Falklands crisis, but she did not veto any part of it.

Not everywhere in Scandinavia do we find the formally tight relationship between the political system and the broadcasting institutions described above. The Swedish broadcasting institution is constituted as a private shareholders' company. Three-fifths of the shares are owned by public organizations, one-fifth by the press, and one-fifth by firms within the media industry. But according to the law, the government decides which company is allowed the monopoly to transmit radio and television programmes, and in practice it is a kind of concession.

In Luxembourg we also find private broadcasting. The Compagnie Luxembourgeoise de Télédiffusion, popularly called 'Radio-Télé-Luxembourg' (RTL), is a private independent company of shareholders having a special agreement with the government about its concession and a monopoly of national radio and television broadcasting. But RTL has no legal monopoly, and the government is looking at the possibilities of setting up a second channel, independent of RTL.

In the Netherlands, broadcasting is organized and designed so as to reflect the political and religious divisions of the society. According to the 1969 Broadcasting Act, time on television is allocated to a number of independent programme-making organizations, their grouping determined according to the number of members they have. Each organization is supposed to represent a distinctive cultural, religious or political stream in the society. NOS is the central organizing body for the system, providing services and technical facilities, including studios. But NOS is only responsible for 20 percent of the time on the air, while the eight private viewer organizations share the rest according to their relative sizes.

Germany has a long tradition of decentralization and regionalism which is clearly mirrored by the broadcasting system. In 1923 civic radio broadcasting made a start. During the Weimar Republic radio programmes were produced by private companies, financed by fees and with very little commercial advertising. Radio stations were later taken over by the 'Post', and in the long run, leading influences on the programme were the 'Post' together with the national and state (Länder) governments. During the Nazi period radio broadcasting was a leading fascist propaganda instrument. After 1945 the occupation forces insisted on starting a new broadcasting policy from scratch. Today the total responsibility for broadcasting — radio and television — belong to the Länder as part of their cultural autonomy. The German broadcasting corporations are organized in such a way that they are open to many outside influences, legal as well as circumstantial, including pressures by parties and lobby groups, but basically they consist of establishments chartered by parliament, owning a (legal or only de facto) monopoly for public broadcasting (Kleinsteuber, 1980).

Programme responsibility

In one way or another all the European broadcasting institutions are by law or proclamation told that they have some kind of programme responsibility. Diversity and impartiality are keywords for the responsibility suggested for the Scandinavian, the British and the Austrian broadcasting. Even the private broadcasting organization in Luxembourg (RTL) refers to such rules attached to their concession in form of objectivity and neutrality. In Germany the Länder responsible for broadcasting are obliged to take care that programming is generally balanced and reflects the existing diversity of public opinion. The Dutch system requires openness, diversity and cooperation and, at the same time, a non-profit orientation. The special Dutch arrangement, with the private organizations running parts of the television and radio broadcasting, explains the emphasis on these rules. The responsibility of NOS includes that of giving access to ideological and religious groups not represented in those organizations able to produce their own programmes.

Generally public broadcasting has been largely and widely expected to use its monopoly position to fulfil social functions, which include giving access to diverse voices and reaching the whole public with information, education and culture. The public service function attached to broadcasting has been strong in most European countries. Public service is also the basic requirement in the new French Act on Audiovisual Communication of July 1982, where radio lost its monopoly, and in the new Swiss Act. The public service concept is expected also in the future to be attached to the European broadcasting.[5]

Financing

The European national broadcasting organizations have different financial bases, but the two major sources are the licence fee paid by the users, and income from time sold to advertisers. Primarily due to rising costs of television production, commercial advertising was accepted as an additional source of income for the Italian RAI, and in 1964 commercial advertising was accepted on the state channels in France (TF1 and A2). In Great Britain, the IBA was from the beginning totally financed by commercial advertising. Licence fees are still the main income for most national European broadcasting institutions as shown in Table 2. Only Luxembourg and Spain were in 1982 dominantly financed by advertising revenue. But incomes from advertisements are considerable and the consequences of increasing commercialization is one of the main issues in relation to broadcasting (see Chapter 11).

In general, listeners and viewers do not want to pay more in licence fees and the political systems, governments, parliaments or ministers, that have to approve the size of the licence fees, have shown increasing unwillingness to accept rises in the fees for public broadcasting. In this way, the public broadcasting institutions which, according to the principles of public service should be financially independent of the political system, depend on the political system. With rising programme costs and demands for greater home production (a pressure experienced both in the south, as in Italy and France and in the north, as in Denmark and Norway) alternative income possibilities are being debated. Pay-television is one of the possibilities most discussed as a way of financing new channels. Pay-television has been introduced in Great Britain, France, Switzerland, the Netherlands and elsewhere in the form of pay-cable.

Public radio channels usually broadcast all day, while the number of hours produced by the different countries for television do vary a lot. Naturally, the number of hours increases with the number of channels, but there is no proportional relation between these two figures.

Regionalization

All the European countries except Luxembourg have some form of regionalization in radio or television production or both. In Ireland experiments within RTE have been introduced on radio. In countries like Denmark, Norway and Sweden the regionally-produced television programmes are aired on the national network, while national radio programmes are sent out on regional network. In the Netherlands there are six regional radio stations, while there are twenty-four regional radios in Sweden and nine in Denmark. Another form of regionalization takes place in Finland where YLE provides local broadcasting in the three largest Finnish cities. Decentralization and regionalization is rather extensive in Spain, with autonomous regions, and also in Germany, where the division into Länder in itself regionalizes the media structure. In Austria ORF altogether sends out radio on thirteen channels of which nine are local programmes. In Great Britain, both BBC and ITV are regionalized (the latter more extensively). In France decentralization is an ongoing process. The third television channel was in 1973 created with 'an allegedly regional vocation' (Kuhn, 1985a:48).

Non-public broadcasting

Besides the nation-wide public broadcasting organizations mentioned above, a number of regional and local non-public stations do exist in Europe. Local radio established outside the public broadcasting has been a great challenge to public broadcasting. Italy is widely known for its great forest of more than 700 private television stations, many of which are organized in networks, and about 2,500 private radio stations.[6] The private radio and television stations live exclusively from commercials. Holland, France and Spain also have many local radio stations, more or less private and sometimes illegal. In all the Scandinavian countries, there are experiments with local radios and television on a non-public, non-profit basis. But in these countries the experiments are regulated by permission from the government, unlike the Italian situation where non-regulation has produced its own form of diversity.

In Germany, private cable experiments have led to the introduction of a private television cable network, in principle covering West Germany from 1985, organized by publishers, and in many of the other countries publishers are eager to get access to the electronic media. Several Länder are presently working on legislation preparing for commercial television, and non-public commercial television is being debated in all European countries not yet having it. Commercials on private radio are much less of an issue.

Actors in respect of public broadcasting

Almost every potential actor in media policy has been active in relation to broadcasting. The importance attached to influencing broadcasting is generally high. Political parties present their ideas in public and in parliament and in those countries which still retain a broadcasting monopoly the main media question discussed in parliaments at the moment is the ending of such monopolies. The control of software has, as mentioned in relation to programme responsibilities, always been of interest in media discussions. And in all European countries except Luxembourg, we find party political concern about the content of broadcasting. Many different actors are working in relation to experiments centred around local radio and television. The press and different grass-roots organizations are active — both hoping for possibilities to join the established electronic media via local broadcasting or cable network. Labour organizations are also interested in getting access. Breaking monopolies can be seen as a breaking of political control, but other goals may be driving forces.

Existing national broadcasting institutions are concerned about their future status in relation to the local and regional experiments, most of them afraid of losing listeners and viewers. Generally active — and not always following the same logic as the national broadcasting institutions — are journalists and their organizations, looking for more and new jobs.

In respect of the new electronic media, the hardware industry is nowadays not very active in relation to radio and television policy as such, but it is definitely not inactive. Introduction of colour television was, for example, a result of an active industry. And in relation to the new transmission possibilities via cables or satellites there is much activity both at the local and the national level.

Issues and future prospects

Breaking the principle of monopoly attached to many of the European broadcasting institutions is one of the main themes in the debate and, more generally, that of private initiatives versus public control (see Chapter 9). Another theme is regionalization, reducing the centrality or the unity of the institution into regions or districts. Diversity versus concentration are the keywords. In all European countries there is an ongoing regionalization. For some institutions it has only reached a stage where some programmes are locally produced or where material is collected from different regional offices. In other cases the regions or the local communities are already independent, 'home' producing and transmitting units. One of the questions discussed in relation to both radio and television is the question of increase in the number of outlets. The discussion goes on in all European countries, independently of whether they have one, two or three channels at the moment.

Commercialization is also discussed in relation to the expansion of the number of channels, due to a general unwillingness on the part of the public to pay more licence fees followed by a lack of will from political bodies to accept proposals for higher licence fees. This theme is treated in Chapter 10.

Alternative ways of financing apart from fees and advertisements are various forms of pay or subscription television. Pay-television is established in Great Britain, France, Switzerland and in the Netherlands in the form of pay-cable (there called subscription television). It is under consideration in the Scandinavian countries. In Sweden, a recent proposal for pay-television has been argued for as a safe way for television to achieve increased resources and continued independence of other financial pressures. But at the same time it is uncertain whether people are willing to pay for more television. This question is especially relevant in a period of increased free offers from the various satellites. In Denmark, policy recommendations have moved from pay-television for a second channel to payment in the form of licence or a licence combined with money from advertisements. The arguments against were much as in Sweden — doubts about future willingness to pay separately for new channels. As a part of experiments with local television, pay-television as a subscription for television has been introduced in Denmark and Switzerland. Pay-per-programme has been discussed in several countries, but not yet introduced.

The overflow of television programmes from communication and direct broadcasting satellites is the challenge that has activated media politicians all over Europe. The impact of the flow of broadcasting from foreign countries will be drastically expanded in the years to come. Besides the national broadcasting problems attached to the existing national media or the expansion of these national media, expansion is the overall problem. Will it be a challenge to the national media structure? Will it drastically change the patterns of listening and viewing? And what will be the cultural and, not least, the eventual political impact of changed media patterns? Some changes must be expected, but not changes in the national pattern proportional to the increase in potential input, as long as the diversity in the flow remains.

The great changes in the future will come when and if transnational organizations really start organizing programme productions which in one way or another will lead to a reduction of national identity. At this moment there are only relatively limited plans presented for transnational activities of any sort other than the satellite flow of national programmes, but increased transnational flow has definitely to be considered as a potential for the future. The Kahn Report from the EEC *Green Paper* on European Television show some potential steps.[7]

Up to now the transnational and international challenge has been formulated by Jeremy Tunstall in the phrase: 'The media are American' (Tunstall, 1977), but in Europe we may ask ourselves: Will we one day be in the situation where we have to say: 'The media in Europe are European and not national any more'? Or will we have to join Jeremy Tunstall in asserting that 'The media are American'? The most recent transnational activity in European broadcasting is the establishment of separate French-speaking and German-speaking television channels using satellite facilities. The language-specific television cooperation opens up for a Europe without frontiers except those laid down by language differences. National broadcasting with public service commitments has been the point of departure for new electronic mass media, the question is whether this situation will continue.

Notes

1. National reports for each of these countries describing the broadcasting organizations are to be published in a separate volume.
2. Arthur Williams (1985) gives more details.
3. Don Sassoon (1985) describes the political struggle.
4. Raymond Kuhn (1985b) describes the political affiliation.
5. See *EBU Review*, 35 (5), 1984 where public service in a number of countries is discussed.
6. This number includes only stations of a certain size. If all private radio stations independent of size are counted there are approximately three times as many, according to RAI (cited by Kuhn, 1985a).
7. Commission of the EEC (1983: 229 and 1983: 300) put forward plans for European television.

References

Commission of the EEC (1983) *Realities and Tendencies in European Television: (The Kahn Report)*. Brussels.

Commission of the EEC (1984) *Television without Frontiers (The Green Paper)*. Brussels.

Kleinsteuber, Hans (1980) *Rundfunkpolitik: Medienpolitische Aspekte von Hörfunk und Fernsehen*. Hamburg: Landeszentrale für politische Bildung.

Kuhn, Raymond (ed.) (1985a) *The Politics of Broadcasting*. Kent: Croom Helm.

Kuhn, Raymond (1985b) 'France: the End of the Government Monopoly', in Raymond Kuhn (ed.), *The Politics of Broadcasting*. Kent: Croom Helm.

Milne, Alastair (1984) 'The Future of Public-Service Broadcasting in Europe', *EBU Review*, 35 (5): 22–4.

Roslau, Blaise (1984) 'Pay-television in Switzerland', *EBU Review*, 35 (2): 33–6.

Sassoon, Don (1985) 'Italy: the Advent of Private Broadcasting', in Raymond Kuhn (ed.), *The Politics of Broadcasting*. Kent: Croom Helm.

Tunstall, Jeremy (1977), *The Media are American*. London: Constable.

Williams, Arthur (1985) 'West Germany: the Search for the Way Forward', in Raymond Kuhn (ed.), *The Politics of Broadcasting*. Kent: Croom Helm.

Chapter 5

Policing the cable*

Cable television, which started in Europe at the beginning of the 1960s in Belgium and the Netherlands, is gradually conquering the Old World. A better reception for all and an end to aerials were the original ideas but the advantages over traditional ether broadcasting were immediately clear. Hardware producers, publishers and other commercial interest groups saw new (and sometimes competing) markets. The scarcity of channels, which had marked television until then, had to make way for abundance. The limit was over and all those involved in politics and economics had to adjust to this new situation in one way or another.

What would governments' role have to be? Would they have to interfere in the interplay between eager commercial interests and an originally public medium such as television? Would governments be forced to regulate the software in order to protect commercially less viable programmes and activities? And what would advertising over cable mean for those countries that traditionally had prohibited commercialization from their public media, mainly to protect the press? Should governments exploit the possibilities of the new media or let cash flow across the border? And were these the only alternatives?

In spite of all these questions, the cabling of a country has become a more-or-less self-fulfilling prophecy. In order not to miss the technical boat and the attached international marketing prospects, cabling has become the thing. Particularly Great Britain, France and Germany, all with a limited number of cable networks at the moment, have initiated ambitious plans which are partly meant as a boost to national industry. But after the original euphoria in these and other European countries, high costs, political and regulatory arguments and commercial weaknesses have cooled things down a bit.

Before we begin to sketch the cable landscape in Europe, we have to deal with some technicalities, because the language of cable is rather confusing, not least because terms are used interchangeably. First of all there is the distinction between shared antenna facilities (also called Master Antenna Television, MATV) and cable networks (also called Community Antenna Television, CATV). In the following we will refer to MATV and CATV or cable networks. The

* Written by Kees Brants.

former only covers a limited number of households in a small area, say a block of flats or a number of houses. The antenna they share usually boosts and relays the programmes it can receive. There are about 20 million MATV homes in Europe. Cable networks connect a whole community and also relay programmes that cannot be received with an ordinary antenna. In some countries, the borderline between the two systems is at 100 connections; in others it is 400 to 500. Cable networks also have the possibility of locally originating programmes and of national programme systems. About 10 percent of the households in Europe (10 million) are connected to CATV, the growth rate being at the moment 10 percent per year. To complicate things further, there is also SMATV, Satellite Master Antenna Television. In this, as yet limited, applied system, there is an antenna at the head-end for providing satellite-delivered cable television programmes to blocks of flats.

Cable television appears in several forms but is roughly based on one of two principles. Firstly, the branch-off or branch-and-tree principle, whereby one cable is placed along the street with a branch off at every door. This cable net is only suitable for a maximum of twelve channels and not suited for an interactive system. Secondly, the star-net principle, whereby every connection is made through an individual connection to a central point. In some countries there exist so-called mini-star-nets with 20–30 channels. An extensive star-net has a capacity of about 200 channels and is suitable for interactive communication.

The latest in cable is optical glass fibre instead of coaxial cable. This advanced cable, based on digital signalling, has a higher quality and gives the opportunity of integrating different information systems (Integrated Services Digital Network, ISDN). Where a star-net is already 50 to 150 percent more expensive than a branch-and-tree system, fibre networks mean an extensive new investment. In practice, combinations of the branch-and-tree and star-net systems offer simple return signalling.[1]

After this short technical excursion, the organization of the cable in the different countries and the services offered are discussed. The emphasis, however, is on the policy-making process, the actors and issues involved in the various national policies and the possible effects of the cable developments on the culture of mass communication in Europe.

The cable landscape

The new medium is mainly a northern and central European phenomenon, with the smaller countries in the lead. Belgium (89 percent of all television households), the Netherlands (80 percent) and Luxembourg (65 percent) could be called the high penetration countries. In Belgium there is a majority of branch-and-tree nets, with a limited number of star-nets. In the Netherlands a mini-star-net covers 45 percent of the country. In both countries there is currently a discussion about whether or not to renew the network, but governments are hesitant because of the high costs involved. The policy is towards some overall compatability of standards and local head-end links. So far, in a few places in Holland (notably in Rotterdam) optical fibre is being installed. The number of channels is usually around twelve, with the more current systems (and those adjusted) rising to twenty to thirty channels. The most advanced system so far (Deltacable), which is only installed in a few places, has 180 channels. In Luxembourg plans exist at the moment for an ISDN.

Although France, Great Britain, Germany and Denmark have a low penetration, they are the most ambitious cabling countries. At the same time the first three countries have the largest European telecommunications industries. The present network in France (only covering 3 percent, with another 38 percent connected to MATV) has a capacity of fifteen channels, but the number of transmitted programmes varies from three to twelve. Germany (about 50 percent MATV) offers a more varied picture, with the new cable networks installed by the Bundespost having a potential capacity of thirty channels. The networks in Great Britain (only covering 13 percent of the households when the present cable policy started) are usually of a much lower capacity, four to six channels, mainly distributing national programmes.

The four countries all pursue an active cabling policy, albeit from different angles. In Germany, with less than 3 percent proper cable networks, the plans are to have half the country cabled by 1990. The centre-right government is in favour of commercialization but also has increased investment funds for the Deutsche Bundespost (PTT) for cabling to about 1 billion DM (£250 million). At the same time, the electronic industry is developing plans to wire the country. Extensive optical fibre networks are not expected before the 1990s. The present plans involve extending and connecting the existing systems. In France, the socialist government tries to keep the finger on the pulse, with an active cabling scheme by which the country should have a mainly optical fibre network by the middle of the 1990s. This scheme became operational in 1984 and has been endorsed by political parties of all persuasions, since it offers good opportunities for national industries and because it is in conjunction with the government's decentralization policy. After the initial optimism, however, progress has been slow and the cabling reality is slowly moving away from the interactive technology. The appearance of semi-illegal, private broadcasting stations might further endanger the ambitious plans.

In the United Kingdom, the government aims to keep its distance in order to let cable be a private and market-led affair. The Thatcher government has already brought about privatization of British Telecom. In its White Paper on cable television, published in 1983, the government showed its wish to develop information technology as a saviour from industrial decline, but at the same time its reluctance to prescribe any particular system: many scenarios have been kept open, as long as they are privately financed and have sufficient capacity for two-way communication. In 1984 the government handed out eleven pilot cable franchises, but since the Chancellor later that year announced the phasing out of capital allowances, many investors in this high-risk business are becoming reluctant.

The last to start, Denmark, seems to be the least bothered by children's diseases (yet). As a booster to its own fibre optical industry, it is planning a 'hybrid' broadband cable network, with partly fibre optics and partly coaxial cable for local distribution. The country, with at present 50 percent mainly MATV cabling, is expected to have a national interactive broadband network by the end of the century.

The other European countries — with the exception of Switzerland with 50 percent connected — have mainly MATV systems or none. The Scandinavian countries are, hesitantly, planning extension or renewal of their networks. Sweden only has a limited number of cable networks which broadcast more than the two channels of the Swedish Broadcasting Corporation. A plan by the Telecommunications Administration to cable the country has been dropped, but a government-appointed mass media committee suggested running trials in which existing MATV networks (at present covering 50 percent of the country), in some forty places, be connected in order to experiment for two years with broadcasting of satellite and locally produced programmes. Unlike Sweden, the Finns are planning, and in fact have started, a limited programme of broadband cabling, mainly in the capital Helsinki. 54 percent of the households are connected to, mainly, MATV cable systems. The Norwegians, with 30 percent MATV networks, have initial plans for further cabling. As far as the other European countries are concerned, Switzerland and Austria have no new plans for renewal of their networks. The former has a fairly high penetration of CATV (50 percent), while in the latter (12 percent) a cabling programme is going on. The same goes for Ireland, with at present over 20 percent CATV. In southern Europe, there is hardly any cable development at all. There are vague expectations in Spain, but only Italy has a few cabled spots; paradoxically, it is the only new medium in that country regulated by government policy. Recently the government has approved plans for a nationwide ISDN network in the late 1980s. However, both PTT and the national broadcasting company, RAI, are hesitant in view of the profitable outburst of private broadcasting since 1976.

Rules and regulations

In most countries in Europe broadcasting is or has been a public affair. The scarcity of channels, and the supposed power of the medium of television, set the scene for some measure of public control. What about the cable, now that the scarcity argument seems less viable with so many channels to choose from? What role do governments and other actors in the different countries play? What regulations are there? What are the developments in these fields and where do pressures, if any, come from?

Who owns and operates the cable?

Cables have to be installed, managed and used, which does not necessarily mean that installation, exploitation and operation are all in the same hands. Quite the opposite, in most countries these functions are separated, with the PTT in a more-or-less central role, be it active, in the sense of operator or installer, or passive, handing out franchises and setting quality rules. If, therefore, we present three types of ownership and control, this is ideally typical and in order to show tendencies and counter-tendencies with regard to the question of public and private control. The installation as well as the management of the cable can be private, public or a mixture of the two. If we present the European countries within this framework, it should be noted that a number of countries operate on the borderlines.

Complete private ownership and installation does not exist at the moment, but Great Britain, Finland, Norway, Denmark, Austria and Luxembourg are either quite close to it or intend to privatize the cable.

In Great Britain at present, the commercial operators form a majority and according to the government's White Paper, investing in cable networks — be they coaxial or glass fibre — should be financed privately and led by the open market, with the restriction that cable providers and operators should be British or EEC and not consist of government, religious or political groups. Eleven franchises have been handed out in 1984 (a similar number is expected in

1985) by a new Cable Authority appointed by the Home Office. Some American firms operate as partners here. Cable providers need a licence from the ministry of industry in consultation with the office of telecommunications. In spite of these regulations the tendency to privatize and denationalize British industry is very strong.

Although Finland has few large cable networks and the government is expected to come forward shortly with cable rules, at the moment it is the most liberal country with regard to the installation and exploitation of cable. Both are in private hands with only a few smaller MATV facilities jointly owned by local governments. In Denmark the government has decided on a nation-wide, thirty-six-channel cable system, with the mainly private MATV systems conveying the programmes to the end-users. In Norway too, private firms rule the cable market but to an increasing degree the PTT operates as a competitor. The PTT has planned to install a broadband net, but the conservative government, which already plans to break the monopoly of the Norwegian broadcasting organization NRK, might well decide otherwise. In Austria the change of government in 1983 meant a more liberal policy. At the moment the role of the PTT is restricted to setting technical demands and the relay of four German programmes. The installation of networks is being done by industry, with the largest network installed by Philips. For the exploitation, a special organization is usually set up in which participate electric companies, local dealers (private as well as public), larger industrial firms and local governments (an obligatory 5 percent). In Luxembourg, known for its commercial broadcasting organization RTL and liberal broadcasting policies, the installation of networks is a private affair under the supervision of the PTT. The few CATV networks in Italy, finally, are also in private hands.

Public ownership in its extreme form is only to be found in the planned network in France. Under Giscard d'Estaing, France had already tried to occupy the third place among the world telecommunication industries. With this industrial ambition in mind, Mitterrand decided in 1982 to cable the country and to organize this publicly. The public organizations TDF and DGT (partly under the supervision of the PTT) supervised the setting up and exploitation of the networks, while local authorities will be entrusted with the running of the teledistribution service. Ownership will be in the hands of the Direction Générale des Télécommunications. The actual installation is done by industrial telecommunication companies, headed by the nationalized CGE and Thomson groups. The initiative for a cable network is supposed to come from local authorities.

A combination of private and public administration is to be found in Germany, Sweden, Switzerland, the Netherlands and Belgium.

In Germany the Bundespost enjoys a monopoly on smallband communication, but not for cable networks. There are several cooperative projects, where private firms or communities do the cabling. In all cases, the DBP regulates and authorizes cable networks and collective antennae; it does not allow the creation of national networks. However, the DBP tries to standardize the cable systems and in this respect is laying the foundations for a national cable network. The CDU-FDP government wants to introduce private television in order to compete with public broadcasting via cable.

The present MATV systems and networks in Sweden do not need authorization for installation and sometimes are owned by those installing them. An exception is the one commercial cable television station in Malmö (with only 1,000 subscribers), which was set up before the 1968 Law prohibited closed-circuit broadcasting. At the moment a concession system is suggested for the exploitation of cable networks through a Cable Board in close connection with the local government.

In Belgium forty-two cable firms exist that need a licence from the PTT-minister. Local governments own the networks, but in practice they have no authority over it. The forty-two firms are either semi-public companies (50 percent), public (35 percent local authorities) or private (17 percent). The distributors are not allowed to connect networks and form a national cable network. The same goes for Switzerland, where two associations of cable distributors exist, the public one usually operating smaller networks and the private larger ones. In the Netherlands the operation of the cable is a local matter with concession from the PTT; 78 percent of the concession holders are local governments and the rest consist of building firms, cooperatives, pension funds, etc. Actual operation of the cable may be in other hands; currently 46 percent is local authority, 10 percent is local utility and 44 percent are private companies. The decentralized organization of the cable was recently criticized by a governmental advisory board, which suggested a stronger hold for the PTT with regard to the installation of the cable.

Financing

The installation and the exploitation of the cable is, as we have seen, a public, private or mixed matter, and so is the actual investment that has to be done by the different bodies. The money has to come from somewhere, but directly or indirectly, it is the consumer who will in the end have to bear the cost. With each new service offered by the cable (pay-television, local programming, interactive services) and with the settlement of copyright disputes, the price goes up. Subscription fees and/or advertising are the ways to finance cable programming.

The subscription fee for the cable varies greatly from one country to another and even within countries. Until recently, in some places in Belgium there was no subscription at all while in France the subscription can be £7 per month. The price is not necessarily linked to the number of services offered, but, on average a ten-channel cable connection costs some £3. In a number of countries, the exploitation of cables is not a profitable business. Notably in Great Britain, Norway, Belgium and the Netherlands some exploiters have financial difficulties. They fear that with the extension of services, subscription fees might become unpayable for some. With one pay-television channel, two new services and, for instance, an adaptor for teletext in a country like Holland, the cable television expenses might well quadruple in the next few years (Brants and Jankowski, 1985).

Copyright payments are only a small token among the amounts the cable subscriber has to pay. So far copyright disputes have only been settled in Belgium, Austria and the Netherlands. Austria was in fact the first country to work out a rather unique arrangement, whereby cable systems have a right to relay foreign services in return for payment of a blanket copyright levy.

The main alternative means through which cable programmes could be financed is through advertising. Pay-television — which will be dealt with separately — has extra possibilities via controlled subscription, advertising and/or sponsoring. In most European countries, advertising on the cable is allowed, although, in most cases, sponsored programmes are not. In the Netherlands, Belgium and the Scandinavian countries advertising is prohibited,[2] although the commercial station in Malmö and recent discussions about sponsored programmes in Norway has stirred the debate. The relaying of commercial programmes via the cable — from commercial broadcasting companies in other countries or satellite — together with the risk of advertising money going abroad seem to be an impetus in these countries to reconsider their non-commercial status.

Programme services distributed

National programmes

The networks in all countries distribute the national programmes offered by the different broadcasting organizations. Most countries require this by law, a regulation both Denmark and France plan to abandon. In the Netherlands only, a so-called 'must carry' rule does not exist at this moment, but in practice the cable distributors observe one. Depending on the number of channels, the majority of networks also distributes a number of foreign programmes which might be picked up directly by the distributors' antennae or by that of the PTT. Restrictions exist in some countries regarding the percentage of foreign programmes, relaying of satellite and commercial programmes. France allows only 30 percent of foreign or peripheral programmes while in Belgium the Flemish have so far refused to send via the cable a planned Dutch-language programme from commercial RTL in Luxembourg, since it will carry advertisements. By law the Belgian cable distributors even have to black out the screens when advertisement blocks from any foreign programmes are on. In reality this never happens. The Swedes plan to ban violent programmes from the cable and any foreign programme with advertising especially aimed at their country. Finland has as yet no legislation, but a parliamentary committee proposed that 40 percent of the programmes should be of Finnish origin, that the programmes should be locally oriented and not contain pornography or violence.

According to the Cable and Broadcasting Bill the Cable Authority in Great Britain must ensure that proper proportions of the programmes originate within the EEC, that news programmes originating in the UK are 'presented with due accuracy and impartiality' and that good taste and decency are not offended. Adult programmes, the euphemism for pornography under the British mastery of understatement, are prohibited too, while rules should prevent the pre-empting by cable of outstanding sporting events (Blumler, 1984:10).

At the moment (mid 1985) there is (limited) reception of Sky Channel in the Netherlands, Great Britain, Switzerland, Norway, Sweden and Finland, while in some of these countries Music Box has been introduced. So far TV5 (and in some places the Russian satellite Gorizont) has a limited reception in France, Switzerland, Belgium, the Netherlands, Norway, Great Britain and in the trial projects in Sweden, but (as can be seen in Chapter 6 on satellites) there are further plans for the European Communication Satellite, Intelsat V and Direct Broadcasting Satellites (DBS). Recently the Dutch government has ruled that inserting subtitles or dubbing the programmes beamed from the satellite is prohibited, while (like the general rule in Sweden) advertising must not be explicitly directed at the Dutch market and the programmes must be broadcast extensively in the country of origin too. The legal status of these regulations however, is disputed.

Community television experiments

Community television experiments are to be found in Belgium, Switzerland, Great Britain, Norway, the Netherlands and Denmark. There are single experiments in Sweden and Finland, in which countries no plans exist at the moment for enlargement. In Germany and France local experiments are taking place in connection with interactive experiments, which will be dealt with below. Fifteen percent of the future French network is expected to be for locally originating programmes.

The thirty-two experiments in Denmark are part of the public experiment with local broadcasting which started in 1983. Some are run by newspapers, some by labour unions, others by voluntary organizations. Apart from money from these organizations, all these experiments are financed through public money (either state or municipal), while a licence is granted by a special board of the ministry of culture. In Switzerland, 258 organizations of varying origin have applied for entrance to the cable, most of which were local stations. In November 1983, thirty-six applicants have started, among them idealistic groups and commercial firms. Seven of these licences are for local television. In the Netherlands, by the end of 1984 a total of fifty stations were cablecasting local radio and television programming. Financing here is through local or regional sources, because the national government is not willing to pay and advertising is not allowed. More than 100 experiments are taking place in Norway at the moment. However, only the one in Oslo has some form of public access and is therefore community television proper.

In Belgium, nine experiments are taking place in the French-speaking half of the country, Wallonia. One station – Canal Emploi — has been set up explicitly as an educational and consciousness-raising service for the large number of unemployed in the industrial and mining city of Liège. A portion of the funding for Canal Emploi comes from the EEC, the rest, as with the other stations, through public means and private subsidies. The Flemish, rather reluctant as far as the new media are concerned, are said to await an integrated media policy before granting permission for local programming.

Thirteen networks in Great Britain were authorized to originate programmes, but in fact few really do. The limited capacity of the old systems gives little room for these community television programmes. Neither the Hunt Report nor the government's White Paper stress local programming.

Pay-television

Although well known in the United States pay-cable or pay-television is relatively new in Europe. For most countries it is hardly an issue in the discussions on media policy; only in Sweden and Belgium (again only in Wallonia) are there plans. Pay-television is actually in existence (mid 1985) only in Germany (with two interactive experiments), Finland (limited to the commercial station Helsinki TV, which is connected to 85,000 households), Denmark (a limited experiment in Copenhagen), Switzerland (130,000 subscribers in Zürich), the Netherlands and Great Britain.

In the latter country, fifteen distributors of cable television provide pay-television. The experiments have had an uncertain start, because only 10 percent rather than the necessary 30 percent of the connected households have subscribed and the major cable companies have backed out. Copyright on films was higher than expected and the subscription fee is around £10, while £5 was planned. Advertising is not allowed on pay-television. In its White Paper on cable television (1983) the government has, however, made room for regular pay-television services.

The Dutch government proposed pay-television in its White Paper of 1983 and in late 1984 eight companies were approved. The two largest firms have merged and started programming at the beginning of 1985. As yet there is grave doubt whether there is financial room for more pay-television operators. The public broadcasting companies are not allowed entrance, but they are allowed to produce for the pay-television companies. Advertising is not allowed; the programming must be financed entirely through subscriptions. In order to protect Dutch culture, a portion of the programming is to be devoted to Dutch cultural issues (in the widest sense of the word): 5 percent in the first year, increasing to 20 percent within six years. Subscription is around 35 Dutch guilders (£8).

Since 1984, Canal Plus in France has provided over-the-air subscription television with sponsored feature films, including horror and soft pornography, banned from the national networks.

Interactive services

Pay-television may be relatively new to Europe, experiments with interactive services are totally in their infant stage.[3] Advanced plans exist in the Netherlands and Great Britain, but in both countries the financial viability is dubious. There is a small experiment in Switzerland (Marsens) and a more extensive one in France (Biarritz). The latter offers view telephone, fifteen television channels, electronic mailing, home shopping, etc. German experiments are well advanced. Two different cable experiments are planned and partly taking place at the same time: ten, very small projects, in which the Bundespost researches the technical side of glass fibre cables, and two pilot projects (and two more planned), in which the social effects of cable are analysed. All projects experiment with view telephone, videotex and an interactive pay-television channel.

The politics of cable policies

So far we have seen the characteristics and scope of cable television in Europe. Where possible, it has been indicated where discussions are taking place and in which directions developments are going. One clear tendency is that the cable — in spite of the financial hardship and be it slowly here and there — is capturing (northern and central) Europe. At the same time, most countries hesitate to invest large sums of money in advanced cable technologies. Another tendency is that, in the development of cable policies, rules and regulations do exist but in most countries, in comparison with broadcasting, are applied with a light hand. In the 1970s governments were still being cautious, while in the 1980s developments are given a freer hand. The aim of this section is to draw a picture of the issues and actors involved, and analyse the trends that are visible in the politics of cable policies in Europe.

Traditionally, in most countries in Europe, broadcasting has been a matter of public control: television was seen as a public service instrument comparable to other welfare institutions. It had an educational and informative function, 'teaching' civil man, giving him the capacity to participate freely and intelligently in a democracy. Although most countries also stressed the entertainment functions of the medium, and the television output seemed to confirm that, education, information and (high) culture were, at least in the eyes of those responsible in politics, the main aims. There are two other reasons why television was mostly under public control. Firstly, there existed a scarcity of channels and where there were too many producers for this restricted market governments were expected to divide and rule. Secondly, television (like radio before it) was seen as a powerful medium, in a position to influence people. Such a powerful medium was best controlled by — in the dominant ideology — a neutral institution such as the state. In some countries the state used this power openly for its own good, as was the case in France; in others, such as the Netherlands and Belgium, the relationship between broadcasting corporations and political parties was so strong that a more-or-less closed political communication system existed. In others again, the state provided opportunities for a relatively free flow.

In some countries, however, private interests were not ignored.

In Luxembourg a commercial system existed from the earliest days, while in Britain, beside the publicly-controlled BBC, an Independent Broadcasting Authority emerged, managing a system financed by advertising. The latter, however, was bound by so many rules and regulations, that a semi-public control situation existed. In addition to these factual situations, political parties of conservative inclination in all countries, by tradition, emphasized private interests. And, in general, control over an informative medium could be said to be not fully compatible with the political culture of, at least, the Western European countries in which freedom of information and the *liberalen Oeffentlichkeit* were treasured by Left and Right.

Public control over broadcasting might be a matter of fact in most countries, but in the politics of cable, several actors competed for the stage. This stage had traditionally been reserved for the government and the broadcasting organizations, but now other actors aspired to at least negotiation status. In the first place and in most countries, initiatives for cabling had come from industrial interest groups. Telecommunication industries saw new markets looming. In the second place, copyright-holders and labour unions were anxious not to see their rights washed away in the general euphoria over economic and technical possibilities. In the third place, local groups and other segmented parts of the public demanded their say, now that cable opened up so many possibilities for so many. Supported by the waves of the participatory ideology of the 1960s and 1970s, they laid their claims for the 1980s. In the fourth place, the traditional media, and notably television, were on the ball, afraid of losing advertising money and their powerful position, particularly in the world of visual communication. In the fifth place, political parties had always been partners in the development of media policies, but this time the different political views and affiliations were no longer hampered by arguments of scarcity of channels. In the sixth place there was the government, not above the different actors, but uncomfortably in-between. Depending on its political stance it leaned towards one or the other. Finally there were the European institutions, notably the European Commission and Parliament, which saw, in the developments of cable and satellite, new impetus towards the unity and economic strength of the Community. In a *Green Paper* they pleaded for opening up the market.

With so many actors and so much at stake it is hardly surprising that public control is gradually losing ground to private initiative. At the moment there seem to be four reasons for this tendency. Firstly, there is an economic reason. Industry had been knocking on the door for such a long time, that it could hardly be left waiting outside any longer. Moreover, telecommunication industries were afraid that they might miss the technical boat and lose the prospects of widening their international markets. For governments there was the extra fear that (advertising or other) money might cross the border into countries where the industrial climate was more prepared to lend a willing ear to commercial wishes.

Secondly, the argument that the scarcity of channels called for public regulation to share out limited air space was being rendered obsolete by technical developments. Although, in most countries, cable was still a shared antenna facility with usually not more than six channels (and quite often less), the sky was said to be the limit. Star-net cable systems in existence in some countries could offer as many as 180 channels, while glass fibre networks which were in an experimental phase in some, and planned in other, countries offered many more opportunities.

Thirdly, in some countries (notably Great Britain and the Netherlands) governments adhered more and more to a policy of 'keeping their distance'. In Europe these policies are conveniently labelled 'Thatcherism' after the 'no-nonsense politics' of the British Prime Minister in which devolution and privatization are keywords. The two mentioned are not the only conservative governments in Europe, but they are the most outspoken in this case. With a reduction in public spending as one of the main policies of these conservative governments, the emphasis is more on industrial than on cultural policy, however 'woolly' the language may be. A fair amount of broadcasting is still seen as a public service but this is not necessarily best guaranteed by public ownership. In some countries (e.g. Belgium), this stance is gradually being taken over by socialist parties.

Finally, there is another economic argument, but this time concerning the exploitation of cable itself. As one CIT report (1984) put it: 'The economics of cable are fragile, the risks speculative and the effects uncertain.' In such a delicate situation light programming, aimed at mass audiences, is the password. Commercialization (advertising, sponsoring, but also privatization of programme making) and an entertainment focus in programme policies are deemed necessary for more revenues, in order to pay back the initial investments in cable technologies and production.

With these tendencies strengthening one another, there are three counter-tendencies at work at the same time. In the first place, the evolution of cable is a threat to the existing media. The cinema, which has already lost ground to the explosion of video rental, might well get the final blow from pay-television. The publishing industry is afraid it will lose advertising revenues when cable is commercially exploited. Public broadcasting suddenly has to compete with foreign stations, satellites, pay-television channels and locally originated programmes. Sometimes these threats are countered by several measures. In some countries the press is allowed access to the cable, but in others it is excluded. In some countries advertising is not allowed on the cable, while in others special measures are taken to ensure that the traditional media are not drowned in the commercial flood.

In the second place, in most countries there exists an implicit or explicit cultural policy, in which the media have quite often played a pivotal role. This could take two forms. Firstly, cable is a costly business for which, in the end, the consumer will have to pay. With subscription fees for the cable itself, pay-television and interactive services, the cable utopia might well be for only the few. Moreover, where the distribution and installation is a market-led undertaking, not all parts of the country will be cabled. So, whereas ether broadcasting is for everyone, cable broadcasting will be exclusively for the (sub)urban areas in most counties. Such developments run counter to principles of both decentralization and equal distribution. Secondly, cable, because of its costliness, tends, as pointed out earlier, to adopt entertainment-focused programme policies. Implicit in most cultural policies is a condemnation of 'mass culture', often visualized as American series, serials and films. In most cable policies there is no restriction such as 'the reasonable proportion' formula in the Netherlands or the 'proper balance' in Great Britain, but some rules were deemed necessary, particularly pertaining to decency, violence and a national character (Finland, Great Britain). Moreover, going for the 'cheap' is an inherent threat to national cultural industries, as the French minister of culture made clear in a letter to the Prime Minister on 20 April 1982:

> The development of our cultural industries . . . is our only guarantee in the long run against worldwide universalisation of the production and diffusion of programs, and implies the necessity of opening up new communication networks (quoted in Vedel, 1984).

As a third counter-tendency, there existed not only anti-mass culture sentiments but also anti-commercial ones. Traditionally Christian Democrats and socialists have, for different reasons, had strong negative feelings about commercialization in general and advertising in particular. For the Christian Democrats it collided with Christian beliefs about profit-making, while for socialists advertising functioned both as a window to, and a manipulating force of, capitalism. But the adherents to both political ideologies could not turn a blind eye to reality. What they prohibited, other countries allowed and industrial money flows where the bedding is good.

In spite of these counter-tendencies, public control is slacker than in relation to broadcasting in general: policing of the cable is only taking place in the sense that policy, rules and regulations exist but merely 'to establish the legal and regulatory framework in which other actors operate' (Blumler 1984:3). In view of this slackening control we finally take a look at the way control is exerted over hardware and software in Europe.

Control over hardware is taking place in its clearest sense in France, where the state exerts all the power to establish an industrial policy which must lead both to the cabling of the country and to the good of the tele-communication industry. In the other European countries, control is either mixed or in private hands. However, in most cases the PTTs have some control over the technical standards. Private control does not necessarily mean government at a distance, because, in spite of their official statements, the Dutch and British governments, for instance, try at best to create an industrial climate for the hardware sector. But, whereas in the UK private industry is supposed to profit from governmental policies, in France it is nationalized industries which do so.

With control over software, privately-controlled cable programming will place emphasis on commercialization for reasons of market orientation and profit-seeking. Publicly-controlled cable programming would stress more the public service possibilities of this medium. One way or another, in Europe there seem to be three particular kinds of regulation as far as the content of cable programming is concerned. In the first place, there is the protection of national culture. France, the Netherlands, Great Britain and Finland all have either a minimum percentage of nationally produced programmes or a maximum of foreign programmes. The question remains, of course, whether in a situation with more than a 100 channels, trying to stop foreign programming from entering the country is not like Don Quixote fighting the windmills. In the second place, some countries have ruled (and others significantly not) that particular types of programmes should be banned. In Great Britain, for instance, pornography is banned, while violent programmes are prohibited in Finland. In the third place, a number of countries do not allow advertising on the cable (or as in the Netherlands, not for the time being), mainly to protect other media.

In view of the high costs involved, the delays of cable construction and installation and the apparent lack of a large market for interactive systems, the initial euphoria that took hold of the hardware industry, has turned into silent reluctance. Current annual Western European spending on CATV, including head-end and subscriber equipment, is approximately $450 million. The optimists expect a rise to $1,100 million by 1990, but the pessimists see large firms in the UK backing out and expect others on the Continent to follow. The new cable systems may be high-tech and high-speed, they argue, but it is also a high-investment, high-risk and long-haul business. In spite of the slackening of control, however, the national governments are the initiators and stimulators of information technology: the paradox of cable policy.

Notes

1. In a few years time microwave distribution systems (MDS), which already exist in the USA, are expected in Europe. At present all European PTTs use point-to-point microwave links for their telephone networks, but these very high frequency signals can also be used for broadcasting a limited number of television channels. Although the reception is limited, the financial advantages over high-cost cabling are enormous.

2. Although advertising on the Dutch cable is not allowed, a number of networks provide Sky Channel and Music Box. This is not prohibited, the present government has decided, since its advertising is not specifically aimed at Dutch viewers.

3. Cable text will be dealt with in Chapter 8 on telematics, while some services will partly be taken up again in Chapter 7 on video.

References

(Apart from the National Reports on which this volume is based)

AGB Research Ltd (1983) *Cable TV and Cable Systems in Western Europe.*

Blumler, J.G. (1984) *The Politics of Cabling Policy in Britain:* Paper presented to an International Forum on the Public Policies of New Communication Technologies. Paris.

Brants, K. and N. Jankowski (1985) 'Cable Television in the Low Countries', in R. Negrine (ed.), *Cable Television and the Future of Broadcasting.* London: Croom Helm.

The Cable and Satellite Europe Yearbook 1985 (and several of the issues of this magazine)

Cable 83: Proceedings of the International Conference on Satellite and Cable TV, London, 1983

CIT Research (1984) *The Economics of Cable.* London, CIT in collaboration with Arthur Anderson.

EBU Review (1984) 'An EBU Survey on Cable Television in Europe', *EBU Review* 35(1):31–42.

Hollins, T. (1984) 'Cable in Britain, the First Ten Years', *Sight and Sound* 53: 86–90.

Vedel, T. (1984) *Local Wiring Policies in France: from Biarritz to Paris*: Paper for Presentation at the Research Forum on Advanced Wired Cities, Washington (DC).

Vos, J. (1983) *Nieuwe Media en Beleid, een Europese Inventarisatie.* Nijmegen, Media-Info.

Whitten, P. (1983) 'Die Zukunft der Kabelkommunikation in Europa', *Media Perspektiven* 4/83: 233–42.

Whitten, P. (1984) 'Kabelkommunikation in West-Europa 1984', *Media Perspektiven* 5/84: 361–71.

Chapter 6

The ups and downs of European satellite development*

The background

The first published proposals for satellite communication go back to 1945 when the physicist Arthur C. Clark suggested a global communication system based on three satellites in geostationary orbit. This orbital distance (36,000 km above the equator) ensures a speed matching that of the earth's rotation. A satellite thus remains above a fixed spot on the earth. Rockets (boosters) were, however, not able to reach these high altitudes until the early 1960s. Satellite technology has primarily been based on military and big business needs and not the PTTs: telecommunication capacity via cable across the Atlantic could handle normal traffic loads. Satellites for remote sensing offer a unique opportunity which no other information system has — mapping geographical features, meteorological developments, etc. Satellites also make possible mobile, global communications between ships and planes and fixed installations. Both these elements are central to military strategy but, once established, they are also usable for civilian communication. Commercial communications have thus followed in military-industrial footsteps.

The satellite acts as an extraterrestrial relay-station. Signals are beamed from one earth station (uplink) to the satellite, where they are received and retransmitted (downlink), on a different frequency, to another earth station. Satellite transmissions are in the gigahertz range and their relatively weak signals are very susceptible to interference from other users of these radio frequencies on earth — notably the microwave systems set up by the PTTs to handle long-haul telephone traffic. A single satellite (platform) has several sets of receivers/transmitters (transponders) and each transponder may be more-or-less directional. In this way, a telecommunications satellite like the ECS-1 may cover all of Western Europe, whereas a national television satellite like UNISAT will be directed towards Britain. This focusing of a transponder beam on a smaller geographical area makes the signal stronger and thereby reduces the demands on receiver equipment.

* Written by Bernt Stubbe Østergaard.

The actors involved

This chapter attempts to trace the ups and downs of European satellite developments. To do this a number of actors are identified and their main objectives are analysed. The following actors and their objectives are crucial in defining where we are now, and where developments are likely to lead us:

Actors and their objectives in relation to satellites

ITU	Global frequency management
INTELSAT	A global satellite communication system
EUTELSAT	Establishing a European satellite communication system
EEC	Strengthen European integration
ESA	Build up European space industry
The European PTTs	Maintain adequate communication capacity and recover satellite investments
EBU	Set up a European television channel
National governments	Ensure participation of national industry
Public broadcasters	Retain share of national viewership
Private channel operators	Reach European viewers
Programme producers	Open new markets

These actors and their interests are central to the issues affecting European media policy which satellites have given rise to.

No single forum exists for the structuring of satellite television broadcasting and integrating it into national or European media policy. Rather, decisions are made on several, partially independent, levels. On the global level, the International Telecommunications Union (ITU) and its specialized body dealing with telecommunication (CCITT), seek to establish international standards and coordinate new services and tariffs. INTELSAT, an international consortium with 108 members, is dedicated to the running of a global satellite communication system. INTELSAT also leases spare satellite capacity for point-to point television transmission. On the European level, industrial interests are represented in the European Space Agency (ESA) and the EEC. European PTTs set up CEPT to ensure cooperation in setting up services and developing administration procedures. CEPT also acts as a form for formulating input to global organizations such as ITU and CCITT. The work of a sub-committee (CCS) of CEPT led to the setting up of the regional European satellite organization, EUTELSAT. It has functions as a regional organization vis-à-vis INTELSAT.

The public broadcasting organizations and their European union (EBU) clearly feel threatened by private commercial channel operators. They seek, on the one hand, to get their existing national programmes onto a satellite — notably German and French broadcasters — and, on the other hand, to set up a Euro-channel for integrated programming (Holland, Italy, Ireland and West Germany). Not all organizations are equally keen on either or both of these options (for instance, the BBC and IBA have shown resistance to the second.

The private operators and the large-scale (until now mostly American) programme producers see new profitable markets in unified European audiences and a chance to break national broadcasting monopolies. A number of national and international consortia of publishers have also been set up. American film producers and distributors are organized in two groups (UCP and TEG) specifically aimed at supplying European channel operators with programme material. On each level, actors try to strengthen their own bargaining positions through alliances with other actors whom they consider necessary to actually getting a revenue-producing service off the ground. However, decision-making is fuzzy — partly because advances in transmission and reception technology are outdating a number of actor agreements and strategies, partly because satellite television will have profound effects on several media policy issues at once, which makes national media policy difficult to plan and to foresee.

Satellite initiatives

The INTELSAT consortium was set up in 1964 in Washington by the USA and nine other industrialized nations to supply members with satellite communication. By 1984, its membership had risen to 108 countries. The Soviet Union and other socialist states established INTERSPUTNIK in 1971 as a countermove, but there is now rising interest in joining INTELSAT. EUTELSAT was set up by the PTTs (of eighteen countries) to strengthen the European space industry, even though INTELSAT had a monopoly position with regard to supplying member countries with satellite communication facilities. INTELSAT has given EUTELSAT permission to provide special services in Europe from 1982 to 1988, but with the ratification of the EUTELSAT Convention, the organization will have established itself on a permanent basis.

The decision to build a European rocket was based on a fear that the Americans or Russians might refuse to launch European satellites — and that the Americans, in particular, might limit the commercial uses to which they could be put to protect their own industry. The European Space Research Organization (ESRO) was first set up in 1964. The participating countries were to produce individual sections of the rocket. It was a failure — no complete rocket was ever built. After a strong French initiative, the European Space Agency (ESA) was created in 1972 and the Ariane launcher programme, organized in Arianespace, was initiated in 1973. French and German firms are dominant partners, while UK industry seems content to specialize in satellite construction. The ESA launched the Orbital Test Satellite (OTS) in 1978. It has proved reliable and long-lasting. Up until the spring of 1984 it has relayed telephony and other point-to-point communication, which since 1981 has also included the British commercial television programme, Sky Channel.

Setting up a satellite system entails not only the positioning of the satellite in space, but also ground facilities for sending and receiving transmissions. Because of the enormous distances involved (the signal has to travel 78,000 km) and the restrictions on size and weight of satellites, determined by existing booster capacity, normal ground facilities have been big and expensive. Typically, receiving antennae (dishes) have been of 12 m diameter and transceiver equipment costing around $2 million. Such facilities for communication satellites have been set up in Europe and run by the PTTs.

The successors to OTS are the European Communication Satellites, ECS–F–1 and ECS–F–2, which were launched in 1983 and 1984. The OTS and ECS are communication satellites with low output power, using the 11–14 GHZ frequencies. What makes them especially attractive to television broadcasters is that their beam covers the whole of Europe.

It was a private UK-based firm, Sky Channel, which launched the concept of satellite television based on advertising revenue in Europe. Using the Orbital Test Satellite (OTS-1), mainly US programmes were used to attract cable television viewers and advertisers. Sky Channel later switched to ECS–1 and was taken over by Rupert Murdoch Enterprises. By mid 1985, this channel could reach over 3 million viewers in Finland, Norway, Holland, Switzerland, Austria and the UK. The ECS–1 launched in 1983 had twelve transponders. Four were pointed towards South-Eastern Europe and the South Atlantic. The other eight are aimed at Western Europe. Nine of the twelve transponders have been leased. West Germany and the UK have leased two each, while Belgium, France, Italy, Holland and Switzerland have leased one each. On the ECS–2, launched in 1984, the Norwegian PTT has leased a transponder, and two transponders are reserved for the exchange of programmes between the European broadcasting organizations within the EBU. The other transponders will be used for traffic in the normal telecommunication network.

Because the communication satellites are an integrated part of the international PTT network, the frequencies alloted to them in the 11–14 GHZ band are also used for other point-to-point PTT communication via microwave links. These links criss-cross Europe, carrying telex, telephone, data and television signals. To operate both systems, communication satellites and microwave links, simultaneously, geographical separation has to be ensured. Reception of signals from the ECS may be disrupted if it takes place within 50–100 km of a microwave link. Also, television programmes beamed via INTELSAT in the 4 GHZ band collide with existing microwave links. Since the late 1960s, INTELSAT has been used in order to relay American programmes to US troops in Germany. To avoid such disruption, and to ensure optimal use of satellite capacity, the PTTs propose to set up satellite receiving-stations at carefully chosen locations. The television signals can then be transmitted via broadband cable to local cable systems.

Communication satellites covering the whole of Europe and operating in the 11–14 GHZ band are not limited to international organizations. France has launched TELECOM-1 in order to transmit satellite multi-services (SMS), and Luxembourg hopes to launch three satellites for commercial television ventures. The first all-French communication satellite, TELECOM-1, built by Matra, was launched in August 1984, having as its main tasks video conferencing and datatransmissions between 2400 bit/s and 2048 Kbit/s. The ground infrastructure is under the ministry of telecommunications (DGT) control. All customers have to rent equipment from the PTT. By the end of 1986 800 uplink installations are planned, offering any customer within 50 km high-capacity cable connection to an uplink. TELECOM-1 will be used to relay television programmes to overseas territories and establish an independent telecom system, something the French military are very interested in. The satellite will also be a part of French plans to digitalize telecommunication and thereby integrate voice, data and other types of traffic in the same network. TELECOM-1 will provide the long-distance capacity. This rapid development in the communication satellite field has for some time overshadowed the ongoing development of national direct broadcasting satellites (DBS).

Advances in the lift capacity of boosters have led to bigger satellites with increased signal strength, and improvements in antennae and receiver technology have reduced the size and costs of ground facilities. Together, these developments have made DBS possible. DBS systems have transmission facilities controlled by

PTTs or broadcasting organizations, but the signal from the satellite can be picked up directly in individual homes or in master antennae (MATV) systems, thus bypassing PTT-controlled cable networks. The earliest television satellites (DBS) beaming programmes directly to viewers were the American ATS–6 in 1975, the Canadian CTS/Hermes in 1976 and the Japanese Yuri in 1978. The first European television satellite will be the German TV–SAT, scheduled for launching in September 1986. The German DBS project, TV–SAT–1, built jointly by Messersmitt-Bolkow-Blohm (MBB) and Aerospatiale, will have four channels. Originally planned by the Social Democrats as a way to control satellite programming, while at the same time creating business opportunities for German industry, the DBS project is now in some confusion because commercial television interests can get transponder leases on the ECS satellites ECS–2 and ECS–3, on INTELSAT and possibly on future privately financed satellite ventures.

Two more DBS projects based on the same type of satellite are the French TDF–1 and the Swedish Tele-X scheduled for 1986 and 1988 respectively. Financing of the Tele-X is however still uncertain. The British Unisat project is running into heavy financial troubles also, but if it comes through it will not be before 1988–9. Unisat will be built by a consortium headed by British Aerospace.

A new Luxembourg satellite project has replaced the CORONET scheme. This time the government has set up the Société Européenne de Satellite (SES). SES will be wholly financed by European investors and hopes to offer thirty-two transponders to private programme producers. The proposed satellite to be used by SES is a 50 Watt (medium strength) Hughes or RCA satellite with sixteen transponders. Choosing a medium-strength satellite reflects the problems still unsolved in the MBB/aerospatiale 230 Watt version. The travelling wave tubes necessary to produce 230 Watt transmitting power have hitherto proved unstable.

Rules and regulations

The television satellites — also called Direct Broadcasting Satellites (DBS) — have opened the way both for national ownership and control and the possibility of reaching a vast audience far beyond the national boundaries. The success of the ATS–6 and the CTS/Hermes led to many countries demanding their share of frequencies and 'slots' in the geostationary orbit. The allocation of frequencies and orbital positioning was made at the ITU's World Administrative Radio Conference (WARC) in Geneva in 1977. DBS communication had already in 1971 been allotted the frequencies from 11.7 to 12.5 gigahertz. Each country, irrespective

TABLE 3
Satellite developments on the European scene, 1980–90

Operational	Launch	Satellite name	Owner	Satellite type	Transmitting strength	No. of TV transponders	Orbit position	Comments
1980	12/80	INTELSAT VF–2	INTELSAT	Com.sat	10 Watt	4	34.5°W	2 transponders used by Spain, 1 between UK & US, 1 used by news agency Visnews.
1983	6/83	ECS–F–1	EUTELSAT	Com.sat	20 Watt	10	13°E	BRD (2), UK (2), I,NL F,SCH,B,LUX. Used by: SAT1, 3Sat, Sky Channel, Filmnet, RAI, Music box, Teleclub, RTL-plus.
	3/82	INTELSAT VF–4	INTELSAT	Com.sat	10 Watt	3	27.5°W	UK: Premiere, Ten, Screen Sport.
1984	8/84	ECS–F–2	EUTELSAT	Com.sat	20 Watt	3	7°E	N, EBU (2).
	8/84	TELECOM-1A	France	Com.sat	20 Watt	2	8°W	No TV at present.
1985	5/81	INTELSAT VF-1	INTELSAT	Com.sat	10 Watt	6	57°E	All transponders leased leased by D for TV.
	4/85	TELECOM-1B	France	Com.sat	20 Watt	1	5°E	Video conferencing.
	9/85	ECS–F–3	EUTELSAT	Com.sat	20 Watt	9	10°E	UK (2), S,DK,N,I (2), T,E. The satellite did not get into orbit.
1986	9/86 planned	TV–SAT–1	Germany	DBS	230 Watt	4	19°W	Much uncertainty about transmitter design. ARD/ZDF, SAT 1, WDR/WAZ.

	11/86 planned	TDF–1	France	DBS	230 Watt	4	19°W	RTL (2). Possibly not operational before 1987.
	perhaps	GDL–1 previously: CORONET	Luxembourg (SES)	DBS but with lower power	45 Watt	16	either 1°E, 10°E, or 21.5°W	Société Européenne de Satellite is now European venture capital based.
1987	no date	TELECOM-1C	France	Com.sat	20 Watt	3	3°E	No current plans.
	no date	GDL–2	Luxembourg (SES)	DBS	45 Watt	Reserve	as GDL-1	SES looks to a fast launch in the hope of RTL interest.
1988	no date	DFS-Kopernikus	Germany	Com.sat	20 Watt	9	23.5°E	Experiments with HDTV.
	no date	Olympus/L-sat	Italy and ESA	DBS	230 Watt	2	19°W	EBU (NOS,ARD,RTE, RAI), I. This will be a very big satellite.
	no date	TV–SAT–2	Germany	DBS	230 Watt	Reserve	19°W	
	no date	TDF–2	France	DBS	230 Watt	Reserve	19°W	
	perhaps	Unisat	UK	DBS	200 Watt	4	31°W	BBC, ITV and private group, but no financial agreement yet.
	no date	Tele-X	Sweden	DBS	230 Watt	2	5°W	NRK/SR/YP Nordic programming.
1989	perhaps	Videosat	France	Com.sat	20 Watt	12	uncertain	No present plans.

of size, got five channels for national programming and a position in the geostationary orbit for a satellite.

The Eastern European countries, especially, were worried at the prospect of foreign satellite programmes beamed directly at them, but at the same time they too felt a need for satellite transmissions. Agreement was reached at the WARC conference on the basic outlines for DBS. The keywords were:

Service-area — the geographical area where a signatory body can demand agreed protection against interference.

Coverage-area — the geographical area within which a signal of a defined quality can be received from a transponder.

The difference between service-area and coverage-area is defined as 'spill-over'. In order to minimize spill-over, the WARC conference set narrow limits on signal strength from DBS. There is however a lower limit to the beam width of 0.6 degrees. This means that small countries will necessarily have quite a large spill-over in proportion to the service-area, because the narrowest possible beam from a transponder will still cover quite a large geographical area.

The USA managed to convince all the delegations in their hemisphere to delay actual positioning until some means of optimizing positions was achieved. This took six years and a lot of computing power, but the result was accepted at an ITU conference in 1983. The European and African delegations at the conference, however, could not reach such an agreement, which meant that partitioning had to take place during the meeting. The result is far from satisfactory, with the West German (BRD) slot placed over the Atlantic (19° W) and the British DBS even further out at 31° W above the coast of Brazil, which is also the position of the Olympus satellite scheduled to transmit RAI and EBU channels.

The slow growth in demand for satellite channel capacity for telecommunications has meant that national PTT members of EUTELSAT have had to invest a lot of money with only small returns. Spare capacity has always been cheaper on INTELSAT satellites than on those of EUTELSAT. This led, in 1981, to a search for new customers outside the circle of PTTs. It turned out that commercial television companies were very interested — almost at any price, because of the Europe-wide coverage. The decision taken in 1982 to allow commercial television onto PTT-owned satellites has never been debated publicly, although it may be the single most important media policy decision since the introduction of television!

Unlike radio programmes broadcast on short-, medium- or

long-wave, television has never been an international broadcasting phenomenon. In all the Continental European countries, border viewing of neighbouring countries' programmes is well known and accepted. But differing national policies on advertising, ownership and media access have up until now prevented the spread of national programming to other countries on a systematic basis. Contributing to this state of affairs is the relative short range of the VHF and UHF signals used to broadcast television, the limited channel capacity and, of course, the existing language barriers. But, besides these constraints, most national Governments see television as an important political instrument for maintaining national coherence. Television, in other words, is seen as a very powerful medium for spreading political messages, even beyond one's borders — something that worries ruling elites in Eastern European countries a great deal. Television is also feared as a channel for foreign (i.e. US) cultural imperialism, something several Western European countries are unhappy about as well. Finally, foreign commercial television is seen as a threat to existing commercial media (mainly newspapers) and potentially affecting consumption patterns in favour of foreign products. It could also affect employment.

Television via satellite relieves channel capacity constraints and permits the geographical spread of signals. So the decision to allocate frequencies to DBS at the WARC conference in 1977 was a very arduous task. To reach consensus, two major restrictions were imposed, the satellite footprint (i.e. coverage-area) should follow national boundaries as closely as technically possible, and frequency allocation and satellite slot should ensure a maximum separation of the Eastern European and Western European broadcasting. The question of advertising has been debated for many years, but no simple or even applicable solutions have emerged. Recently the Commission of the EEC, representing Europe-wide integration and multinational industry, has come out in favour of international television advertising[1] and the Council of Europe (COE) has suggested quite liberal guidelines for such activities (see Chapter 3). But WARC and COE decisions are now of less importance after the PTTs' decision to give commercial television access to the communication satellite transponders, and from there to reach Europe-wide audiences.

Media policy in all European countries must now face the fact that a number of new media operators are emerging whose primary aim is to generate advertising revenue from low-cost entertainment, often repeated, with low take-up and high 'churn'. The cheapest sources of programmes are American. There will be little encouragement of local (i.e. national) film/television production industry. This development will also lead to frequent bankruptcies among operators. The potential effects on national media interests are extensive: traditional advertising media may lose revenue; public broadcasting may lose viewers and licence or advertising money; national film/television production may lose markets; cinemas may lose audiences; and PTT plans for national cable networks may be thrown into disarray.

The decision to allow commercial television onto vacant transponders, once taken, however, has led to a speeding up of satellite development in EUTELSAT. Thus in 1982, communication satellites owned and controlled by the national PTT suddenly changed the balance in relation to the agreements reached at the WARC in 1977. However, channel leases on the ECS are short-term and television transmissions have to give priority to telecommunication needs. If, in other words, data transmission, video conferencing, etc., expands rapidly they may push the commercial television operators out. To this must be added that the ECS–F–1 acts as a back-up to ECS–F–2. If the F–2 is damaged, telecommunication traffic is transferred to the F–1. In this situation, a national medium-power satellite system, SES, which the Luxembourg Government is supporting, may attract customers who want to broadcast commercial television and be sure they can stay on, irrespective of developments in the field of telecommunication. This project has, however, like its predecessor, CORONET, not attracted sufficient venture capital. EUTELSAT plans to launch an F–3 communication satellite in autumn 1985 with nine transponders reserved for television broadcasting. This launching was unsuccessful.

Internationalization of broadcasting by way of satellites

On the European level, a very strong lobby of media actors including major publishers, electronics manufacturers, advertising interests and programme producers are pushing for cross-frontier broadcasting. In the recently published EEC *Green Paper*,[1] cross-border broadcasting is seen as a significant contribution to European unification and the development of the EEC. DBS is seen as offering many more services than terrestrial-based systems on a pan-European basis. This however must not degenerate to Dallas-type programming from the USA. Development of DBS is dependent on reaching a common standard of transmission. With Britain and the EBU advocating one standard C–MAC and France/Germany choosing D2–MAC, this is still contestable. D2–MAC is a simpler standard which is compatible with existing video-recorders.

On the programme side, the EEC finds that increased advertising will stimulate sales, but that it must rest on aligning national policies; and that household investments in programme viewing will pave the way for massive investments in new information systems and software development. The most likely programme content in international broadcasting seems to be: films; video-music; sports; news; children's programmes; and general entertainment. The main existing suppliers of much of this content are as follows:

Hollywood

Two Hollywood distribution organizations, United Cable Programmes Ltd. (MGM/United Artists, Paramount and Universal Pictures) and the Television Entertainment Group (Columbia Pictures, Goldcrest, 20th Century Fox and Home Box Office) have interests in European satellite television. The two groups together have about 4,000 movies in stock. However only some 110 new films come out of Hollywood per year. With something like 100 television transmitting transponders over Europe by 1990, a lot more material will be needed.

National public broadcasting organizations

A number of established broadcasting corperations are planning to put their programme on satellite — BBC, ITV, Canal Plus, ZDF, NOS to mention a few. They will use their normal programmes product. Also the European Broadcasting Union (EBU) wants to be in on the act with a transponder on the ECS–2 for pan-European productions.

Publishing houses

Some of Europe's biggest publishing enterprises are going into the satellite television market, most in either pay-television or advertising-based operations. This group includes Bertelsmann, Springer, Bauer, Esselte and Rupert Murdoch. A number of publishers have set up joint ventures with firms already in the electronic media field, whereas others with sufficient capital have set up their own programme production units. Several examples illustrate this. The biggest publishers in Germany — Springer and Bertelsmann — have set up a pay-television company, with the US company Home Box Office holding a minority share. Rupert Murdoch, the Australian newspaper tycoon, has brought Sky Channel, the first European commercial satellite channel. The biggest book publisher in Europe, Bertelsmann, is cooperating with Radio Luxembourg in setting up a commercial German language satellite programme on the TDF–1. In Germany, 135 newspapers are cooperating with Bauer and Springer, in producing a channel to go on the German TV–SAT (see also Chapter 3 above).

Main issues

Summing up the ongoing development in the satellite field, a number of important media policy issues are raised. They concern content, control and financing.

The ECS development may open the way for a massive dose of Americana. Thus, in an attempt to avoid US/USSR supremacy in space (at least over Europe) the issue of cultural integrity is raised. Britain, which sees itself as a programme exporter, does not feel threatened by this development, and France, which already for some years has been satelliting programmes to North Africa, the overseas French dominions, and the French Canadians, is prepared as well. The only other government looking forward to such conditions is the Grand Duchy of Luxembourg, where Radio Luxembourg will have a French- and a German-language channel on the French TDF–1 — this will be Radio Luxembourg taking off into space. On top of that, the Luxembourg government is trying to get into the business with its own SES scheme.

Cultural integrity was not on the agenda, when the European PTTs in EUTELSAT decided to give commercial television interests access to the whole Western European television viewing population. Cultural integrity will certainly be affected by the results. Whether this is seen as a good or a bad thing depends on the eye of the beholder. The EEC sees it as a contribution to European unification, and the increase in advertising as leading to an increase in demand and thereby industrial output and inter-regional competitiveness. Opposition on the cultural level comes from cultural workers, intellectuals and other media such as books and newspapers who may lose readers and therefore also a local cultural identity.

There was little need for more channels or frequencies for normal PTT services when the first satellites went up, and the PTTs had great difficulty in finding traffic they could divert via a satellite. Satellites were part of the national and European military/industrial policy. But the development of private communication satellite systems (the American SBS) indicated that satellites could pose a threat to the European PTTs' monopoly, forcing them to offer private business the same services as their American counterparts. As yet this threat has not materialized. The price of satellite communication is still daunting but the financial formula created by CORONET/SES may turn out to secure enough backing to get off the ground.

Several countries in Europe are working on plans for laying down a nationwide broadband cable system to extend the tasks of the existing telephone network and ultimately enable picture communication between individual users. With the initiation of the EEC RACE programme these plans have moved to a pan-European level. This is a very expensive idea, taking at least thirty years to achieve, and one way of financing some of the expense is to let the national PTTs put television programmes from other countries into the cable — but that means limitations on the use of private parabolic antennae. Thus DBS is open for anyone while ECS-transmitted programmes must be transmitted via PTT installations. This may be very difficult to do, if non-scrambled programmes are up there waiting for anyone to tap them. In France, for example, there seems to be conflict between satellite developments and the national cabling plan, which calls for the cabling of 1.5 million homes by 1985 and the rest within this century. Such a cabling makes DBS satellites somewhat superfluous because television signals can be sent directly via cable or via communication satellites to cable head-ends. Cable and satellites will surely continue to co-exist. Usage will depend on capacity, pricing and programme content. Whereas satellite television was originally intended to be channelled via DBS with a (mainly) national coverage, and therefore be controllable by national authorities, it seems likely now that commercial satellite television will go via the European Communication Satellites (ECS) covering the whole of Europe. This is, of course, very attractive to many advertisers. The drawback is that relatively large parabolic antennae and expensive receivers are needed for the ECS signal reception compared to the DBS. But technological advances and the increase in the size of master antennae facilities (MATV) are solving those problems. This development makes it very difficult for national advertising policies to prevail in countries where the state traditionally has monopolized television broadcasting while the printed news media are privately owned, and to a large extent financed via advertising. This is the case in the Scandinavian countries and Germany. With private interests gaining access to television viewers, the public opinion process is changed, because private news media usually have Conservative owners while the public broadcasting leans toward the Social Democrats. In other countries like Italy the different major political parties each dominate one of the national channels, ensuring them access to the voters.

The sharp increase in number of channels will, of course, affect prices of programmes and programme producers' sales strategies. With more buyers on the market, prices will rise and with a number of new selective audience screenings systems — pay-television, video cassettes, CATV — programme producers will wait until the last possible moment before selling programmes to public broadcasting.

The dominant media structure in Western Europe has in the 1960s and 1970s been characterized by private commercial printed media, public broadcasting and commercial television licensed by the state. In the printed media concentration of interests has led to fewer, but larger, corporations both in books and magazines and in newspapers. With the coming of satellite television, channel operators and the greater part of their viewers no longer live in the same country or under the same jurisdiction. National media policies seeking to regulate media control are no longer possible. The original hope of controlling national broadcasting through control of channels on national DBS is no longer realistic, because of available capacity on ECS and even INTELSAT. Regulation is thus only possible in the cable networks (CATV or MATV head-ends). Here restrictions on cross-ownership, securing access for local programming, etc., may come in.

Irrespective of implemented national policy, viewing moves towards privately run, commercially financed television programmes. High licence fees to public broadcasters will become more unpopular. The traditional hold on viewers exercised by political party control of television will falter. One recourse may be to strengthen local/regional cable television programming and wait for the shake-out among the numerous commercial channels. Another possibility is that public media may disappear or at least lose importance. The political implications are a strengthening of conservative views predominant in the privately owned media.

Conclusions

The developmental drive with regard to satellites has come primarily from military and industrial interests. Specifically regarding communication satellites, these emerge as the computer industry and telecommunication industry are integrated. The microprocessor development was originally propelled by the need to reduce weight, size, heat dissipation, etc. But miniaturization has now itself created wholly new services. Developing a satellite sector in Europe has now become a show-case for European technology, but with some uncertainty concerning services to be carried. The development of DBS systems with very powerful transmitters may turn out to be a blind alley. This is partly due to problems with developing the necessary equipment, partly to the spread of cable systems, which reduces the need for individual antennae. For the individual household costs are about even — joining a cable television system or buying DBS-receiving equipment might both cost £300–600. New plans from EUTELSAT operate with a second generation DBS with transponders each with 100 Watt transmitters, somewhat less than the 230 Watt transmitters of the first generation. With the advent of commercial communication satellites, the PTT monopoly on point-to-point communications will be broken, and the PTTs themselves are moving into broadcasting systems. The intricate system of frequency distribution and access is challenged as more actors demand access. With the creation of regional, European, organizations, European space efforts managed to get off the ground. Now, more and more, national efforts are taking over. The EEC is highly involved in trying to ensure that national research programmes are in accordance with international, or at least European, standards. The ESPRIT programme aims to give the European information technology industry the basis necessary to be competitive on the world market. The programme has five subprogrammes — advanced microelectronics, software technologies, advanced information handling, office automation systems and the integration of computers in industrial production. Beyond that the new RACE program (Research in Advanced Communication technology in Europe) aims at the introduction of broadband services, including television in a digital network (broadband ISDN) covering all of Western Europe (see above, pp. 30–31).

Whether or not Europe will develop a satellite sector flexible and cheap enough to cater for broadcasting and telecommunication needs is not so much a question of the technological base, but rather of organization and financing. Satellite systems are inherently international, but so long as national industries play such an important role in shaping policy then consensus is unlikely. The problems are not overcome by investing more resources in research and development.

Television programmes beamed from communication or DBS satellites are creating a European market. The EEC Commission and EBU are vigorously in favour of this development. National media structures are being changed by a mixture of national and international industrial policies. Ongoing experiments with new satellite services now taking place all over Europe have, however, run into great difficulties with regard to user financing and most of the projects depend heavily on state support. We are witnessing the quantitative escalation of the information society concept, but dangerously little research has been done on information needs in relation to living and working conditions on the European level.

Note

1. Commission of the EEC (1984) *Television without Frontiers (The Green Paper)*. Brussels.

Chapter 7

Home video — a maturing medium*

During the 1960s, videotape recorders were developed in Europe and the USA with a consumer market in mind. None of the products presented, however, became a success. In the middle of the 1970s, the home video product of today, the videocassette recorder, was launched by European and Japanese manufacturers. The full emergence of home video equipment did not come until around 1980. As an alternative to videocassette recorders, videodisc players were developed. The latter product has so far been much less successful than the former.

The most general issues of home video are those of copyright and smuggling, the latter being caused by price differences between countries sometimes produced by taxes and levies. An issue of growing concern is the content, especially regarding the occurrence of violence on video. Media policy moves have been taken in many European countries on that issue. Gradually, the supply of pre-recorded cassettes has improved, and there now seem to be two different markets: one for pre-recorded cassettes (the software) and one for the video recorders (the hardware), each of some concern to the legislature. All together this sums up to a question of control.

Diffusion and applications of home video

Home video started as a confusing variety of products, creating uncertainty in the industry and among the ultimate consumers. There were discs, there were cassettes, and moreover different disc and cassette technologies. This problem was easiest to overcome in countries like the UK, with rental traditions in home electronics, and a strong rental market for home video soon appeared.

Distribution channels for videocassette recorders were available, although the retailers had to choose among the systems and there were few retailers for the business of renting and selling pre-recorded and blank cassettes. In most countries, given the general absence of control, the number of videocassette retailers grew quickly.

In the beginning, the manufacturers of videocassette recorders offered only the service of black-and-white recording and replaying. This imperfection was probably of minor importance, since the most significant determinant of demand is likely to have been availability

* Written by Marjan Flick, Karl Erik Gustafsson and Olav Vaagland.

of colour television sets. In households owning only a black-and-white television set, colour videocassette recorders cannot be fully exploited. Whether videocassette recorders can promote the sales of colour television sets is an interesting question, but impossible to answer without comparative surveys.

The initial phase of video use can be characterized by institutional application (in the mid 1970s). This means that video recorders and cameras were bought and used by institutions like schools, hospitals, training centres, etc. The foremost purpose was filming individual or group behaviour, which afterwards could be evaluated by the group, the therapist, etc. So an important part of the video equipment was the camera. This is obviously not the case in the later, booming home use of the video equipment, that is until recently, when the home video has become an alternative to traditional home movie-making on Super 8 or Single 8 film.

TABLE 4
Videocassette recorder penetration, 1982 and 1983, in Western Europe

Country	Population 1981 ('000)	VCR ownership as % of TV licence-holders[1] 1982	VCR ownership as % of TV licence-holders[1] 1983
Austria	7,510	3.8	6.6
Belgium	9,861	6.4	8.1
Denmark	5,122	8.7	14.4
Finland	4,801	2.9	4.0
France	53,963	5.8	9.5
Greece	9,707	1.5	4.1
Ireland	3,440	12.5	17.3
Italy	57,197	1.3	2.0
Netherlands	14,246	9.4	13.0
Norway	4,100	11.9	15.0
Spain	37,654	2.8	4.5
Sweden	8,324	15.5	18.1
Switzerland	6,473	10.1	12.9
United Kingdom	55,833	19.2	30.5
West Germany	61,666	12.0	17.6

Sources: a) TV licences: *Media Perspektiven* 7/1984; b) VCR ownership: 1982 – *Intermedia* 4–5/1983; 1983 – *Screen Digest*, June/1984.

[1] Base for licence-holder total is 1983.

The United Kingdom had (mid-1985) the largest total number of videocassette recorders as well as the largest coverage: close to every third television set is used as a home video component. The large household penetration of videocassette recorders in the UK is said to be caused by the strong rental market, which existed prior to the home video. The rental market accounts for about half of the penetration. Other nations with strong or sizable rental markets are Ireland, Denmark and Norway. In most instances, the rental market was created by the home video. The rental system not only reduces initial confusion among consumers since the rental companies bear the risks of technological uncertainty. By buying large numbers of videocassette recorders, rental companies can also demand quantity discounts and in that way offer low rental fees. While rental systems may promote penetration in more than one way in the early stages of evolution of the industry, they can be more vulnerable to sudden decreases in demand in later stages.

Sweden and West Germany also have rather high penetration figures, although in both countries the rental market is not strong and buying is by far the dominant means of acquisition. Italy has apparently the lowest degree of penetration, one reason for this being the heavy taxation on electronic equipment (36 percent including VAT). Another important reason for the low figure may be that the provision of electronic entertainment and information is close to saturation, thanks to the wide availability of private television channels.

In accounts of video use in different countries, the main finding is that home video is used as a complement to broadcast television. The videocassette recorder implies an extension of off-air broadcasting. It is used as a time-shifting device. Surveys in countries like the UK, Ireland and Sweden report that about 75 percent of home video viewing consists of off-air recordings. The highest percentage reported — 85 percent time-shift viewing — concerns Belgium. Due to the many channels available, the degree of video penetration is relatively low, but home video households in Belgium, all the same, use their video devices for time-shifting. In other countries time-shift viewing may be negligible. In Norway, for instance, with only one channel and where a relatively small proportion of the population can receive foreign television channels, rather little use is made of videocassette recorders for time-shifting (25 percent). In Denmark, on the other hand, where also only one (Danish) channel is available, time-shift viewing is probably close to 60 percent. This is, of course, due to the fact that most Danes may receive two or more foreign channels.

The supply of pre-recorded cassettes was initially limited in a double sense, both as to the number of titles and their variety. As the main use of home video has remained recording off-air television, the limited supply did not seem to be a problem in recruiting buyers. The narrow, biased, range of titles available (mostly films portraying violence and sex) may even have increased the demand for home video among certain groups with a special interest in that kind of content. In some countries, it was only when the amount and variety of pre-recorded videocassettes increased, that the sales boom of videocassette recorders came. In those countries the videocassette recorders are mainly utilized as a substitute or supplement to ordinary television, or even as cinema. Again, Norway, with little time-shift viewing and with a buoyant rental market for pre-recorded cassettes, would be typical.

Although the number of titles available is clearly an important factor in the penetration of the videocassette recorders, other factors may be just as decisive. The number of television channels available is surely of importance. Where there are few channels and many titles within reach, one would expect high penetration, mainly for watching pre-recorded cassettes. On the other hand, in countries with many television channels, it would also be reasonable to assume rapid and high penetration of videocassette recorders, but in these cases primarily for time-shift viewing. When — or if — the DBSs become operative, this will probably be the situation in most countries. So far, it is impossible to say anything conclusive in this matter. There are examples of multichannel countries with high penetration of videocassette recorders (UK) as well as with low penetration (Italy). Very likely there are other factors than availability of channels or cassettes which will influence the rate of penetration in different countries, e.g. costs, standard of living, patterns of social life, and, of course, the extent to which the authorities have put restrictions on the contents of the cassettes or on the distribution system, or laid financial restraints on software or hardware.

Control

As is sometimes the case with new media or other kinds of technology, regulations or legislation do not appear until after the diffusion of the technology has reached a certain level, or a certain pattern of use is established. In most countries this is also the case with the videocassette recorder. We could, of course, attribute this to the lack of a coherent media policy, but we could just as well say it is caused by the rapid technological development, which politicians have not been very able to cope with. Accordingly, the regulation, both of the distribution of videocassette recorders and the use of the equipment or the content of the software, has so far been rather lax or casual.

Control may be divided into at least two spheres: public control and private initiative. Until recently, questions of public regulation or control have not been put on the public policy agenda. We may say that private initiative has reigned in most European countries, concerning both the spread of the recorders and indirectly their use, and the content of the software. The emphasis has been on self-regulation, based on adjustment to the market. This has in some countries led to a flourishing business, on both the software and the hardware sides. One reason why public control has lately become an issue is the wish to avoid possible negative consequences for already established media or national media industries; another is the question of 'protecting' the audience from undesirable influences. There are reasons to believe that public control will be further emphasized in the future. It is possible to categorize the notion of control as concerning either content or money, or a combination of both. The copyright question, especially, hints at both the content and the financial aspects.

Content

Some countries have announced a new attitude towards the contents of videocassettes; others have already implemented new laws or regulations. The areas which so far have given rise to the most concern have been to do with sex and violence. There are general laws in most countries against pornography and violence on television and cinema. Harmonizing the rules for videocassettes with these has recently become a common issue: censorship for movies should apply to video as well. This is the case, for instance, in Norway. Other countries have chosen other solutions, like making laws applicable to video alone. In Sweden this led to a law against violence on video in 1982, Finland introduced such a law in 1983 and Britain legislated for a classification system in 1985. These are examples of rather restrictive attitudes towards the content, and the result is negative sanctions.

On the other hand, the vast supply of second- and third-class videocassettes in the countries most concerned with the content raised the issue of positive measures to upgrade the quality. In some countries, public broadcasting bodies have been engaged in producing cassettes of broadcast standard as an alternative to cassettes of low-grade content. Other producers of quality content have been, for instance, book-clubs. These actions may be labelled positive countermeasures.

To illustrate the difference in attitudes towards these questions, Denmark may be chosen as an example. Here, the Government Commission on Mass Media discussed whether Denmark should follow the Swedes and forbid some kinds of content. Violence, perverse sex and commercials were the categories discussed. The majority of the members of the commission voted against any kind of ban, and recommended instead the production and distribution of alternative, supplementary video programmes financed by a so-called video fund.

Questions of copyright

All copying devices create copyright problems: copy machines for printed material, sound recorders for sound, and video recorders for moving pictures. In countries where there has been little pressure for control of content — advertising, violence, and so on — at least matters of copyright have been discussed. This makes the copyright question one of the most general of the video policy issues. All the same, these discussions have not led to any initiatives in the form of laws and regulations. One of the main problems in relation to copyright is smuggling and cassette piracy. In some countries unlawful copying is estimated to be relatively high, although the parties involved in the open trade try to stop it. Videogram associations in countries like Ireland, the Netherlands and Norway, for instance, are campaigning to prosecute pirates.

One measure against cassette piracy could be to register all cassettes. In Spain all pre-recorded cassettes have to be licensed by the Ministry of Culture. In Norway a central registration — asked for by the retailers to get a clear picture of the copyright problems — has been suggested. The most effective measure would probably be to demand a spoiler device on every tape.

Another solution to the copyright question would be controlled distribution of the cassettes. The copyright issue was, for instance, raised in Sweden when Swedish Television was to start distributing cassettes. It took a very long time to reach an agreement with the journalists but, finally, under the threat of a law, a solution was reached. These cassettes, made by television journalists, were to be distributed through mail order. An agreement was made between Swedish Television and the Swedish Postal Administration in 1983 on an alternative distribution channel. A catalogue would be printed and from that people could order by phone or mail cassettes they wanted to rent. Within 24 hours the cassettes would be delivered either to a post office nearby, or by a rural postman. In November 1983 the mail order system started in two provinces of Sweden. So far, the results are mixed, and new attempts are being made along the same lines.

As an alternative, controlled distribution of videocassettes by public libraries has been discussed. Even today the distribution of videocassettes is very much like that of books: the options are renting or buying. In Norway and Sweden there are plans based on the public libraries' participation in distributing the cassettes, although on a rather small scale. In Norway even booksellers have been suggested as a distribution channel. Up to now, none of these proposals have been implemented.

In Italy, Mondadori, the largest publishing house, has established a department of 'electronic books' which publishes educational, professional and entertainment (non-violent) videocassettes. In the same way, the RAI has entered the video market by selling educational cassettes, and has plans for producing high-quality and highly spectacular software. One reason for this is to get a share of the international market, by way of joint ventures with foreign television companies.

To summarize this part, we may conclude that very little has been done in Europe to solve the problems raised by the copyright issue, apart from a few attempts at developing new channels for distribution, and with a very limited effect.

Financial regulation

The other main measure undertaken by some governments in Western Europe to control and direct the development of home video is of a financial nature. This may again be divided in two, depending on whether it is for fiscal or cultural motives. Taxation or other financial means of control may be imposed as a way of implementing certain regulations, or just to obtain income for the state. Very often these measures are interwoven, with both financial and cultural motives working at the same time.

In some ways the use of videocassette recorders is an extremely private or individual activity, even if much of the viewing typically takes place in company with others. It is private in the sense that it is the user her- or himself who decides what to see at what time.

Even financially speaking, video is rather special. There is, for instance, no need for any kind of superstructure, such as a transmitter, or special premises, such as cinemas, for those who want to make money in the video business. Getting a foothold in the market for selling or renting pre-recorded videocassettes is in most countries rather easy, while establishing an enterprise for renting or selling the recorders may be only a little more cumbersome. In spite of this, there are some possibilities for the authorities or politicians to pinpoint issues in order to follow some kinds of media policies. In addition to proposing laws or regulations concerning, for instance, the content of the cassettes, politicians may control the spread and use of videocassette recorders by imposing taxes on the equipment. In some countries this would be done to protect a national industry. Naturally, this most concerns countries with a big electronics industry, such as France, West Germany, the Netherlands and the UK. In some countries, e.g. France, the goal is not only to protect, but also to promote the home electronics industry. This of course is an industrial policy, rather than a cultural or media policy. Nonetheless, the implications have consequences for these policy arenas too.

European manufacturers of videocassette recorders, headed by Philips, at first competed with the Japanese manufacturers on the European market. Delayed introduction of its 'second generation' home video equipment made Philips lose ground to the Japanese formats. Other measures had to be taken to control the Japanese expansion, or the European production of videocassette recorders would have declined and unemployment increased. Therefore import barriers were introduced. In November 1982, Philips and Grundig filed charges with the EEC against the Japanese manufacturers for price-dumping videocassette recorders in Europe. The Japanese products were sold at prices below their production costs, at least according to Philips and Grundig. In February 1983 an agreement was made with the Japanese manufacturers, the so-called Tokyo Agreement. For a period of three years not more than 4.55 million videocassette recorders annually could be imported from Japan or assembled by Japanese companies in Europe. The corresponding figure for 1982 was 4.9 million units.

Other countries use taxation as a manoeuvre against inflation and economic recession. In Italy there is a tax of 16 percent on top of the 20 percent VAT. This is not a protectionistic measure, as there is practically no national production of electronic consumer goods. Countries like Norway and Sweden have introduced taxes on video equipment, founded on both fiscal and cultural arguments. In Sweden this led to a drop in the sales of videocassette recorders to a level of just about 50 percent of the previous year, mainly due to hoarding before the regulations were brought in.

In the same manner taxes or levies may be imposed on the cassettes, either pre-recorded or blank ones. The reasoning behind this could be the same as with the recorders, but in addition there may be an idea of protecting the national broadcasting companies or movie industry, or of taking into consideration outdated copyright laws. In this case the levy must be fed back to the copyright-holders in some way. A few countries have regulations which take care of this.

Home video in relation to other media

New media are often compared with existing media. Home video has had its period of discussion about possible negative effects on other media. Gradually the primary tensions created have been unravelled.

Home video vs public television broadcasting

Initially home video was regarded as a threat to public broadcasting, at least by the broadcasting organizations. Now, home video is no longer looked upon as a dangerous competitor, as it was in the beginning. Broadcast television and home video are to a degree dependent on the same market, and the broadcasting companies therefore are interested in surpervising this market. For instance, both the Norwegian Broadcasting Corporation (NRK) and the Swedish Broadcasting Corporation (SVT) have made surveys on home video a standard activity, and ARD and ZDF in West Germany will add studies on the use of videocassette recorders to their continuous audience research.

Instead, the public broadcasting organizations have used the expansion of home video equipment as an argument for more financial resources — increased licence fees, and so on. They say that the videocassette producers raise the prices on copyrights, and that these companies can get exclusive rights. The broadcasting companies are also arguing that they have a right to arrangements for sports news reporting, regardless of what rights video companies have acquired. In some countries these questions are still unsolved.

Countermoves have been suggested by the public broadcasting companies: for instance, the companies could change programme policy and offer more live programmes. They might introduce pay-television or pay-per-view as a means of paying more for the copyrights. The question is whether pay-per-view systems would finally bring off-air broadcasting and home video into a state of competition. If popular movies are reserved for pay-television, then time-shifting recording might lose popularity.

It is said that time-shifting has had only limited effects on the time people watch television, although pre-recorded cassettes increase in number. The most remarkable change is that light viewers may become heavy viewers by the time-shifting function, while there seems to be no change in viewing time for the heavy viewers.

Gradually the public broadcasting companies have entered the pre-recorded cassette market, by releasing their programmes on videocassettes. However, no figures on the potential of that business are available. Recording off-air has not been regarded as a copyright infringement in Europe as it has in the USA. In January 1984 the US Supreme Court chose the European way. On the other hand, the issue of a levy on the sales price of blank tapes has been raised in many European countries in connection with off-air recording.

In all European countries there are restrictions on advertising on television. In three countries there is a ban: Denmark, Norway and Sweden. As long as home video was regarded as a competitor to public television, it was debated whether the same rules should apply to home video. In the Scandinavian countries, this issue seems to have declined in interest. The potential of home video as an advertising medium — spot advertising on pre-recorded tapes or in the video magazines (vidzines), and sponsorship — has been re-evaluated. In countries with regulations on advertising on television, like Finland and West Germany, there are discussions on the different treatment of public broadcasting and home video.

Home video vs press
Relationships between home video and the press have aroused interest in countries with press subsidy policies against concentration. In the Scandinavian countries one of the reasons for the ban on advertising on radio and television is that the daily press might lose advertising revenue. The daily press, being to a large extent financed by advertising, might be sensitive to competition in the advertising market from new media. Therefore, a ban on advertising on videocassettes has in some countries been demanded from the publishers. In other countries this has not been an issue at all.

Regardless of what will happen to the ban on advertising on videocassettes, as proposed by some publishers, there is little reason to believe it would become a serious problem. There are two reasons for this: first, the videodiscs, so far not a success, are probably more suited for advertising than the cassettes. Second, videocassette recorders are equipped with a speed scan device, so the viewer can zip through the commercial interruptions. Instead, publishers (e.g. Mondadori), have entered the video market and a number of multimedia companies have added video business to their traditional businesses.

Home video vs cinema
Although there is a lack of quantitative data, the effects of home video on cinema going have been discussed in some countries. Some (e.g. the UK) report very significant effects. The negative effects are unevenly distributed: big cities are not affected, but the countryside is. Total figures on cinema attendance conceal this fact. In some countries action has been taken to protect cinema against competition from video, e.g. Switzerland, where four cantons have forbidden video screening in restaurants and dance-halls.

In Norway it has been suggested by a Government commission that the rules for video should be harmonized with those for the cinema. One reason for this could be that there has been no regulation of video content, as there has been for years on movies. This might have led to a greater propensity among politicians to change the old Cinema Act. Cinemas are a municipal concern in Norway. The commission suggested that persons or companies interested in commercial screening, selling or hiring must have a concession. This concession should be paid for and the income used to support local culture, be it cinema, video, or something else.

One important group of actors is the movie producers. For instance the MPAA (the Movie Producers' Association of America) has applied heavy pressure to gain access to the European market for their movies. Already the European market is dominated by American productions, the USA generally speaking having a coverage of about 60 percent. To get a share like that, one procedure has been to sell movies in blocs: to obtain a new and popular movie, you have to buy a number of (old) B-movies as well.

Summary

In the past one-and-a-half decades, video seems to have matured as an entertainment medium, mainly for home use. The main uses of video are now time-shift viewing and watching pre-recorded cassettes. Two factors seem to be decisive for these uses, the number of available television channels and the existence of a rental market. In countries with a large number of television channels like Denmark or the Netherlands, the use of video to record one favourite show, while you are watching your other favourite show, makes sense. On the other hand, in countries with only one television channel, like Norway, one can imagine that there exists an urgent need for some variation in the menu. So in countries like Norway and Iceland, video is mainly used to watch pre-recorded cassettes, and this of course is dependent on a sufficient supply of video films. The UK, then, is the country where there exist both several television channels and great use of pre-recorded cassettes. The quick penetration of video in the British market is connected with the existence and effective operation of a rental market for television sets.

Summarizing on policy for video, we can discern two aspects, a cultural one and a financial one. The copyright question partakes of both. There does not seem to exist a uniform policy in this field; the measures that are taken seem accidental. The Scandinavian countries appear to be the most concerned, especially about violent and pornographic videocassettes. As far as industrial policy is concerned, those countries which have a large electronics industry themselves have been trying to protect their national industries. They have not been wholly successful, since the Japanese electronics industry for a great part has taken over the market.

When we consider video in relation to other media, we can conclude that video covers by-and-large the same market as television broadcasting and the cinema, but after an initial phase of fear of competition, there now seem to be only small problems.

The concluding remarks on video policy-making can be that video is not really a policy area, and that video is almost totally based on the market. Structures of distribution are largely unregulated, although there is a (growing) tendency to regulate content, in much the same way and degree as cinema film.

References

Darkow, M. (1984) 'Video in the Federal Republic of Germany', *EBU Review*, 4/1984.

Gustafsson, K.E. (1984) 'Forecasting Mass Media Development', *EBU Review*, 4/1984.

Howkins, J. (1982) *New Technologies, New Policies*, London: British Film Institute, the Broadcasting Research Unit.

Hulten, O. (1982) 'The Use of Video in Swedish Homes', *EBU Review*, September 1982.

Hulten, O. (1984) 'The Video Trend in Scandinavia and Finland', *Nordicom Review*, 1/1984.

InterMedia (1983) 'Video around the World', *InterMedia*, 4–5/1983.

Meyn, H. (1984) 'Die Neuen Medien — neue Chancen und Risken', in *Berlin: Politik kurz und aktuell, 41*. Berlin: Landeszentral für Bildungsarbeit.

Porter, M.E. (1980) *Competitive Strategy: Techniques for Analyzing Industries and Competitors*. New York: The Free Press.

Radevagen, T. and Zielinski, S. (1982) 'Video-Software-Annäherungs-versuche an einen neuen Markt', *Media Perspektiven*, 3/1982.

Radevagen, T. and Zielinski, S. (1984) 'Video-Software 1984 — Strukturen des Marktes und Tendenzes des Angebotes', *Media Perspektiven*, 5/1984.

Roe, K. (1981) *Video and Youth: New Patterns of Media Use*. Lund: The Department of Sociology, University of Lund.

Screen Digest (1984) 'Video Manufacturing and Market Reports', *Screen Digest*, June 1984.

Chapter 8
Mass telematics: facts and fiction*

Basic features of telematics

Among the new media that have, or are going to have, major impacts on the economic world and on people's lifestyles telematics undoubtedly occupies a primary position. In fact, telematics can be seen as the terminal point of the entire new media system: messages carried by broadcasting or by satellites and cables will be supplied to users by means of telematic media, such as electronic mail, videotex, teletext, videoconference, homebanking and the like.

The 'new television' (through DBS or homevideo), despite the fact that it enjoys more attention from public opinion because of the perspective of an enormous European television offer (about thirty-six national broadcast television channels) and audience (more than 300 million) has less of a revoluntary potential than telematics in the 'electronic village' of the 1990s. The 'new television' is just a more powerful or extended version of the 'old' television: the basic structure of its content (fiction, news, entertainment) is likely to change very little. In addition, it is not certain that it is going to influence radically either viewing habits or ratings.

Telematics, on the other hand, is a completely new adventure, liable to stimulate unprecedented social and economic demands and behaviours on a wide scale. Everything is new: the medium and the content; the hardware and the software; the offer and the demand. No wonder that one speaks of the 'telematic revolution', likening it to the industrial revolution in the extent and scope of its effects. Telematics, however, is also an ambiguous concept, a term used to mean different things: the medium; the networks; and the services in general. The origin of the term partially accounts for the confusion. It is, in fact, a combination of the words telecommunication and informatics, i.e. two fields which were independent until technological progress opened new possibilities for their mutual integration. Here we shall take as the correct meaning the one stemming from the official definition by ITU (1980–1):

> a set of services, different from the traditional telegraphic and telephonic ones, which can be provided to the users by a telecommunications net and which allow public and private information and data to be sent and received.

* Written by Gianpietro Mazzoleni.

The focus on the character of the 'service' of telematics — which distinguishes it from other new media like the DBS satellites and cable that have rather an instrumental character as means of transmission — does not exclude its being a medium in the traditional sense of the word. Like telephone and television, telematics is a means of communication between a sender and a receiver. However, while the telephone is always a medium between a single sender and a single receiver, and television is always a medium between an organized sender and a collective receiver, telematics can have both characteristics, depending on the type of service that it provides. Such a distinction is based on a sociological criterion, the same one that helps us to delimit our analysis and accounts for its title, 'mass' telematics.

Consistent with the scope of the book we take into account only the telematic services that enter into the realm of mass communication. According to McQuail (1983: 34–5), one can speak of *mass* medium when its 'message is not unique, variable and unpredictable, but often "manufactured", standardized, always "multiplied"'; when the receiver is — at least potentially — part of a large and heterogeneous audience; and when the relationship between the sender and the receiver is impersonal. Clearly telefax, the tele-conference, the teletex, telemedicine, homebanking and similar telematic services lack at least one of these conditions, whereas teletext and videotex are the only two telematic media that could answer to all the necessary criteria for consideration as mass media.

The content of teletext does not differ in principle from any normal television message; it is centrally manufactured by organizations and broadcast to a heterogeneous and potentially large group of users. The content of videotex has identical characteristics to that of teletext but, either for technical reasons (its distribution is via telephone cables) or for economic reasons (high service costs for consumers), its receivers are more limited in number. Even so, its messages are immediately available to a potentially undifferentiated audience. Moreover the interactivity of videotex is absolutely impersonal, given the standardized nature of the symbolic commodities being exchanged, and, especially, because of the formal nature of the user's interlocutor. In sum, telematics as a whole is a bridge between the sector of telecommunications and that of mass communication, for it belongs at the same time to both.

Incidentally, this is the reason why in different countries the telematic media are at times objects of specific telecommunication policy-making, and at times subject to broadcast media legislation. Such a duality is especially true for the two mass telematic services — teletext and videotex. The fact that policies regarding both these media are part of broader policy-making touching other electronic media, be they old or new, is an indication of the existence, at least on the intentional level, of an integrated approach on the part of several actors to the problems raised by what we may call the challenge of the coming electronic media revolution. A deeper analysis of the global effort of the European countries will tell us whether or not it has succeeded in moving from the projectual level to the construction of an effective, comprehensive media policy.

The origin and development of teletext and videotex

By teletext is meant a television broadcast of paged information that the user can call, select and visualize on a television screen. Videotex carries information through cables to users who can interact with data banks and visualize the required content on a special video-terminal.[1] These two telematic media have registered a rapid — but so far not intensive — diffusion in the countries of Western Europe, where they have different names. Teletext and videotex are in fact the standard names fixed by international bodies such as ITU and CEPT. Here follows, for each medium, a summary description of its development and of the policy-making regarding it.

Teletext

In Europe teletext was first developed in the early 1970s by British research, promoted by the BBC and IBA. The original purpose of that experiment had a limited scope: to help the impaired of hearing to follow the regular television programmes. Soon both researchers and promoters realized that the new technique brought with it several other potentialities. Accordingly, the social rationale behind the former politics turned into an industrial one, through the development of a totally new medium, the standard of which was fixed in 1974 and 1976 by the British Radio Equipment Manufacturers' Association. The BBC in 1976 and the IBA in 1981 inaugurated the regular teletext services called respectively CEEFAX and ORACLE. The BBC and IBA offer similar contents, differentiated according to their institutional orientation: more 'public service' on BBC, more commercial on independent television. As with their regular television broadcasts, only the IBA teletext carries advertising.

Practically in the same period — but independently — France developed its own teletext with a completely different policy approach: not broadcasting institutions but other media enterprises were primary actors; not specific social purposes, but a broad plan of mass informatics. In fact, ANTIOPE, the French teletext, is just a token of a complex telematic system, the Didon (Diffusion de données). In both countries teletext falls under broadcast legislation. No problems were raised in the United Kingdom where two existing broadcasting organizations were involved. In France, in order to allow other communication enterprises to conduct experiments, a piece of legislation had to be modified by means of 'dérogations' to the monopoly. However, licences were granted to the enterprises only on a provisional and revocable basis. Advertising was allowed by the French parliament in 1982, in order to guarantee adequate financing of the service. ANTIOPE has several functional identities (e.g. Antiope-Antenne 2, Antiope-Météo, Antiope-Route), called 'magazines' which are coordinated by a central public agency, the TDF (Télediffusion de France), which also takes care of their actual transmission. Access to the magazines takes different charge patterns, according to the nature of information requested. Magazines reserved for a profession or for closed users' groups (CUG) are charged, the public service-oriented magazines are free. The French government has intensively favoured the export policies of the hardware and software industries in order to promote national technical standards in direct competition with the British ones.

Teletext has had a reasonably fast, but still modest, diffusion in the rest of Europe. After the United Kingdom and France — the pioneers — some countries introduced it soon, others a bit later, depending on the domestic industrial and political conditions. In all cases, relatively long periods of testing preceded the final adoption. The decision to introduce teletext, and to choose the appropriate standard was mostly taken independently by the broadcasting organizations (West Germany, Finland, the Netherlands, Denmark). Policies worked out by public authorities (government and/or parliament) have in some cases (Italy, Sweden, Norway) guided the broadcasters' operational policies, for instance by imposing a pre-test period.

It is interesting to note that it was mainly in the northern countries that the service was initiated for overtly socially-oriented purposes, e.g. for the hard of hearing. Other European countries introduced teletext simply as a supplementary information medium for general use within a framework of new media development policies. Because of its technical characteristics, such as over-air transmission, teletext falls everywhere under broadcasting laws and regulations; it has, accordingly, been entrusted to the existing television organizations. Participation in management of teletext for enterprises other than broadcasting organizations is generally limited to the supply of contents. Such enterprises are mostly newspapers and press agencies which are the traditional producers of information. Their collaboration is a regular feature in the majority of the European countries, except the United Kingdom, Italy, Austria and the Netherlands where the press is not involved, the information being directly provided by the managing organizations (respectively, BBC and IBA, RAI, ORF, NOS).

The reactions of the users to teletext services are the best indicators of the success or lack of success of this new medium. There is no consistent pattern in the various countries, for the simple reason that some are far ahead with penetration and others are still testing. In certain countries opinion research shows consumers to be fairly dissatisfied either with the content or with the graphics, in some others fairly satisfied, and in a majority of countries openly satisfied. The main reason for high satisfaction — which, incidentally, is positively correlated with high penetration rates[2] — seems to be on economic grounds: teletext, unlike videotex, does not represent an extra burden on the family budget, as it is mostly offered free of charge. The only cost which users have to bear is the buying of decoders. However, thanks to governmental policies regarding the manufacturing of television sets with built-in teletext facilities, that cost can only decrease to a great extent in the near future.

Videotex

The history of videotex is similar to that of teletext, at least with regard to its technological development. Again the United Kingdom and France were the first to work on it in the early 1970s. The British Post Office Research Centre developed the PRESTEL system in 1970, while France enlarged the potentialities of ANTIOPE, the same system it developed for teletext. Unlike teletext, however, videotex does not originate in strictly social motivations, such as subtitling for the deaf. From the very beginning, the British Post Office's aim was of an industrial-economic nature: to make computerized information available to a large public via telephone networks. This basic goal has been pursued in the policies for videotex of all the remaining countries, where it has gradually taken on a predominantly commercial character.

The PRESTEL service became operative in 1979 in the United Kingdom, and TELETEL in 1983 in France. In the rest of Europe videotex has been tested extensively in the period between 1979 and 1984, but not all the countries had introduced it by the end of 1984. The reasons for such differences lie mainly in the relatively modest success — as far as penetration is concerned — in the countries where it had been already inaugurated, leading to caution in other experimenting countries in planning its regular start. Some countries simply made up their policies a lot later than others (e.g. Italy, Spain). Just as teletext is a broadcast medium falling under broadcast legislation, so videotex is a medium that stands within the domain of telecommunications. Accordingly, it is almost everywhere managed or controlled by the PTTs.

Unlike the broadcasting organizations with teletext, the telecommunications authorities and institutions, be they public or private, do not directly provide the content carried by the videotex medium. This task is generally entrusted to information providers of very different kinds: travel agencies, stock exchange, real estate, insurance companies, specialized data banks, banks, and the like. The most outstanding actors of the information-providing business are, though, the newspapers. From the very beginning, the press looked upon the new medium either with preoccupation — since it was seen as a threat to their information monopoly — or with great interest by the publishers who saw videotex as an extraordinary instrument for enlarging the readership of their newspapers and a source of profit. So, the press sector engaged intensively in all the pre-operational experiments, in some cases as key policy contributors and primary actors. Their enthusiasm cooled as soon as they realized that because of the slow penetration of videotex their investments would not pay off. Nevertheless newspapers have not given up completely. In some countries various publishers have created associations of information providers.

The even smaller success of videotex, by comparison with teletext, is certainly the result of economic reasons above any other. The terminals, keyboards and decoders are expensive gadgets, and the tariffs for the services offered are still out of reach of the mass public. This accounts for the unplanned but continuing specialization of the two media: teletext for the home and individual users; videotex for business or collective consumers.

Key issues in policies for mass telematics

Among the several issues raised by the processes of policy-making in the broad field of the new media and by the interplay of different actors, a few deserve a closer look. They are crucial for any survey of the comprehensiveness and suitability of the official policies worked out in Western European countries by governments, industries, commercial agencies and cultural institutions faced with the challenges raised by the 'telematic revolution' to their political, industrial, economic and social establishments. In a continent where monopoly control of electronic media and telecommunications is the rule, it is of great interest to point to any major or minor change, for instance, towards a deregulatory approach to the new media. Moreover, the economic and industrial sectors are heavily engaged in the development of telematics, and are directly bearing the thrust coming from worldwide competition. How do they adjust? What direction do their policies take? The rapid introduction of telematics is bound to have an impact on cultural patterns in all countries. What measures do governments and media organizations take in order to control a balanced transition to new patterns?

Teletext policy issues

Liberalize or not? As previously observed, teletext as a broadcasting medium follows the broadcasting monopoly structures which exist in each country. Some are very strict (France, Italy, Sweden), some are looser (the United Kingdom, West Germany, the Netherlands, Switzerland). So, significantly in all countries, it is governments that have entrusted the public broadcasting organizations with the task of initiating experiments, and have eventually authorized the same organizations to run a regular service. The only exceptions are the United Kingdom — whose government authorized both the public and the commercial services — and Finland, where experiments were freely conducted by either public or private entrepreneurs, mainly publishers. On the matter of the legal monopoly, the various governments do not vary according to their political colour: all (except the United Kingdom) maintain the public monopoly control over the service and do not show signs of deregulatory attitudes. Even the temporary 'dérogations' (1972, 1974, 1978) from the broadcasting monopoly granted by the French government in order to allow an experimental teletext service are far from being a signal of any loosening of the legal monopoly: they seem rather to be the proverbial exceptions that confirm the rule. No significant opposition by other actors (parties, industry, unions, etc.) to the legitimacy of the political power of monopolizing teletext is recorded in the countries under study.

By contrast, a wide variety of policy attitudes and styles is observable when one examines the issue of access. It can be said that governments, once having ensured their legal control (i.e. right to dictate norms) over this broadcasting service, show permissiveness towards private initiatives. To be sure, such permissiveness is not always self-generated but often induced by several pressures from interested actors. Access to teletext, nevertheless, is not to be confused with access to the running of the service, but simply a chance to participate in the provision of contents offered by the service. Given the informational characteristics of teletext, it is natural, as noted above, that the most interested are the newspapers. These are explicitly excluded from the running of the service in the United Kingdom and the Netherlands, and implicitly so in the remaining countries, but in almost all they are given access as information providers, and especially in France, Sweden and Switzerland. In West Germany and Austria, access for publishers was assured by government policies, but because of conflicts with broadcasting organizations, the press pulled out.

Economic-industrial issues. It has been pointed out that teletext was first developed by British research as an attempt to solve the difficulties of the deaf in following the regular television broadcasts. The policy issues were thus of a social nature at the beginning, but soon became industrial. By contrast, French development of ANTIOPE was industrial from the start. The philosophy which had inspired British and French teletext policies soon became predominantly industry-oriented: they favoured the adoption of national standards by the domestic electronics industry and the conquest of international markets. British industry registered a large success in the export of the CEEFAX–ORACLE systems and of the related hardware. Practically all Western European countries adopted the British standard. The French success was more limited, at least in Western Europe. One can say that there exists a sort of industrial monopoly of teletext technology, strongly held by the two pioneer countries. In view of this dependency on foreign technology, the introduction of teletext by the rest of the Western European countries is only partially to be explained in terms of domestic industrial development. Of course, domestic electronics firms do build teletext hardware for the internal market, but the relatively low demand for this new telematic medium means low profitability and little positive effect on employment.

The uncertain demand from users. Teletext, relative to videotex, is a medium that does not seem to raise dramatic commercialization problems in Europe. This does not mean that the economic side of the teletext enterprise has been disregarded. Despite the efforts made by the broadcasting organizations of many countries to advertise the service, its penetration is generally far from being achieved on any large scale. The United Kingdom, France, Sweden and the Netherlands are the only countries where one can speak of some success, even if there remain a lot of unsolved problems concerning the limited transmission capabilities of teletext. The initial difference between countries in the attitude of consumers is also quite significant. On a hypothetical attitude scale, West Germany ranked lowest: the experiments run by the two broadcasting organizations, ARD and ZDF, in a few cities had not aroused the enthusiasm of the potential users. Italy ranked somewhere in the middle: there had been some positive reaction from the sample of home consumers, and, on the contrary, much less interest from business. On the top of the scale we find the Netherlands where 95 percent of users had declared themselves enthused (data from Syfret, 1983).

It needs to be underlined, however, that crucial obstacles to the commercialization attempts by broadcasters and to an exact evaluation of consumers' interests are represented by: delays on the part of governments in choosing standards; the scarcity of decoders on the market; the high costs both of running a regular service and of the adjusted television sets; the low quality of software offered.

Focusing, in particular, on the problem of cost, the various countries have developed different policies, conditioned in some degree by the legal traditions of broadcasting. In the United Kingdom, the BBC teletext is one of the many services offered by the public corporation and its costs are covered by the same licence fees collected for television, since no advertising is allowed; ITV teletext, on the contrary, covers the costs through advertising (15 percent of the transmitted 'pages'). In France, parliament ruled in 1982 that the teletext service could be financed by advertising. In Italy, no decision has been taken by the government on advertising, but RAI is seeking authorization to carry advertisements. In Finland, the full-channel teletext is run by a company and has no financial problems, even if advertising is not allowed. In Switzerland, the service costs are covered by licence fees, advertising and by the information providers. In West Germany, Italy, Sweden, Austria and the Netherlands, the regular television licence fees appear to be the only source of revenue for teletext.

Overall, we can say that the solution to the financial issue raised by the introduction of the new medium in most Western European countries lies in the old scheme of the licence fee. Admission of advertising is still a policy followed by only a minority of countries. One of the main (not always manifest) reasons why advertising is not allowed by national policies is the protection of press interests (as in Sweden).

Decentralization. The issue of decentralization, in the sense of a structure of teletext service tied to the levels of more local realities (such as regionalization), appears as a specific topic of governmental or organizational (i.e. of broadcasting corporations) policy. The United Kingdom, France and Italy, that is large countries with more evident problems of geographically and culturally differentiated audiences, have plans for regionalization of teletext. West Germany already has a decentralized broadcasting system and, accordingly, a regionalized teletext service.

With regard to decentralization as a process, thus implying some form of deregulation, we do not observe any substantial sign of movement in this direction, except, again, in the United Kingdom. A form of decentralization with very peculiar features could be registered in Italy, where lack of specific legislation on commercial broadcasting makes formally impossible, but practically possible the establishment of teletext services by local and regional television channels. The case of the Netherlands seems somewhat contradictory: official media policies show a tendency to favour decentralization, but at the same time the sole control by the NOS of teletext is seen as a 'safeguard against fragmentation of editorial policy' (WRR, 1982: 40).

The cultural question. The question of what content should be carried by the teletext service in the different countries has never represented a critical issue of policy-making. Teletext has been considered by the majority of countries as a carrier of information (in the broader sense: news, public utilities, etc.) and of entertainment. No country has decided negatively; in other words none has issued regulations banning, for example, entertainment. The real question, instead, is how to fill the service, given so many technical, economic and social difficulties that for years have kept the teletext far from becoming a popular new medium, compared, for instance, to video.

However the issue which is by far the most discussed and also the source of most disputes between actors involved in the teletext business, is whether a too extensive and more sophisticated informational content may damage newspaper reading patterns. Governmental actors have kept out of such disputes which have involved, instead, broadcasting organizations and publishers.[3] The former hold that the structural characteristics of teletext (synthetical pages) do not satisfy all the information needs of the users; the latter, however, hold that people can get used to this content because it is fast, cheap and updated. A compromise between the two opposed interests has been found in some countries by entrusting (in part at least) to the publishers the task of information provision in the form of newspages.

On a further analytical level, the cultural issue has also to do with the diversification of content. Countries like the United Kingdom, France, Belgium, pursue a line of differentiation of the service, following four patterns:

1. differentiation stemming from the existence of different teletext services (e.g. in the United Kingdom BBC offers mostly news and public utility, ITV emphasizes business and entertainment);
2. differentiation fulfilling varied needs of the audience (e.g. in France TDF offers specialized magazines to specialized targets);
3. differentiation tied to language diversity (e.g. in Belgium the French-speaking channel and the Flemish one use diversified content that is consumed by bilingual audiences);
4. differentiation linked to the above-mentioned regionalization of the teletext service, that is, to an offer calibrated according to geographically-bound demand.

In most of the smaller countries, the theme of diversification of content does not appear to have been on the agendas of the main actors.

Videotex policy issues

The question of public control. As a telecommunication medium videotex follows the regulatory pattern of the TLC/PTT organizations which exist in the various countries. In Western Europe one finds a wide spectrum of legal schemes from strict public control to total non-regulation. Accordingly, policies for videotex are either worked out in monopolistic or liberalized milieux. For example, the choice of videotex standard was made by the PTT central authorities in those countries where the monopoly philosophy prevails.

At the extreme poles of the spectrum we find Italy as a jealous defender of public monopoly, and the United Kingdom, where British Telecom has been largely privatized by the Conservative government. The Italian SIP, the public telephone company, is the only organization authorized by the government to manage the telematic net and to run the videotex service. No private videotex is allowed. In the United Kingdom, major consequences of the privatization of British Telecom were the end of its complete control of standards and the possibility of competition for private videotex. The remaining countries lie somewhere close to one of the two extreme poles, some with mixed forms of monopoly-laissez-faire policies.

There is no sign of conflicts of policy as between different primary and relevant actors in the videotex sector in any of the countries, as far as the issue of control is concerned. The coming of telematic services does not seem to have particularly shaken the traditional TLC power map. Deregulatory pressures are a general feature of the new media field, rather than of videotex alone. In the videotex case, hardware and software industries did not challenge the existing political control patterns. The hardware firms' main interest appears to be directed towards liberalization of the terminal market, while the software organizations look for the widest circulation of information and data on the public videotex networks. Both these goals are regular achievements in all countries, with few or no restrictions being imposed by governments on demands of industry over the amount of the information supplied by the information providers.

In line with the lack of conflict on the control issue, the related question of the participation in videotex is similarly non-problematic. There exists no limit to the number of information providers, even if the managing institutions do, in some countries, hold some power to screen applications, mostly to assess the legality of the content offered. The links between different data banks and between private and/or publicly owned computers are regularly assured by the videotex in all of the countries.

Uncertainties in the industrial and commercial domains. As has been observed, the videotex medium has a relevant industrial background, especially in the United Kingdom and France where the governments or governmental agencies issued specific development plans. The philosophy of such policies was essentially the promotion of national industry. The policies for the introduction of videotex in the rest of Europe appear less industrially-oriented, but still economically-oriented. Telematic media are in fact universally seen as boosting factors of national economic growth. It is emblematic of this fact that not a single Western European country lacks a plan for videotex. The relative success of videotex penetration in some countries and lack of success in others has undoubtedly diminished the enthusiasm of the late 1970s and early 1980s. The limited penetration was at the beginning attributed to the inability of the hardware industry to provide enough decoders and terminals. Other reasons of a commercial nature appear instead to be responsible, as shown by the fact that the penetration rates have not risen substantially as soon as the hardware became abundantly available to the potential markets.

Despite the optimistic projections made by the PTTs and by the videotex managing organizations, one observes a widespread hesitation by hard- and software industries to invest capital in the videotex adventure. They might in the future — if penetration is successful — but at present they show a wait-and-see attitude, even in the two countries (United Kingdom and France) that between them enjoy the fortunate situation of having a monopoly of the videotex systems exported to all Western European and neighbouring countries. In the United Kingdom, for instance, Eastern Counties Newspapers and the *Financial Times*, which had engaged in the PRESTEL since the beginning, decided in 1982 to cut their videotex investments. In France, the situation appears less dramatic, thanks to the PTTs' bid to provide all the telephone users with MINITEL-Annuaire Electronique, which is, actually, something quite different from normal videotex.

For the aforesaid reasons, commercialization seems to be the key issue of videotex-related policies in Western Europe. Unlike teletext — which had taken on the nature of a further broadcasting service with its financing mostly covered by the television licences — videotex is an independent telecommunication service, requiring a specific financing that has ultimately to be drawn from tariffs and advertising. Accordingly, the success of the medium — in terms of its mass diffusion — lies to a great extent in the type of tariff and advertising policies worked out by the various interested actors. As far as the tariffs are concerned, there exist three different charge-patterns: for supplying information (together with the costs of preparing the software by the information providers), for telephone time, and for information consumption. Each can be a matter of policy-making and of negotiation between actors, including the consumers' associations — where they exist. Keeping the production of the access to information costs low and liberalizing advertising on videotex is the most successful formula. Against this, high tariffs for access to the service and to different kinds of expensive information plus a ban on advertising is a pattern that is scarcely likely to promote the fortunes of videotex. In between one finds a mixed pattern of high access-costs matched by a fairly large freedom for advertising. The majority of countries fall in to the last pattern, which appears to be the most viable in Western Europe.

From a strictly economic point of view, low tariffs are only possible once the number of users becomes very large. On the other hand, the penetration of videotex could receive a big push from a low tariff policy. The dilemma is undoubtedly hard to resolve. Thus one finds actors engaged in all sorts of alternative promotion practices, such as the Deutsche Bundespost giving free decoders to 5,500 Düsseldorfers and Berliners at the end of the experimental phase of the Bildschirmtext. The problem of whether to have advertising or not on videotex has, moreover, been a thorny one in a number of countries. The newspaper business was alarmed at the introduction of the service, fearing the loss of a good slice of the advertising cake, and above all, the collapse of press circulation.

There have been some conflicts between publishers and videotex managing organizations, ending in compromises (as in West Germany) because the former recognized the futility of a 'conservative' resistance to a new medium. Given the impasse on the commercialization issue, the mid-1980s' picture in Western European countries was of an increasing specialization of the videotex service, with business and industry as crucial users, but without any sign of its reaching a mass public.

Overview

The slow growth of mass telematics in the Western European countries is an undeniable fact. How should we interpret it? From this rapid review of policy-making and policy issues in the teletext and videotex sectors, we can infer that mass telematics does not appear to be at the top of the long-term strategies of either governmental or economic-industrial policy-makers. The scarce engagement, with few outstanding exceptions, in any active promotion of the telematic media by any of the interested actors, the reluctance of capital to invest, the absence of a comprehensive plan for telematics by the EEC (but see Chapter 3, pp. 30–31), are but three indications of the weakness of the mass telematic media if compared to the substantial achievements of other new media. A further explanatory factor is to be found in the prevailing industrial philosophy of the few ad hoc policies worked out in the previous decade. One can expect, as a matter of course, that the United Kingdom and France will pursue industrial goals because they invented the videotex and teletex hard- and software and had to conquer the domestic and foreign markets. It is less clear why the remaining countries, which after all depended on British and French technology, in a frontierless flow of goods assured by the EEC for most of them, privileged industrial interests over the cultural and social ones. The consequence cannot be other than a surplus on the offer side — with negative fall-out on profitability of the industrial activities themselves — and a sluggish demand both for the services and for the technical means. Free from any obligation to feed domestic industrial appetites, the political authorities of the mass-telematic systems purchasing countries had the opportunity to stimulate, by appropriate policies, the social and cultural demand for the new media. The attitude of policy-makers in the test periods does not appear particularly dynamic in that sense, with the effect of leaving the mass of potential users indifferent vis-à-vis the new media — as several surveys have revealed.

Thus, in the mid-1980s we have the paradoxical situation of a great availability of advanced technology largely unexploited by a rigid consumers' market. The gap between offer and demand raises serious doubts about the actual meaning of the 'telematic revolution'. As long as the policy-makers and interested actors do not fill this gap, the expected rapid change in the cultural patterns and in the lifestyles in the post-industrial world, may just be wishful thinking.

Notes

1. Technical details are not given here. They can be easily found in several specialized and popular publications.

2. At the end of 1984 there were 2,400,000 teletext sets in the UK and 1,500,000 in West Germany that is in the two countries where recent (1984) research shows consumers to be most satisfied (data from EBU Teletext Seminar, Vienna, March 1985).

3. Except the German government which allegedly delayed the experiments of teletext as a political concession to newspapers.

References

McQuail, Denis (1983) *Mass Communication Theory*. London: Sage.

Syfret, T. *Television Today and Television Tomorrow*. London: J. Walter-Thompson.

Wetenschappelijke Raad voor het Regeringsbeleid (WRR) (1982) *A Coherent Media Policy*. The Hague.

Chapter 9

Breaking the broadcasting monopoly*

In a comparative perspective, there has until recently been a characteristic West European model for the organization of national broadcasting (radio and television). The model is distinctly different from the American model, as well as from the postwar East European model. This does not imply that the organization of the broadcasting system is the same in all countries, but the similarities clearly overshadow the differences. In its ideal-typical form, the West European model consists of a nationwide public monopoly which, although controlled by the state in matters concerning organization and finances, is still fairly independent in its programming policy. In the American model, the public monopoly is not known, and in the East European model the public monopoly is considered a tool for state and party interests.

One of the most clear-cut effects of the new developments in media technology has been a dissolution of the West European broadcasting model. In a number of countries, the monopoly is already broken, and there are more upheavals to come. The purpose of this chapter is to analyse this change. We will examine some central features of the monopoly system and look at the conditions under which it has been established, maintained and finally abolished. We also discuss the new organizational structures that seem to emerge.

The 'monopoly' concept and its application

The concept of 'monopoly' is borrowed from economics. A standard textbook definition could be the following:

> A pure monopoly exists when there is one producer in a market. There are no direct competitors or rivals, either in the popular or technical sense. However, the policies of a monopolist may be constrained by the indirect competition of all commodities for the consumer's dollar and of reasonably adequate substitute goods, and by the threat of competition if market entry is possible (Ferguson, 1969: 253).

In a traditional market theory, monopolies are the undesirable results of competition between suppliers of goods or services. The European broadcasting monopolies are the planned results of

*Written by Asle Rolland and Helge Østbye.

political decisions. When a sector of the economy has been monopolized by market forces, it is no longer subject to consumers' control. When monopolized by political decisions, it may indirectly be maintained or abolished by the consumers, acting as voters.

Thus, we may distinguish between monopolies established by market forces and those established through a political process. A market-based monopoly undermines the very idea of the consumers' influence on the quality of the product. The underlying logic of the broadcasting monopolies, on the other hand, lies in the consent of the established political elites, which in turn are the representatives of the consumers, acting as voters.

The relationship between the broadcasting monopolies and their audiences depends on the relative importance of broadcasting politics in the general political debate and on the ability of the political process to represent the views of voters. If the electorate articulates demands concerning the monopoly's policy and these demands are widespread and intense, or if such demands are strong in some important parties, this will lead to pressure on the broadcasting institution from the audience. If, on the other hand, the political parties' aggregate interests tend to cut across audience attitudes or if media politics is of little importance, the audience will have limited influence on the decisions made by the political elites in media politics.

The West European broadcasting model has been adapted to quite different sociopolitical and economic conditions. It had served a number of political purposes, and the means employed have not always been the same. But even though the monopoly concept has been used differently in different settings, some features seem to be almost universal.

If we look at the various elements of the communication process, we find that monopoly rights are restricted to transmission only, and do not cover the production of content or the reception of the signals. A broadcasting monopoly means that only one institution is allowed to send from a given territory. Where production is concerned, each broadcasting institution may be located somewhere on a continuum from automony to dependence on other producers, the position being determined by factors like economy — the transmission hours must be filled with cheap foreign material — or political demands, for instance, to support and promote the national culture (see Chapter 1). When it comes to the reception of signals, there is no requirement to use the services offered by the monopolies, nor is there any prohibition against tuning in to foreign stations. But the monopoly's basic financial form, the licence fee, implies that the initial way of thinking at least involved a generic cohesion between a monopoly of what was to be sent and of what would be received. In some countries there was talk of a monopoly to cover even radio receivers, just as the PTT monopolies covered telephone sets.

Any broadcasting monopoly must have a geographical definition. Most European countries established nationwide monopolies, with one institution serving the whole nation. These institutions have, subsequently, very often started regional broadcasting. This is the original British Broadcasting Corporation model, which countries like France, Italy and the Scandinavian countries adopted. But there are exceptions to this definition of the monopoly, particularly where cultural and linguistic conditions within the country made centralization difficult. In countries like Belgium and Switzerland, each linguistic group got their own broadcasting service. To the extent that the linguistic groups live in separate areas, this model will create formal or de facto regional monopolies. Audience figures indicate even that people from the different Swiss and Belgian language groups, when supplementing the national television channel(s) in their own language, prefer foreign channels in their own language to national channels in a 'foreign' language. In Norway, where the two official languages are very similar, one programme could serve both linguistic groups.

There are other deviations from the ideal-typical monopolistic concept. West Germany is a federal republic where the states, Länder, were made responsible for broadcasting. Hence, West Germany has regional monopolies, which, in turn, have been 'added up' to form national television networks.

In the United Kingdom and Greece, duopolies have emerged. In Greece, EIR was established in 1945 as a continuation of the public company from 1936. The second company was gradually established by the Armed Forces in the postwar period, and changed in 1982 to a second state-controlled broadcasting company, independent of EIR. In the UK, the independent television companies (within the IBA group) were formally established as regional companies, but most of the programmes are transmitted nationally. The programming policies of the two bodies, BBC and IBA, are almost identical.

An interesting hybrid is found in Finland, a mono-duopoly model. The national broadcasting corporation, YLE, sells a substantial part of its programme time to a private company, MTV, which gets its revenues from commercials and is responsible for its own programming on YLE's network.

In Italy, there is a monopoly for national broadcasting, but local radio and television is allowed for private companies. The Italian case draws our attention to differences between the legalities and the actual performance. Legally, RAI has a monopoly on national television in Italy, but the government has been able neither to regulate private broadcasting, nor to enforce RAI's monopoly on nationwide broadcasts. As a result, the private stations have organized themselves into national networks. The Swedish Broadcasting Act indicates the possibility of several broadcasting companies, but here the monopoly is established through a formal agreement between the government and the broadcasting company. During the period of this agreement, the monopoly is protected by civil law, and thereby less likely to be changed than if it had been part of a law that could be changed within a few weeks. In Norway, the Broadcasting Act gives NRK a legal monopoly, from which the government is allowed to give only limited exceptions. But since the government has allowed 120 local television stations and 330 local radio stations to operate, the reality of the monopoly has disappeared.

We often find a close resemblance between the control system for broadcasting, and other structures developed to compete with conflicting interests in pluralistic societies. In multilingual countries like Belgium or Switzerland, each language has its own service, and in a consociational democracy like the Netherlands, the major 'pillars' of the society are reflected in the separate, independent broadcasting organizations coordinated by the Dutch Broadcasting Foundation, NOS. The highly centralized French governing structure was transferred to the broadcasting system. The British idea of broadcasting as a public service — guiding BBC as well as the IBA activities and exported to many of the West European countries — is clearly modelled after the rules for neutrality and impartiality governing the civil service in general. In other countries, there are formal or informal procedures for the sharing of political control over broadcasting management, the staff of different channels, and so forth.

Whether all these different organizations can be subsumed under an operational definition of monopoly is doubtful. For those accustomed to a strict interpretation of the concept, some of the national models seem pretty competitive. But the actual use of the concept in the various political debates is not governed by the requirements of comparative research. In actual usage, the monopoly concept is one of those political tools that actors define according to the goals they have and the issues at stake. Therefore, the objective definition and subjective perception of a monopoly situation may not coincide at all. What appears as monopoly in one context, may seem competitive from another point of view. To a certain degree, this depends on different evaluations of what is actually the effect of a broadcasting monopoly. For some actors, monopoly constrains the freedom of speech and limits pluralism. For others, it is the only way of guaranteeing a fair, even and balanced programme. In West Germany there has been an important debate on the advantages and disadvantages of 'pluralism from within' (Binnenpluralismus) as compared to 'pluralism from outside' (Aussenpluralismus).

From an audience point of view, satisfactory 'demonopolization' may be obtained simply by allowing any other voice than the one authorized by a single broadcasting headquarters. Even competition between channels and programming departments, or decentralization within the organization, may lead to the desired freedom of choice or pluralism. Tendencies in this direction have been noticed within the existing broadcasting monopolies during the last decades. As a response to public demands and extended competition in the audience market (radio vs television, pirate radio stations, increasing number of national channels, increase in reception of listening and viewing from neighbouring countries, cable networks, satellites, video, etc.), even the broadcasting monopolies have changed their programmes, decentralized and increased the number of channels in order to attract a broader audience.

On the production side, we find interest groups or companies applying in vain for a licence to send, either in order to have their views disseminated or to earn money. To them, any limitation of access may appear as a monopolistic protection of those who got there first. All broadcasting models will appear monopolistic to newcomers since there will have to be restrictions on the establishment of new enterprises.

The broadcasting monopoly model may be contrasted to a complementary competitive model. But we must bear in mind that there is an asymmetry between these models, since the monopoly may be total, while the competition is always limited, due to a limited number of possible channels. And it is not always clear what they are competing about. Audience attention is an important part of this, but what is the reward for success and failure? If one company is financed by a licence fee while the other(s) are supported by advertising, they are in a sense not fighting for the same money. If one is guided by objectivity principles while the other(s) preach their gospel subjectively, they are not fighting for the same effects, etc.

Establishing monopolies

The establishment of broadcasting monopolies in all of West Europe is more than a historical contingency. There is a number of common reasons, of which some will be discussed here. Probably the most important factor is the need for regulation of broadcasting.

A monopoly is frequently the preferred solution for the exploitation of limited natural resources and situations in which production or distribution of the commodity make for substantially higher prices if competition is allowed. The classical economists called this a 'natural monopoly' (Ferguson, 1969: 255). Broadcasting is based on techniques for the utilization of electromagnetic waves in the air. When first discovered, the waves were used for wireless telegraphy. Wired telegraph and telephone systems were usually organized in national or local monopolies, and electronic communication of this kind cannot function without traffic regulations. Thus, broadcasting satisfies any requirements for speaking of 'natural monopolies' based on the utilization of natural resources.

Radio as a mass medium started in the USA. The first regular transmissions took place in 1920, with the Westinghouse Company acting as initiator. The company's motive was to stimulate the sale of home receivers of their own make. Within a few years, there was an almost explosive diffusion of radio stations, and in 1923 there were more than 500 major stations and approximately 1,400 small stations all over the country. The establishment of new stations was left to free enterprise, with no entrance regulations. In 1923 'every spot on the frequency band was occupied, some by several stations. The broadcast band could not be extended without severely infringing upon other important kinds of radio and wireless operations' (DeFleur, 1970). Finally, in 1927, the worst chaos was brought under control by the Dill-White Radio Act, which introduced the Federal Radio Commission (later the Federal Communications Commission or FCC) as the regulatory body.

The Norwegian-American sociologist, Thorstein Veblen, introduced in 1915 the idea known as 'the advantage of backwardness'. He showed that Germany would soon surpass Britain as the leading industrial country in Europe, since the latter had 'the penalty for taking the lead' (Veblen, 1966). If Veblen had written his book only a few years later, he could have introduced broadcasting as another proof of his theory. In the years following the first broadcasts in 1920, influential actors like European PTT directors returned from visits to the USA, expressing their shock over the chaos the Americans had created. Thus, in the case of organizing broadcasting, the Europeans had the advantage of *not* taking the lead.

The American experience had shown that broadcast communication could not function without traffic regulations, otherwise the whole communication process would collapse. The European latecomers were determined not to repeat the mistakes made by the innovators.

Among the countries that learned their American lesson was the UK. The BBC was established in 1922 and national monopolies followed very soon in a lot of countries (Italy in 1924, Sweden in 1925 and Ireland, Denmark and Finland in 1926). In other countries private radio, with some public regulation, existed for some years, but were then converted into public corporations (the Netherlands in 1930, Norway in 1933, Greece in 1936 and France in 1945).

To this diffusion process explanation, we will add those instances where a foreign solution was imposed upon the recipient country. In postwar Germany, the decentralized model for broadcasting is to a large extent the result of the fear the Allied Forces felt of a united and strong Germany. Each of the four occupation zones got a broadcasting system similar to the system of the country that controlled that zone.

Most countries had to hand a potential 'model' for the organization of broadcasting. The national telecommunication structure was normally organized as, or integrated in, national monopolies. From the very beginning, broadcasting was considered a telecommunication activity (rather than, for instance, something like newspapers or magazines), to be regulated by the telecommunication authorities. In France, for instance, the telecommunication monopoly was extended to include radio transmission as early as in 1923.

The same PTT authorities and their strong international bodies — the International Telegraph Union dates back to the 1860s — took firm control over the regulation of traffic between countries. Radio waves were used for point-to-point communication for several decades before radio turned into broadcasting. The basic regulatory framework was already available in the Radio Convention of 1906, made by the International Radio Union established the same year. (In 1932 the International Telegraph Union and the International Radio Union merged into the International Telecommunications Union, ITU.) The need for international regulations was stronger in Europe, with many countries within a relatively small area, than in most other parts of the world.

For all countries, the choice between broadcasting models was partly determined by the results of international conferences concerning allocation and reallocation of frequencies, whereby the number of channels available for each country has been decided. With a very limited number of channels available, an overwhelming majority of the European countries reserved the channel(s) for a public institution. The only exception turned out to be Luxembourg. Radio Tele Luxembourg, RTL, is a private corporation controlled by foreign capital. The broadcasting company is by far the Grand Duchy's biggest taxpayer.

The need for national and international co-ordination in the broadcasting sector draws our attention to a more general point in political theory: the state's authority rests on its ability to make binding decisions concerning the reallocation of limited resources. Without regulation, broadcasting cannot function. If there is no public regulation, private regulations will appear. Particularly in the interface between international order and national claims, regulation can hardly be left to private bodies without undermining the state's authority. But also at the national level, a government's determination and ability to enforce its decisions is of some importance.

Finally, there was a demand for national networks and unifying forces at a time when the resources were scarce and the nation-building processes in most European countries called for integration of different social and geographical segments of the population. Broadcasting is often referred to as a part of the infrastructure tying internally heterogeneous nations together. Many of the new broadcasting monopolies saw daylight during the great depression.

Maintaining or breaking the monopolies

It was stated at the outset of the chapter that broadcasting models are established, maintained and eventually abolished, by decisions made in the political system, and only indirectly by actions taken in the market. This implies that the monopoly structure will be preserved as long as political alliances mustered in favour of it are stronger than those against.

It was also stated that the development of new electronic communication techniques has started a disruption of the monopoly model. This implies that there have been a number of decision-making points in the past where politicians might have chosen *not* to maintain the monopoly. One such point was, of course, the establishment of television as a dominant new medium. But for a long time, most European broadcasting monopolies were widely accepted. Like most organizations, they had been growing. The monopolies were originally established to produce and transmit radio programmes. They normally started with only one radio channel, and gradually increased their number. The introduction of television did not change anything; television was incorporated within the same organizational structure, often financed by money from licences paid by the radio owners.

Technological change is not, in itself, sufficient to break down the monopolistic model. Neither is an increase in the country's capacity for electronic mass communication. Independent of this, there must be widespread (at least in politically influential circles) dissatisfaction with the monopoly, either due to its programming policy or for more ideological reasons. But if there is a very small number of channels (frequencies) allotted to the country, if money is short, and so forth, there is still a pretty good chance that monopoly will survive.

Among the actors mustered in favour of a monopoly solution, we of course find the broadcasting institutions themselves. Since broadcasting is based on advanced communication technology, they have also had the advantage of monopolizing the national know-how, and have thus been able to tell politicians what they should do on 'purely factual grounds'. In addition, they have also found support in organizations like the European Broadcasting Union (EBU), or by referring to the way things are done 'elsewhere'. But the limits of the institutions' knowledge, may set boundaries to their expansion. The incorporation of television and (later) teletext into the original radio monopolies was eased by the fact that these technologies had been developed within the existing broadcasting framework. But the broadcasting institutions were left out of the discussion concerning videocassettes, videotex, cables and to some extent satellites, since these media were based on technologies different from those of basic radio and television.

The alliance between the broadcasting and the telecommunication monopolies may, for some time, have been an advantage for both. But the recent development of cabling may lead to a competition between the two institutions.

It is usually assumed that any monopoly will fight to prevent any invasion of its territory by a competitor. However, according to one student of monopoly, Hirschman (1970), there is a category of 'lazy monopolies' for which this may not hold true. A lazy monopoly is one which, rather than using its position to exploit its customers, fails by producing inferior goods at unnecessarily high costs. According to Hirschman, a lazy monopoly may actually prefer to have some limited competition in order to provide what he calls an 'exit option' for the most quality-conscious and vocal customers (those who exercise 'voice'), thus removing pressure and allowing the old, lazy ways to go on. This description may well fit the case of some European broadcasting organizations, at least from certain points of view. The evidence is to be found in complaints about high licence fees and low programme quality. In general, the broadcasting monopolies have tried to trade off their different vocal critics against each other. This has been possible because most criticism comes from elites and there are different opinions about what constitutes 'high-quality' content. The danger for lazy monopolies which allow limited competition to ease pressure (e.g. from religious critics of secular programming) is that it can breach the principle of monopoly and open the way to large-scale desertion of audiences. In general the more elite 'exit options' are the safest and this may also apply to local programming exceptions as well. On the whole, it had to be said that the European broadcasting monopolies have not shown themselves to be lazy in encouraging 'exit options', but have fought hard to maintain their status.

The opportunity to keep broadcasting under control is probably a major reason for the fact the broad coalitions have been established in favour of monopoly. Some fifteen years ago, Norway's leading conservative media philosopher argued that nothing could be more democratic than broadcasting monopolies because of their vulnerability to 'voice' (in the sense used above). A decade later, as Minister of Culture, he broke the monopoly on grounds that nothing could be more undemocratic (Bakke, 1981).

Over the years, the broadcasting monopolies have been concerned about the use of voice by their most 'quality-conscious customers'. Such individuals and pressure groups can influence major decisions concerning organization and finance of the broadcasting institutions, since they have easy access to the political channels. On the other hand, the monopolies have been protected from direct pressure from the audience, since the revenues are not directly related to the size of the audience. Therefore, they have developed a 'social responsibility' model for their programming. The main principles of this model can be summarized as follows:

- Media should accept and fulfil certain obligations to society.
- These obligations are mainly to be met by setting high professional standards of informativeness, truth, accuracy, objectivity and balance.
- In accepting and applying these obligations, media should be self-regulating within the framework of law and established institutions.
- The media should avoid whatever might lead to crime, violence or civil disorder or give offence to ethnic or religious minorities.
- The media as a whole should be pluralistic and reflect the diversity of their society, giving access to various points of view and to rights to reply.
- Society and the public, following the first named principle, have a right to expect high standards of performance and intervention can be justified to secure the, or a, public good. (McQuail, 1983.)

Obviously, an institution with goals like these will receive a lot of sympathy among cultural and political elites. It is equally obvious that it will have problems in a competitive market based on audience demands.

However, the preservation of monopolies is more dependent on coalitions established outside the realm of broadcasting, than by any action taken by the broadcasting institutions themselves. As long as significant actors find their interests better served by a monopoly than by a competitive model, the system will not be altered. This includes situations where the monopoly is preferred as the 'lesser of evils', or serves as the acceptable compromise between strongly conflicting interests. A labour government with weak support from the press may not be satisfied with the treatment it gets from the broadcasting institution — and it does need support to counteract the bourgeois newspapers — but it may still prefer the monopoly to 'independent', bourgeois radio and television channels. A bourgeois government based on support from liberalistic business interests as well as conservative segments of the society, may be in favour of both commercial and paternalistic broadcasting. A possible (and common) compromise is to allow advertisements within the existing public service monopoly.

It seems that the following three developments in media technology have been particularly important for the break-up of broadcasting monopolies:

— *satellite transmission and video explosion*, which increases the number of channels and programmes that are beyond national control,
— *cheaper transmission equipment*, which enables even less wealthy actors ('ideal' or commercial) on the local level to start broadcasting, and
— *cable transmission and FM radio*, both making a higher number of broadcasting channels available at the local level, and thus within the country as a whole.

There are some differences in the timing of these events. FM transmission was introduced decades ago, and there has been a gradual increase of cable television systems. On the other hand, the video explosion and the launching of communication satellites with television channels (and the plans for direct broadcasting satellites) represent more dramatic steps in the development. Thus, media technology has led to an increase in the number of electronic communication channels available.

The development of community antennae into larger cable networks that transmit programmes from neighbouring countries has reduced the importance of the monopolies, seen from the audience's point of view; they now have alternatives to their own monopoly. But as long as the alternatives from the neighbouring countries were produced according to the same general principles, the national monopolies were not really threatened. The real challenge has come from the video explosion, the 'treats' from satellite television, and the development of cable networks from community antennae into programme-producing units.

Furthermore, the new technology has other capacities than just an increase in the number of channels. As long as each European country had only one or a very limited number of television channels allotted to it, hardly anyone thought of creating organizations for multinational or local television programming. With the advent of satellite transponders and cable channels, there was suddenly a strong interest in these organizational forms. New technology has also led to improved utilization of existing communicational means, creating new media like teletext and videotex. The importance of the supply may be compared to any (economic) activity based on the exploitation of limited resources. Once new resources are found, the political system must decide what to do with them. They cannot be handled over to the market forces, because the market presupposes free enterprise and supreme control by the consumers while, in the case of limited resources, the freedom to establish new enterprises is prevented by those who came there first.

Hence the politicians must decide who should be licensed to take part in the exploitation of new resources, who should operate the new channels and manage the new media. Should the original radio monopolies, already expanded to cover television, continue to grow into teletext, videotex, cable television and satellite broadcasting monopolies? Or should the field now be opened to private entrepreneurs? Who should own and operate the second, third, fourth, etc., channel that we now can afford? To what extent and in what form should competition between private enterprises be allowed: local, regional, national or international? Should private business and public institutions compete, or should there be a division of labour between them?

In this discussion, the fact that broadcasting also has something to do with culture becomes important. The setting of the old broadcasting companies has been that of a highly centralized institution, with most of the input to the system coming from social, cultural and political elites, and not from the audience. To some extent, the underlying dissatisfaction with the monopoly system is caused by this. The case of the UK can illustrate this point. Tunstall (1983: 33–4) argues that one of the reasons why it was possible to break BBC's television monopoly in 1955 was a widespread dissatisfaction with BBC's highbrow programming policy.

There were broad coalitions behind the broadcasting monopolies. The core of these coalitions consisted of the intellectual establishment and liberal and social democratic parties. It seems, however, that the coalition behind the monopoly will rapidly become vulnerable if two or more of the following interest groups (segments) manage to establish an alliance:

— Commercial interests that want advertising, etc.
— Groups with sufficient economic resources to establish their own channels
— Groups that feel their views are not properly represented in radio and television (sender interests)
— Groups that feel their interests are not properly satisfied by the programmes in radio and television (audience interests)

Again, the breakdown of the BBC television monopoly gives a good illustration. In addition to the above mentioned dissatisfaction with BBC, there was, at the elite level probably, a coalition between profit-oriented businessmen in the Conservative party and ideologically oriented conservatives who wanted competition and freedom of choice (for a more detailed discussion, see Tunstall, 1983: 38). The same coalition is now found in Norway, perhaps with the same result.

New organizational forms of broadcasting

Many actors have interests in the field of broadcasting. Regardless of public policy, some actors will have access to the broadcasting media while others are left out. These kinds of decisions can be taken by public decision-making bodies (like parliaments, governments, municipal councils, etc.), by the economy (even though the equipment for transmission has become cheaper, it is still too expensive for most organizations to run their own radio channels, and television is many times as expensive), or by the public (which has a limited amount of time to spend on mass media, and which will select among available channels according to economic resources, interests, etc.). There will have to be a discussion on the principles of selection. The lack of a formal decision on this issue has the same kind of consequences as a formal decision.

What will follow the old monopolies? One part of the answer lies in the factors that have undermined them — the development of new organizational forms for the transmission of broadcasting. The old monopolies were national institutions. National borders defined their extension. The new developments seem to reduce the importance of the state as a unit for the dissemination of messages. Two conflicting tendencies can be observed: decentralization and internationalization.

Local radio and local television — via the air or cable — have had a very rapid growth in most West European countries during the last few years. These local channels very often bring locally-oriented programmes. Over time, this local orientation may increase the importance of the local communities, and give them more political and cultural importance at the expense of the state.

On the other hand, satellite broadcasting and, to some extent, video and extended cable transmission of programmes from neighbouring countries internationalize the message people will receive. Language, rather than nation, may be important in the choice of programmes. This, too, may reduce the importance of the nation.

Conclusion

In most countries of Western Europe, the original broadcasting monopoly has been broken in varying degrees and in varying ways and the process of demonopolization is continuing, perhaps quite rapidly, in the mid-1980s, when this book is being written. As noted in the outset, the key feature of the politically established European broadcasting monopoly was a monopoly of radio and television transmission, within the national boundaries. This was supported by a compulsory licence which tied the receivers to the transmission monopoly in a certain way. It was also generally the case that the transmission monopoly, especially because of the costs involved with television, brought with it a de facto production monopoly.

The changes which have taken place were sometimes dramatic, as in Italy where, in effect, an entirely new privately financed and operated national television network was established within a few years of the challenge to the state monopoly in the mid-1970s. More commonly, as in Germany, the Netherlands, France and Belgium, the process has been represented mainly by the legalization of television transmission outside the established public system, using cable networks (and sometimes satellite transmission) and financed by non-licence revenue, whether from subscription or advertising. Characteristically, the new services are supplementary to, but often competing with, the public services. Nearly everywhere, the changes in the situation of the transmission monopoly have been accompanied, often preceded, by an erosion of the original de facto production control and also the control of reception. Changes in market conditions and technology outside national governmental control have played their part in weakening the support and wings of the original monopolies.

The old broadcasting institutions have, in most countries, remained surprisingly unchanged in their goals and structure. They have acquired competition, but have been able to retain the licence system, while their competitors have to fight for limited new money from advertising and subscribers. The ex-monopolies may well be vitalized by competition in the audience market and are likely to undergo an adaption of goals, so that commercialism in some guises will show itself even in the socially responsible public service institutions. They have so far shown a capacity to survive, as long as the coalitions behind them have remained reasonably firm. Nevertheless, they have entered a new phase, with an unpredictable future, during which the forces leading to break-up or modification will not go away and may gather momentum.

References

This chapter is based mainly on information extracted from the 'National Reports' written for the Project. In addition to these, there are a few other references.

Bakke, Halvard (1980) *Står NRK-monopolet for fall*. Oslo: Cappelen.

DeFleur, Melvin L. (1970) *Theories of Mass Communication*. New York: McKay.

Ferguson, C.E. (1969) *Microeconomic Theory*. Homewood (Ill.): Irvin.

Hirschman, Albert O. (1970) *Exit, Voice and Loyalty*. Cambridge (Mass.): Harvard University Press.

McQuail, Denis (1983) *Mass Communication Theory*. London: Sage.

Tunstall, Jeremy (1983) *The Media in Britain*. London: Constable.

Veblen, Thorstein (1966) *Imperial Germany and the Industrial Revolution*. Ann Arbor (Mich.): Ann Arbor Paperbacks.

Chapter 10
Culture at stake*

Introduction

The technological developments which are currently under way involve drastic changes in processes and systems for collecting, storing and distributing information. Until now, the purpose for introducing new machines and techniques has primarily been stated in economic, technical and organizational terms. Thus, it is said that machines will save manpower and salaries, and they will also facilitate the transference of vast amounts of information. Business will no longer be 'as usual'; rather it will be performed via computer terminals and in teleconferences, reducing the amount of both time and money which are necessary for conducting negotiations and reaching an agreement. As for citizens, it is expected that they will obtain more and easier access to information about public affairs, thus having better opportunities to participate in a democratic society.

Industry, as producers of both hardware and software, and the business community as users of the same, have for several years pushed technological development forwards and they have also, to a great extent, defined the relevant issues in the public and political debate. Cultural aspects have been quite sporadic in their appearance in the political debate about the social consquences of new technology, including the electronic media.

The purpose of the present chapter, therefore, is to describe the extent to which cultural aspects have been included in political debates about new media technology. Firstly, a general theoretical framework for a cultural analysis is presented and, later, this is applied to media policy in the countries which are included in this study.

Culture, media technology and society – a theoretical framework

The phrase 'cultural aspects of new media technology' implies a causal relationship between technology and culture. Such a notion should at once be challenged as involving too simple a framework for understanding the processes behind innovation of new technology and its implications for society. Technological developments take place within certain social structures, and will in turn effect changes in the same social structures.

---

* Written by Marit Bakke.

The same reciprocal relationship applies to media technology and culture. Both phenomena must be seen as reflections and consequences of certain social structures. Thus, descriptions of specific societies and significant structural dimensions serve two purposes: they help us to understand how media have developed and have put their mark on the present media structure, and they give a basis for evaluating the extent to which cultural issues have been relevant in the public and political debate about new media technology. This chapter will, on the basis of information received about each country participating in the project, try to identify those cultural issues which have been and currently are being seen by various actors as relevant, crucial and important in relation to the new media technology.

But first the concept 'culture' has to be explained. This is not the place to make a detailed description of the manifold interpretations of culture. Generally, there are two extreme definitions: (a) the anthropological one in which culture is 'whole ways of life', and (b) 'works of art' according to an aesthetic approach.[1] For our purpose the first approach is too broad, while the second is too narrow.

In this chapter the concept culture will be treated as having two elements:

1. values, ideas, meanings, beliefs (i.e. content)
2. the way, or the social order in which, values, ideas, meanings, beliefs are exchanged, i.e. the communication order or network.

The second element refers to relationships and networks, and not to the concrete means used for transferring different types of symbols and signs. The means belong to the technical part of our subject, i.e. they comprise the new media technology which we will be looking at: satellite, cable, video, teletext and videotex. The relevance of distinguishing between media as something technical on the one hand and communication networks as something social on the other hand, can be illustrated by Mumford's (1963: 13) statement that the clock was an almost 'inevitable product' of monastic daily life in the middle ages, representing both regularity and accuracy. The theoretical framework for the analysis can now be summarized in Figure 1.

From the figure three questions can be derived which will form the basis for later analysis. Regarding the content element the question is: What do or should we communicate about? And regarding the network, the question is: How do or should we communicate? It is the thesis of this chapter that the answers to those two questions will vary according to the specific media technology we are looking at. Thus the third question is: In what

FIGURE 1
Theoretical framework for the analysis of cultural aspects of new media technology

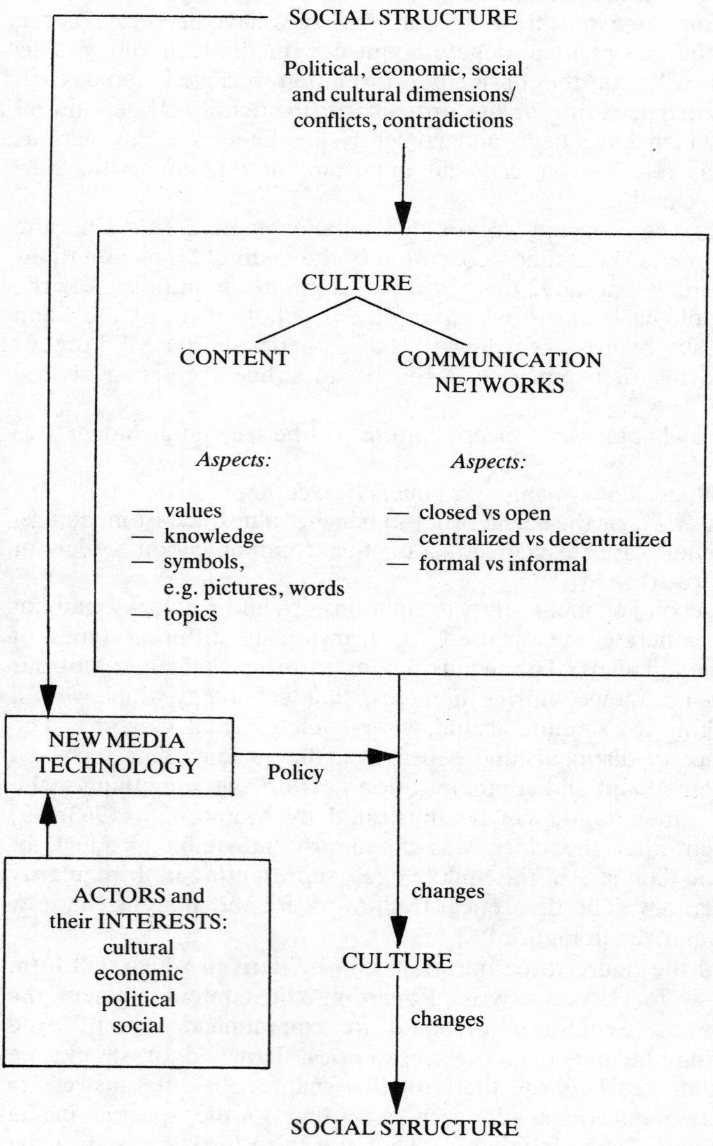

way will the new media technology affect the communication networks and the content transmitted via these networks? This, then, is the key issue in the overall theme of culture and media technology. However, since the media technology under scrutiny are indeed new, we are not yet able to tell what the effects are. What we can do, is to look at to what extent various actors have used culturally related arguments either in favour of, or against, certain media technological developments. Which actors express concern with respect to specific cultural aspects? Which actors take policy initiatives, and who makes decisions?

Cultural aspects of European media policy

In the theoretical framework presented in Figure 1, culture was defined as comprising content and communication networks. In addition, our crucial question has been stated as possible cultural effects of new media technology.

Figure 2 shows the four main issues which have been brought up in respect of media content: identity; quality; balance/diversity; and commercialism. The figure then lists the European countries in which one or more of the four issues have been salient, and it also shows how the relevance of each issue is based on certain structural characteristics or dimensions.

Content aspects

Starting with the content element, we can describe those aspects which various actors consider may be influenced during the development of media technology. Afterwards, we can look at factors on which changes in the content may depend, especially access and control.

There are two kinds of involvement by actors: on the one hand there is concern and advocacy expressed in various ways from 'outside', as it were and, on the other hand, there are decisions which are made explicit in regulations and laws by those in control. The following actors have, thus, participated in the media policy-making process: government (via commissions, proposals, regulations, laws, etc.), political parties, voluntary associations, software producers (film industry, video and broadcasting companies, etc.) and minority groups.

Identity is probably the dominant cultural issue in almost all countries, caused by the prospect of a multitude of satellite-transmitted foreign programmes. However, there are differences between countries, depending upon the degree to which foreign programmes are regarded as a threat to local, regional or national identity. The regional level is relevant in France, Germany and

FIGURE 2
Cultural issues related to media content

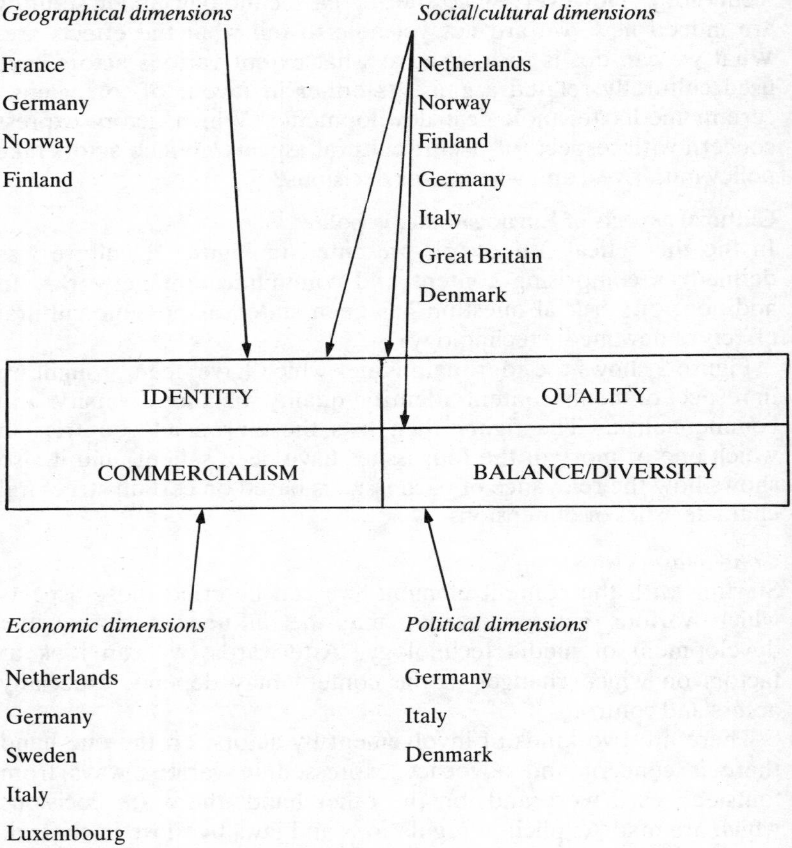

Norway. In France regional movements have been arguing for possibilities to preserve their cultural identity, partly against the centralizing influence from Paris, partly against foreign programmes. In Germany the federal constitution leaves all aspects of culture to the Länder. Here, all political parties regard media content as important for promoting Länder identity and cultural autonomy. In the third country, Norway, two forces act in support for regionalism. On the one hand there is the traditional geographical centre–periphery division and, on the other hand, the recent drive by the bourgeois government for decentralization, which is also part of a strategy for breaking the broadcasting monopoly. A decentralized media structure is regarded as the means for maintaining and developing these regional identities, and cable systems may strengthen this trend.

A concern about national cultural identity has particularly been expressed in Italy, the Netherlands, France, Finland and Denmark, with governments as the most ardent defender of this aspect. The French government has talked about the 'English language imperialism', while the Italian government is concerned about 'cultural colonization'. Naturally, the launching of a series of satellites can generally be seen as a serious threat to a nationally-oriented cultural policy. And satellite transmissions combined with local and regional cable-television will in a few years time offer impressive communication networks, which will be very difficult to control. The import of foreign video programmes is also seen as quite problematic and, so far a few countermeasures have been tried (see Chapter 7).

In 1982 the French government stated that the general objectives of broadcasting should be to defend the national culture and encourage programmes which presented local life. The development and regulation of cable has played a central role in the government's media policy. A general rule for programming on cable-television was decided upon in April 1984, in which the government stated that at most 30 percent of total programme time might be of foreign origin. In an attempt to control the amount of foreign video programmes, the government has imposed restrictions on the import of video hardware, e.g. a high tax and particular technical specifications. The government has also tried to encourage associations and cultural industries to establish a multimedia group which could compete with the huge production from American companies.

Since 1978, the Dutch government had tried to revise the Broadcasting Act, partly in order to be able to cope with the increasing flow of foreign programmes. In a 1983 memorandum the Cabinet stated that the general goal for its media policy was to protect the national culture. The following year, in June 1984, a government memorandum for satellite and cable-television transmissions proposed that at least 5 percent of total programme time should present national cultural material, and that the percentage should increase to 20 percent during a five-year period. Most political parties are in favour of some kind of control of foreign programmes, and only the Liberal party is against restrictions.

In Italy, it is particularly the left parties which have pushed the cultural influence of foreign software as an issue in the political debate about media. However, the situation is still characterized by non-decision. Since 1983, there have, however, been plans for a law which would demand that between 15 and 30 percent of the total programme time should be self-production, i.e. national programmes, as a condition for private broadcasting stations to obtain a licence. In Finland, the government has proposed a law according to which at least 40 percent of cable-television programming should be of Finnish origin.

After having seen that some European countries are quite concerned about foreign threats to regional and national cultural identity, we may ask what is the basis for this concern. Is there a general uncertainty and scepticism with respect to foreign influence as such, or is there a real fear that the import of foreign television programmes will be even larger than at present, thus challenging the existing value pattern? Some evidence on the actual situation is available. Table 5 provides estimates of the amount of total programme time which each country included in this study imported from abroad in 1983 (the first column). The second column shows whether there has been an increase or decrease in the amount of imported programmes, and the third column tells how many countries the programmes are imported from.

The table invites one comment in particular — two of the countries in which concern has been expressed about 'cultural imperialism', France and Italy, rank quite low with respect to amount of imported programmes, respectively 19 percent and 18 percent. The import to the Netherlands is also fairly limited, at 25 percent. Is the attitude described above then based on scepticism towards foreign influence in general, rather than reflecting a genuine concern about national identity? The problem of foreign influence may be related to the fact that between 1973 and 1983 the amount of imported programmes had increased significantly in France and in Italy.

According to Table 5, Denmark and Finland are the two countries which do in fact have grounds for being worried about threats to their national cultural identity, importing respectively 43 percent and 37 percent of total television time. However, they both import from many different countries, thus reducing the risk of receiving a limited set of cultural values. In fact we might argue, on this basis, that certain countries are more internationally oriented than others. Thus Sweden, Denmark, BRT in Belgium, Finland, Norway and the Netherlands import programmmes from between nine and twelve different countries. To this observation must, however, be added that the USA contributes a relatively large share

TABLE 5
Television imports in European programming

European countries ranked according to proportion of imported television programmes in 1983; change since 1973, shown as proportion of total programme time on national networks; number of significant importing countries; amount of imported movies in 1983, in percent of total movie programme time.

	1983[1]	Change between 1973 and 1983		Number of significant importing countries[2]	Movies
		+/−	No information		
Denmark	43		x	11	91
Austria	43		x	5	90
Finland	37	−3		9	85
Sweden	35	+2		12	65
Spain	33		x	6	87
Norway	30	−9		9	75
Belgium					
RTBF	29		x	7	94
BRT	28		x	11	93
UK, Channel 4	26		x	7	100
Netherlands	25	+2		9	100
W. Germany,					
ZDF	21	−9		6	30
France	19	+8		7	53
Italy	18	+5		5	74
UK					
BBC	15	+3		5	69
ITV	14	+1		2	31
W. Germany					
ARD	14	−9		2	54

Source: Varis, Tapio (1984) *Flow of Television Programmes in Western Europe: Data during January 31–February 13, 1983*. Tampere.

[1] Cable programmes are not included.

[2] Only countries contributing more than 1 percent of the imported programmes are counted.

of the imports, from 20 percent in Norway to 34 percent in the Netherlands and Belgium, BRT. USA is the primary importing country to fourteen of the national networks which are included in Table 5. Great Britain ranks second in eight of the national networks, and it is only in Norway (32 percent) and Denmark (27 percent) where most of the imported programme time has British origin. The percentage of imported programme time is definitely largest with respect to movies, and the amount is presented in the last column in Table 5.[2]

There is no doubt that the issue of national identity is present in most European countries' media policy debate. However, so far the issue has primarily been raised by governments in public reports and proposals. Left-wing parties have been more sporadic actors. In relation to the issue of identity, it is also interesting to note that there are indeed indications of a transnational or, rather, a European identity. And it can be found in Luxembourg. Luxembourg is the only country in which media policy is aimed at establishing pan-European television programmes and where national identity is missing as a cultural issue in the political debate. However, national economic interests can clearly be identified with respect to the production of hardware (see Chapter 12).

A similar, although less strong indication of a European orientation can be found in the British government's proposal regarding cable television. The transmission licences are to be given by the centralized Cable Authority, partly on the basis of the companies' plans for bringing news and information from and about countries within the EEC.

A transnational orientation was the basis for the plans for a Nordic satellite, the so-called NORDSAT. The main actor was the Nordic Council of Ministers, and in 1978 it commissioned a group to look particularly at the cultural implications of satellites. In 1979 a joint report (NUA 1979: 6) expressed agreement among the Nordic governments (in Denmark, Finland, Iceland, Norway and Sweden) that the purpose of NORDSAT would be to support the work otherwise being done for Nordic cultural integration. This could partly be done via the exchange of nationally-produced programmes, but an important means to this end would be the new jobs and wider distribution opportunities for artists and other cultural workers.

In 1981 a minority in the Danish Media Commission voted in favour of NORDSAT, giving cultural cooperation as one of the most relevant arguments. Only by participating in joint ventures would it be possible to counterbalance the expected flow of foreign programmes transmitted via satellites, thus supporting the development of a Nordic identity. A majority of the Commission members rejected the plans for economic reasons. Also the Norwegian government found the price too high and withdrew from the plans. Instead the Finnish and Norwegian governments have expressed interest in taking part in a Swedish communication satellite, the Tele-X (see Chapter 6).

TV5 is another transnational media initiative with a broadcasting organization as the main actor. The station started broadcasting in 1984, being sponsored and run jointly by French-speaking stations in three countries (the three state-owned channels in France, RTB (Belgium) and Telévision Suisse Romande (Switzerland)). Its main purpose is to promote the French language in an effort to counterbalance the strong English influence via satellite-transmitted programmes. In the long run this initiative may result in a European channel.

Quality. So much for the issue of identity, now we turn to the issue of quality. The different actors have separate definitions and interpretations of quality. Generally governments emphasize traditional 'high-cultural' standards, while actors such as private, commercial broadcasting and liberal (right-wing) parties interpret quality as 'that which the audience likes', i.e. content which is preferred by a majority, so-called popular content.

Quality has been explicitly stated as a media policy issue in Great Britain and Italy. Indeed a number of British commissions of enquiry reports (e.g. Annan) have emphasized that the media have a national image-building (representation) and cultivating function. Within Britain public media should strive to keep high cultural standards, thus trying to keep the public from consuming mediocre mass culture. In relation to other countries, the government sees it as important that England, particularly London, is presented as a world media centre, particularly with respect to producing software of high cultural quality. Therefore, any means which can strengthen Britain's position on the international software market are encouraged, like producing television programmes and facilitating satellite transmission. Unisat 1 — the first planned operational Direct Broadcasting Satellite in Europe — is one example of such image-building activity. In the early 1950s part of the government in the Netherlands opposed the introduction of television because it was feared that television would mean a degradation of culture. A similar concern about cultural standards has also been expressed by the present government with respect to the content which is and will be transmitted via cable and satellites.

An indirect demand for high quality may be said to be found in regulations banning violence, pornography and blasphemy in video and television programmes. Such laws exist in Finland, Norway, Sweden and Italy. In Germany part of the CDU Party has argued in favour of initiatives which can protect the family institution and religious values, and the protection of cultural standards is an important issue for the Dutch government.

Balance/diversity. The issue about quality is partly related to two other cultural aspects, balance and diversity. According to Figure 2, balance and diversity as cultural issues are related to either political or social dimensions in the societies' social structure. The political dimension is relevant in the case of Germany and Italy. Thus a Federal Constitutional Court decision in 1981 stated that the 'Länder' are obliged to guarantee that programme content generally reflects the existing diversity of public opinion. In Italy one of the reasons for supporting the publicly run broadcasting company (RAI) is that it is said to be best suited to safeguard political-ideological diversity. This issue is particularly relevant in face of the uncontrolled growth of local broadcasting and the expected increase in satellite transmissions.

There are other countries in which balance and diversity are seen as cultural issues based on social and not only on political structural dimensions, i.e. in the Netherlands, Norway, Finland, Sweden and Italy. This is particularly the case in the Netherlands. Already in 1930 the Dutch government ruled that only broadcasting corporations representing existing political, religious or ideological pillars in society would be allowed on radio. The Broadcasting Act of 1969 stated that broadcasting time should be allocated to the organization according to number of members (in practice, the number of subscribers to specific broadcasting magazines). Because of the growth of pirate radio stations, the government's great concern has also been to control and secure the religious and ideological diversity at regional and local level. The general secularization process during the 1960s had also contributed to impair the 'pillarized' basis for programme-making and distribution. The 1969 Act also dealt with another aspect of diversity by ruling that broadcast content should be reasonably balanced between entertainment, culture, information and education.

In other countries, diversity is often a question of having programmes which convey the ideas and values of different ethnic and language groups, e.g. Swedish in Finland, Finnish in Sweden, Lappish and New Norwegian in Norway, French, German and Serbian in Italy, Flemish and French in Belgium and Catalan in Spain.

Government has been the one type of actor which has felt most responsible for securing diversity in broadcast content. In those European countries where radio and television are state monopolies, diversity is built into programme regulations. Along with the current demonopolization process in several countries (see Chapter 9), the governments' strategy for guaranteeing diversity is apparently to grant broadcasting licences to a broad spectrum of private interest groups.

Commercialism is the last element which we shall consider in relation to content aspects of culture. Although commercialism is treated more thoroughly in Chapter 11, its cultural implications necessitate some comments also in this chapter. While the issue of diversity is based on the idea of fair representation of interests and values among the population, commercialism is related to success in the audience market. Thus commercialism is connected with economic interests, particularly possibilities for revenues from advertising and from the selling of media software.

The problem can be stated quite succinctly. The new media technology will drastically expand the possibilities for transmissions across long distances, i.e. to new and larger audiences. They will also increase the content volume, i.e. amount of programmes and various kinds of information, which may be transmitted. Thus there are two markets: one for regular programmes (media software), and one for advertisements. The cultural implications can naturally be seen in the extent to which these two markets are coordinated. The more advertising is allowed either during programmes or in separate blocs between programmes, the greater the incentive for trying to avoid controversial or 'boring' programmes. And if we look at just the programme side, it may be expected that, to the extent that companies are established in order to produce and distribute television programmes, there will be a drive for large markets, which, in turn, most probably puts a premium on non-controversial content. In this way, the issue of commercialism is definitely connected with the quality issue.

Technical developments introduce some contradictions in national media policies, more strongly in some countries than in others. On the one hand, it is evident that, except for Luxembourg, national identity plays an important role in all European countries' media policy, particularly for the state. On the other hand, the new media technology rapidly presents technical 'necessities', thus more-or-less forcing an international perspective on media policy. The contradiction between national values and technical potential is further emphasized by the fact that the networks offer more transmission capacity than it is possible to fill with national production. The problem arises in relation to the expansion of home video, and to the increasing number of television channels and satellite transmissions. As long as it is impossible to supply the video market or supply television time with home production, the solution will be to import software. This is already the case in Italy, and is partly the reason why left-wing parties have brought up cultural 'imperialism' as an issue in the political debate.

The relationship between advertising and programme content is an issue in most European countries, particularly in those countries where advertising is not yet allowed in broadcasting, i.e. in Belgium, Denmark, Sweden and Norway. In Sweden industrial interests in the 1960s argued for establishing TV2 which would carry commercials. Nothing came of the compaign, partly because the government wanted to protect the economic basis of the press. There has been similar pressure on the governments in the other two Scandinavian countries, but so far advertising is not allowed. However, the issue is a salient one in the ongoing debate about media policy. The bourgeois parties use it as an element in the general policy for breaking the state broadcasting monopoly. At the local level, these parties are joined by some of the private groups which are involved in experiments with local radio, and which regard advertising as one way of financing both the experiments and, later on, permanent local radio.

Since the middle of the 1950s, the CDU, in particular, pressed for commercial television in Germany. Advertising was allowed in 1956, but through rules made in 1961, 1971 and 1981 the Constitutional Court has put severe restrictions on commercial television.

Communication network aspects

Some of the cultural aspects related to content which have been discussed in the preceding section partly depend upon characteristics of the communication network. In this section we shall particularly look at two network elements which have cultural implications, access and control. Thus we can briefly state the proposition: the kind of content, i.e. ideas, values, topics and knowledge, which is presented via the media, depends upon who has access to media channels and/or who is in a position to control the content which is transmitted.

Electronic media are characterized by quite complicated technical equipment, a fact which has at least two consequences. First, not everyone has enough money to invest in the material which is necessary for transmissions via radio, television, cable, etc. Thus we find that electronic media in Europe are either state-owned or financed by private companies. Also, the more advanced the technique, the more centralized does it tend to be in organization. Secondly, not everyone has the necessary knowledge to make the most of electronic media's possibilities. Usually private citizens must leave the control of the product's final presentation to professional media people. Thus technique, economy and professional knowledge are factors which clearly limit the possibilities for access and control by various groups or individuals. The question is how have public or private owners of electronic communication channels coped with this problem.

All countries included in the study have general government statements regarding 'freedom of speech' and 'free flow of information'. In addition there are some specific regulations with respect to access for different groups. Regulations of this kind have been established partly as a consequence of the government's principle of diversity, but they have also been pushed by various minority and ethnic groups. The Dutch system has already been described, where the state has prescribed forms of access based on religious-ideological pillars in the society. However, the increase in the number of pirate radio stations has represented a threat to the government's attempt at securing its chosen form of diversity on the air. A similar problem may arise in France, where an Act of 1982 legalized free stations, giving associations and cultural industries the possibility to produce and transmit programmes. This system should not jeopardize the government's stated policy that media should be a 'service publique'.

In Germany, access for minority groups is somewhat limited, not for technical, but for political, reasons. As described earlier, the German media system is closely connected with the political party system. This means that access to a greater extent is defined according to political than to ethnic and social differences, with the 'Länder' governments as the major actors. The Italian media structure includes special radio and television broadcasting stations for French, German and Serbian minorities, thus giving these groups direct access to communication channels and control of programmes. The Finnish media system contains possibilities for a similar arrangement, by allowing any organization to apply for a broadcasting licence. In Norway, the Broadcasting Law states that a certain amount of programme time should be presented in New Norwegian, the dialect-based second language. Since people speaking New Norwegian often also represent religious and temperance movements, the language rule indirectly secures access for these two sets of values. Although the regulation is a formal one, these pressure groups quite actively check the programmes in order to make sure that the rule is followed. The expansion of local radio has meant that many groups have obtained easier access to electronic media. Thus public access is guaranteed in the Swedish local 'Everyman's Radio', and in Denmark religious and various voluntary organizations have regular programmes on local radio. According to a Norwegian law from 1982 institutions and organizations can produce and transmit programmes at the local level.

When we talk about access to electronic media in a cultural perspective, cultural workers and artists must be mentioned separately. Today cultural activities are regarded as being separate from economic, political and social institutions. Thus culture is no longer an integrated part of everyday life as it used to be in the days of artisans, guilds, etc., in feudal societies. Crafts, music, etc. were basically made for immediate use, and artists' work was supported by patrons who regarded it as an integral part of the routine activities at a court or in a nobleman's household. Thus the cultural workers and artists did not have to depend upon success in a market. Along with changes towards a market economy, the relationship between the cultural producers, their products and the audience also shifted; from being fairly direct and personal the exchange became more complex and anonymous. The new electronic media contribute to this process. On the one hand, electronic media have increased the distance between cultural workers and the public, and turned it into a more anonymous relationship. On the other hand, the cultural workers and artists have less possibility to control the production and distribution process.

Naturally satellites represent the most extreme communication network, leaving the programme originator with no control whatsoever over the distribution process. Once a television programme is made, the rest is left to the international trade of software buying and selling. Even this may be difficult to control and will be more so, considering the expanding video market and various plans for European television satellites (see Chapter 6). One aspect of this development is the question of copyright, which is treated as a specific issue by the Council of Europe, the Nordic Council and the EEC Commission (see Chapter 3).

Concern about cultural workers can be found in a few countries' discussion on media policy. In 1983 President Mitterrand said that he was worried about the decrease in French artistic and intellectual production. Also within the cultural community itself, misgivings have been expressed (e.g. by authors) about the way they are treated by mass media, particularly television. In Great Britain the production of software is partly seen as one way to support the British film industry, both by the government and by the industry itself.

While satellite transmissions may give diversity in programme output, decentralized media structures at both regional and local level may be the best means for diversity of access and control. This is also reflected in several countries' media policy. During the 1970s and during the first years of the 1980s, regulations and laws involving decentralizing measures were passed in France, the Netherlands, Sweden, Norway, Denmark, Italy and Luxembourg. In Luxembourg's case, the argument from RTL was that free radios should be local in order to keep RTL's monopoly on programmes intended for foreign audiences. In all other countries demands for local media reflect genuine interests by various pressure groups — religious in the Netherlands, Norway and Sweden; ethnic in Spain and Italy; cultural-ideological in the Netherlands and Norway; linguistic in Belgium, Finland, Norway and Sweden; geographical (regional) in France and Norway. Indeed in France the official media policy has decentralization as the key word, partly in order to encourage regional and local integration. In Germany we are once more faced with the dominant role which the Länder play in the media structure — there are just a few local television stations (in Berlin and Hamburg) and very few local radio stations. In Finland, the public broadcasting company, YLE, is negative towards local radio, while private companies and trade unions are positive.

It is evident that the various new media technologies have different implications for the degree and kind of access and control. Cable is generally regarded as an excellent means in a decentralization process. However, due to the big investments necessary for the installation of cable, which will have to be financed by market principles (i.e. according to the number of subscribers), cable systems will tend to be limited to the urban parts of a country. Such a development will be against a principle of equality with respect to the distribution of information, entertainment and cultural programmes.

On the other hand satellites encourage plans for transnational communication networks, giving new opportunities for corporations which are interested in producing software. The risk is that mediocre programmes will dominate and set limits to the cultural policy which the government of any one country may have. Luxembourg is, as described earlier in this chapter, the only European country which does not have national identity or decentralization as central elements in the media policy. On the contrary, official media policy is based upon interests for the European market. Consequently, plans for expanding satellite transmissions to neighbouring countries are given first priority. This includes both the technical means — the hardware — and the production of software.

Telematics may be the most influential means for changing communication networks. Through the combination of several techniques it will be possible to exchange huge quantities of information. So far, government and representatives from the commercial sector have shown interest in this development, the former for reasons related to the public-versus-private-control issue, the latter primarily for economic reasons. A general concern — as, e.g., expressed in Italy — is the role of telematics with respect to moving society towards a post-industrial era. Culturally, this may imply less personal communication, linguistic changes involving standard phrasing, increased use of abbreviations, etc. So far, we know very little about such possible consequences.

New media technology gives rise to yet another general comment concerning cultural policy, one which has to do with what cultural activity really is. If consumption of cultural programmes in, e.g., radio and television is regarded as equally 'cultural' with the very making of such programmes, new media technology contains vast possibilities for increasing the public's level of cultural activity, If, on the other hand, taking part in cultural life excludes the consumption of products in the media market and, on the contrary, means being involved in activities which emanate from people's own experiences, then the new electronic media will indeed be detrimental to cultural life in the years to come. This question has not, however, been dealt with in the political debate.

Media technology and integration

The way in which the title of this chapter is phrased indicates a separateness between culture and media technology — that they are two different entities. Actually this may not always be the case. In fact communication networks can be looked upon as constituting one particular aspect of a society's culture. This interpretation can often be found in studies of national development, in which efforts to establish mass media structures are regarded as part of a nation-building process. For instance, Deutsch (1966) applies the word 'integration' to processes comprising the exchange of goods, symbols and messages, and he identifies three types: communicative, normative and functional.

Communicative integration refers to the means which are used for exchanging information and messages, i.e. technical networks. Thus we may characterize the culture of Western European countries as a technical one, because a considerable part of the information exchange both within and between countries, is done via formal, technical devices. Normative integration has the usual connotation, i.e. symbols and values which are manifestly expressed (e.g., through media content), and which are generally agreed upon by people within certain boundaries. The playing of national anthems before football matches and flag-flying on independence days both express some degree of normative integration. The third integrative aspect — functional — entails the division of labour, e.g. between the hardware and software sides of media industry.

If we apply Deutsch's concepts on the European scene with respect to the new media technology, the problem can be stated in terms of a dilemma between normative integration on the national level or on the international/transnational level. National integration is explicitly said by governments in most countries to be one of the goals for mass media transmissions. Reactions to the prospect of transnational integration are more uncertain and mixed. So far the state's attitude in France, Italy and the Nordic countries is sceptical. Both Italian and French politicians talk about 'cultural colonization' to the detriment of national and regional/local identity. It is difficult to judge whether the scepticism is based on concern for the international 'community' or fear of American domination, or both, i.e. that the international cultural community will be established according to American criteria. In either case, national values will be at stake.

Hartmann (1980) states the problem in terms of a change in the classical phrase 'Who says what to whom with what effect?' into 'Who is communicating to whom and in whose interests?' In whose interest is *Dallas*? The question becomes even more relevant as we can observe the merging and integration of different media institutions. The process has already started in several European countries, involving newspapers, cable and local television companies. The co-operation between the Luxembourg government, Murdoch in Australia and Bertelsmann, is the most prominent example.

The situation which confronts us is very similar to what has already taken place with respect to an international market in which both news, and natural resources and commodities have been exchanged. The problem has been seen in terms of dominance and dependence. Expressions like 'the new international economic order' and 'the new international information order' reflect the acceptance that an ongoing 'natural' process may have to be changed. The imbalance in the exchange of news across countries has been well documented in several studies. The music recording industry gives another example of the existence not only of an international communicative integration, but also of a normative integration. The tendency is most conspicuous within pop music, with the Beatles and Abba as the most significant examples.

Three trends seem possible with respect to the cultural order both at the national and international level: mass culture, cultural domination, and cultural diversity. The first two have been discussed in several books and articles, for instance in the MacBride report (Unesco, 1980, p. 32).

> In setting up ever more powerful, homogeneous and centralized networks, there is a danger of accentuating the centralization of the public or institutional sources of information, of strengthening inequali-

> ties and imbalances, and of increasing the sense of irresponsibility and powerlessness both in individuals and communities. ... by intensifying competition, it may lead to the standardization of content and, at the international level, accentuate cultural dependence by increasing the use of imported programmes.

What then can be observed on the European media scene? If cable networks and satellite transmission are combined we have a situation where McLuhan's expression 'the global village' seems at least technically appropriate. The first steps towards a European media community have already been taken, particularly by EBU. The Sky Channel is already transmitting to Norway, and the EEC has plans for a European television, satellite and cable channel.

At the same time as we see tendencies towards technical integration, there are trends towards some kind of division of labour. On the one hand there is a pronounced French policy to develop an independent electronics industry. On the other hand British companies are producing documentaries and entertainment programmes for an international software market. Both trends are encouraged by government bodies. Both public and private media organizations have demonstrated an interest in developing new media technology. To these must be added the European PTTs, which partly cooperate through EUTELSAT. So far, however, transnational actors have primarily been interested in building technical networks, although the copyright issue is, as mentioned on pp. 35–8 above, regarded as a real problem.

It is noteworthy that only politicians and public commissions have reflected upon the potential cultural effects of new electronic media, while private actors like media industry and publishing companies have mainly emphasized economic aspects.

Now it would be naïve to conclude that it is only purely cultural considerations which have motivated governments and various minority and ethnic groups to bring cultural issues into the political debate about the new media. Although the concern about cultural issues is genuine, it must also be seen as having both economic and political aspects. For instance, the French government's emphasis on national culture can partly be seen as pretext for defending and promoting the national electronics industry. The same kind of twofold motivation is also relevant with respect to the British government's use of culturally based arguments, i.e. by promoting quality programmes for export to other countries the government at the same time gives an incentive to the British software industry.

Loss of control may be seen as another issue which implicitly lies behind cultural considerations. Thus a great influx of satellite programmes will make state regulations about broadcasting licences and advertising obsolete and irrelevant. Such a combination of cultural aspects with the issue of control is at least indicated by both the government and left-wing parties in France, the Netherlands, Finland and Luxembourg.

Conclusion

In this chapter we have identified some cultural issues in the political media debate in Europe. However, having the technical means does not automatically guarantee that certain messages reach people, in the sense that they are accepted by the audience. This is, of course, the crucial point when we want to evaluate the extent to which the existence of technical networks influences some cultural factors at the local, national and transnational/international level.

However, technical developments and changes are taking place. The easiest trends to identify are the technical integration regarding distribution networks (i.e. communicative integration in Deutsch's terms), and a potential division of labour regarding production of media hardware and software respectively.

The communication networks seem to expand particularly at the local and the transnational levels. Adding the attitudes which are expressed in the various countries' official media policy, it seems reasonable to make a general statement: the development of media technology is no longer a process involving national integration and identity building. Instead, it contributes to two opposite trends: on the one hand decentralization and on the other hand internationalization or transnationalization. The major actors which favour a decentralization process are: local groups which support specific interests, regional and local media groups, left-wing parties and the government in some European countries. On the other hand, the transnational aspect is emphasized by actors such as the electronics industry (supported by the government in France), private companies which are producing television programmes (supported by the government in Great Britain), and the government in Luxembourg.

It is much more difficult to evaluate the new electronic media's implications for people's values, or for normative integration in Deutsch's terms. First, it depends upon who will own and control the hardware, who will have access to various media and thus try to influence the content in radio and television programmes or different kinds of information which can be transmitted via videotex and teletext. Secondly, the extent to which new electronic media really will have an impact on attitudes, opinions and values very much depends upon how mass media and people's everyday interpersonal communication are linked. How will new media technology's more anonymous form fit into already existing communication patterns, which are usually characterized by being informal and a two-way exchange? Also, how will the content be 'in tune' with the common man's interests and everyday experiences?

Two possible tendencies with respect to media content can be identified: on the one hand non-controversial entertainment for a mass audience, and on the other hand, specialized programmes or information packages for diversified audiences. It does not demand much imagination to picture two communication communities, each being based on common interests between producers and consumers; one entertainment-oriented and another information-oriented. Each 'cultural community' risks being squeezed between purely technical networks and a basically market-oriented software-producing industry. The key question remains without a clear answer: 'do we really have grounds for considering there to be a coherent and homogeneous global — or European — cultural village?

Notes

1. In his book *Culture*, Raymond Williams (1981) gives a general and thorough introduction to different theoretical approaches to culture and cultural studies.
2. Caution is needed in interpreting this table, since the figures relate to content rather than audience attention and only deal with the 'offer' of national channels in each country.

References

This chapter is based mainly on information extracted from the 'National Reports' written for the Project. In addition, there are a few other references.

Allen, Irving Lewis (1977) 'Social Integration as an Organizing Principle', in George Gerbner (ed.), *Mass Media Policies in Changing Cultures*. New York: Wiley 235–50.

Deutsch, Karl W. (1966) *Nationalism and Social Communication: an Inquiry into the Foundations of Nationality*. 2nd ed. Cambridge: MIT Press.

Eisenstadt, S.N. (1981) 'Cultural Orientations and Center-Periphery in Europe in a Comparative Perspective', in Per Torsvik (ed.), *Mobilization, Center-Periphery Structures and Nation-Building*, pp. 94–107, Oslo: Universitetsforlaget.

Hartmann, Paul (1980) 'Cross-Cultural and International Communication: Content, Values, Effect'. Report of the 4th Session of the IAMCR Conference 1978, in *Mass Media and National Cultures*, Leicester: IAMCR.

Mumford, Lewis (1963) *Technics and Civilization*, New York: Harcourt, Brace & World.

NUA 1979: 6 Band 1 og 2. *Nordisk radio och television via satellit. Kultur- och programpolitisk delrapport*, København: Nordisk Ministerrad.

Slack, Jennifer Daryl (1984) *Communication Technologies and Society: Conceptions of Causality and the Politics of Technological Intervention*, Norwood (New Jersey): Ablex Publishing.

Unesco (1980). *Many Voices, One World: the MacBride Report*. London: Kogan Page, Paris: Unesco.

Varis, Tapio (1984) *Flow of Television Programmes in Western Europe: Summary of the Basic Data during January 31–February 13, 1983: Report 14/1984*. Tampere: Peace Research Institute and University of Tampere.

Williams, Raymond (1981) *Culture*. London: Fontana.

Williams, Raymond (1983) *Keywords: a Vocabulary of Culture and Society*. London: Fontana.

Chapter 11
Commercialization*

The concept

Arising in part from consideration of cultural policy, and certainly provoked by efforts to develop new means of communication for reasons of industrial policy, is a set of concerns which are conveniently referred to by the term 'commercialism' or, to describe the process at work, 'commercialization'. This process is what cultural policy seeks, amongst other things, to resist although it (commercialism) is generally only a means to achieve some economic benefit rather than an end pursued for its own sake. These have been loaded, even emotive, terms in discussions of media policy in Europe, with mainly pejorative connotations. For the most part, these negative associations stem either from an idealist view of culture and communication as spiritual goods which should not be sullied by the market place or traded for profit, or from a political objection to capitalism and the power of a business class, which might be reinforced by control of mass media. In between, there is a more pragmatic and probably more widely-held view that more commercialism in mass communication inevitably intensifies competition for large audiences and, under conditions of channel 'scarcity', leads to a neglect of those minority interests and tastes, in both cultural and political spheres, which are protected by current public service systems. More important, perhaps, is the argument that much current programming in European television in the sphere of culture and information, which is designed to reach quite large audiences, is not really, and could not be economic without subsidy or market protection of one kind or another.

There are variants of both the idealist/culturalist and the political-economic positions and variations between countries in the weight which one or the other version is given in policy debates. For instance, an 'idealist' anti-commercialism may either have a nationalistic (possibly anti-American) basis or stem from aesthetic and cultural considerations. Political opposition to commercialism can range from a fully worked-out Marxist position, according to which the means of opinion — and consciousness-formation — should not be allowed to fall into the hands of a powerful business class, to a view that pluralistic democracy requires guarantees of access to groups and interests which cannot afford to buy

* Written by Denis McQuail.

communication channels and that the general public interest requires some limit to the commercial exploitation of communication media.

Television was introduced in most European countries in the postwar period either under the influence of more progressive governments or continuing the public service tradition of radio broadcasting, without much change. There was, in any case, a rather similar hesitation on the part of possible commerical interests to that which had originally allowed radio to fall into public hands. Most European countries had become accustomed to extensive public control and the keynote of the time was planned social reconstruction after the war. In many countries, there were sufficient opportunities for commercial development in other media sectors and limited funds for advertising in a medium which did not, initially, reach a mass public. The development costs were thus carried by the public sector and a de facto division of media spheres of activity between public and private sectors was tacitly accepted. The political and cultural forces ranged against private exploitation of broadcasting were strong and the main available model of commercialism, that prevailing in the USA, was not viewed with much favour by most social and political elites.

Since the postwar recovery in Europe during the 1950s, the issue has been less one-sided and the pressure to allow more 'commercialism' of various kinds has increased. After an initial development phase, television became institutionalized with a rather more widespread (though still subsidiary and strictly regulated) commercial element than had been true of radio in prewar Europe, partly because of changed political circumstances, partly for economic reasons — television is simply much more expensive. It is the resulting systems which are now being challenged by technological developments. The general arguments against commercialism have remained much the same for at least forty years, although the balance between them has changed and a summary of these arguments can serve in place of definition of the concept. The essence of commercialism is the production and supply of information and culture within a market structure, for profit. This is held by critics to have a number of varied, mainly negative, consequences.

Firstly, it advances concentration of ownership and control in private hands, thus tending to a monopoly situation without any mechanism of independent and democratic accountability. Secondly, the commercial producer or supplier is held to have no personal or moral concern with the product or its wider consequences. Commercial communication systems operate primarily on the basis of the long-term interest of the senders and of those who finance them, rather than of the receivers, and one may speak of manipulation or exploitation of the latter by the former. At best commercial systems are neutral about what they carry and at worst they may advance the interests of a propertied class and thus conservative or reactionary forces. Thirdly, there is a widely held view that, in the market for culture and information, a version of Gresham's Law prevails, such that the bad tends to drive out the good. There are two main reasons for supposing this to occur. One is that profit maximization leads to competition for the largest possible audiences and, under conditions of limited channels, this reduces the offer of content likely to appeal to cultural and political minorities, which are too small and differentiated for profitable servicing. Another reason is that commercial competition requires minimization of costs. In respect of culture and information, cost-cutting is likely to be more harmful to the quality of production than in material production, where standards are easier to monitor, where raw-material substitution is easier and where automatization can increase productivity. Decline in cultural and informational standards is less easy to demonstrate and attempts at efficiency can threaten intrinsic properties of originality, complexity and diversity.

There is, fourthly, a very specific objection to commercialism in European television in the argument that it upsets the delicate balance of the operation by which public broadcasting authorities have tried to achieve both cultural (society-originated) goals and mass consumer satisfaction. Other, more theoretical or more polemical, arguments are also often deployed about the consequences of cultural production within a purely commercial system. These perceived consequences include: the promotion of 'consumerism', materialism, hedonism, escapism and passivity; the dissemination of a misleading or very incomplete view of social reality; public conformism and conservatism; the submission of content to the influence of advertisers; the weakening of working-class solidarity; a lower degree of internal freedom and creativity for producers of culture.

In general, commercialism has often been equated with conscience-less encouragement of popular prejudice and the wish for easy, immediate gratification or worse (pornography, vicarious violence, etc.). In this version, it offends against the work ethic and ideals of social and moral improvement, which tend to favour values and ends such as: the public good over private pleasure; the freedom and creativity of the cultural/information producer; education, truth and social improvement; diversity of viewpoint and cultural expression; the national or regional language or culture.

This litany of evils does tend to obscure the fact that there are positive things said in the debate about media policy on behalf of free enterprise and the market, if not of something called 'commercialism'. These can be summarized in four main points. Commercialism can produce rapid exploitation of the technology and of human potential and make benefits available more widely to individuals than either public control or planned development. Secondly, the moral neutrality of commerce is regarded as a positive virtue by comparison with any kind of public interference in culture and information. In theory, market forces (including demand) will decide what is carried in communication channels, rather than political and moral judgements by self-appointed guardians. Thirdly, commercial competition can lead to an upgrading of quality of some services, since it may increase the finances available and use these more efficiently. Profitable operations are also likely to be able to support high-cost services to small audiences (some of whom may be profitable to reach for certain advertisers). There is a much wider argument linking freedom of economic activity with freedom of expression and political action. The alternative to commercialism, in this view, is ultimately state control, uniformity and stagnation, if not totalitarianism. Thus, for those who advocate free-market exploitation of media, the key word is not commercialism, but several others, including freedom, pluralism, diversity, choice and change.

In this presentation of the case against and for commercialism, more space has been given to the former than to the latter, despite the fact that for many (possibly a majority — but it varies from country to country) of the potential audience, commercial exploitation of media is unproblematic in principle and for many actors — potential as well as commercial — it is regarded as normal in a free society. The reason for this imbalance here, however, is that in the European debate, commercialism *is* regarded as problematic by many significant actors and this view is institutionalized in public television systems which keep commerce at a distance or under tight control. The debate thus reflects arguments in defence of a status quo.

The forms of commercialism

The above version of commercialism, as seen especially by its opponents, tends to be based on the worst case and involves the most wide-ranging assumptions about the likely consequences of operating media within a market system. For the most part one can observe only rather modest tendencies which are held back by a good many other forces in any communication system, including: the traditions of particular sectors of the cultural production industry, such as book publishing; the professionalism and dedication of media producers; the existence of many, potentially profitable, minority audiences within the mass public; various forms of direct or indirect subsidy. In the case of television and other electronic media, commercialism has appeared in Europe in several forms, few of which correspond to the unrestrained exploitation of a mass market implied in the picture sketched above. These forms can, even so, be described as ranging from 'strongest' to a 'weakest' version of commercialization.

The former would be a system, financed entirely by private capital, receiving income only from advertising or sponsorship, run as a business and without any close public regulation of content. There is a little radio broadcasting of this kind already in Europe but, aside from the long-standing 'deviant' case of Luxembourg and some recent innovations involving satellites, it is, so far, virtually unknown in Europe. A second, much weaker, commercial model is represented by a privately financed operation run within a structure of public regulation as part of a wider system. Current examples are Independent Broadcasting in Britain and MTV in Finland. A third commercial variant is the model of subscription television, which can be offered over cable systems and, in principle, DBS, where consumers pay directly for the whole service, or component parts, either with or without an advertising 'subsidy'. A fourth, and currently commoner, variant is that of public service broadcasting, partly financed by selling time to advertisers between programmes. Finally, we might identify a weak version of commercialization, in which private finance or advertising is not directly involved, but which refers to the 'dilution' of cultural and informational content by public service broadcasters in the interests of maximizing audiences or saving money, as a result of competition of different kinds or because of economic and political pressure. This may be the 'weakest' version, but it may also be regarded as the most widespread and insidious form at present. It is almost impossible to prevent and there is little doubt that the financial and political position of many broadcasting bodies in Europe, always somewhat exposed, has weakened a good deal over the last decade and opened the way for more indirect commercialism.

The current debate about commercialization is somewhat confused by the existence of these variants and, in particular, by the distinction between two basic models of television provision — one advertising-supported, the other subscription-supported — and by the supposed threat from 'indirect' commercialization process as a result of competition. In general, the model of subscription finance (pay per channel) has found most favour in plans for cable expansion, partly because it does not require mass markets and has acceptable precedents in the distribution systems of books, films and music, partly because it avoids the most visible commercial element — the advertising message, with its potentially exploitative, mendacious or misleading aspects. It also causes less upset to other commercial media. What is often neglected, however, is that subscription television can rarely cover the cost of much original programming, so that 'cultural dilution' is no less likely than with 'stronger' versions of commercial operation.

The status quo of European broadcast media in respect of commercialism

Until now the traditional European electronic media (mainly television and radio) have been largely non-commercial, or under the influence or control of public service regulations and traditions. The countries under review can be assigned, according to a number of criteria, to a given position on a continuum of 'commercialism'. This is the status quo referred to in the heading. Relative position on this continuum provides a baseline against which to assess plans and prospects for future commercialism and gives some measure of explanation of the direction and substance of current policy-making. It is sufficient to consider countries in groups classified as either 'high', 'medium' or 'low' in the degree of broadcasting commercialism so far reached.

Approximate position may be established by reference to relative dependence on advertising revenue (see Table 2 above, p. 46): the amount of advertising on television in terms of air-time; the share of television in total national advertising expenditure; or the proportion of GNP equivalent in television advertising expenditure. However, a consideration of the structural arrangements for commercial access to, or support for, television is more explanatory and leads to much the same results. The main aim of the following brief sketches is to locate the various national situations in respect of commercialism. Planned or possible developments are considered separately later. New forms of electronic media have, until recently, been either too small in scope, or too subordinate to the public 'regime' to have contributed much to 'commercialism', as yet. The main exception is video (see Chapter 7).

Group I: countries with relatively 'high' commercialization

Britain. The location of Britain in this group can be justified either by reference to figures for the share of advertising time on television or television's share of total advertising expenditure. On both, Britain ranked high at the start of the decade (AGB, 1983). This leading position stems from the fact that Britain is the only European country to have a television service fully financed by advertising revenue, with two complete channels (ITV and C4) and a daily Breakfast TV channel (TV AM), as well as the two BBC channels, supported by licence revenue. Until now, sponsorship has not been allowed in Independent television.

Figures of the kind referred to above do not tell the whole story about the extent and character of commercialism which obtains. The private sector of British television is quite closely regulated by law (administered by the IBA) as to the amount and kind and placing of advertising and as to the rest of its output as well.

This situation reflects both a tradition of elite distaste for commercialism and also political objections when commercial television was established in 1954. A further aspect of the British case is the intense competition for audiences between the BBC and the IBA which has led to charges that both reduce their cultural standards and fail to meet public service responsibilities. In other words, the mixed system is held by some to give indirect as well as direct impetus to 'commercialism' in the weaker sense of more popular, undemanding programmes at peak hours.

Italy. Italy takes its place in this group by virtue of the de facto establishment of private (local) television stations in 1975, following a successful challenge to the constitutional validity of the RAI monopoly. The numerous local stations have now developed into a small number of quasi-national channels, which offer full programme services in competition with the two RAI national channels. There still remain many small local additional channels. All this provision is financed entirely by advertising revenue and by 1982 the revenue exceeded that obtained by the RAI from advertising. The amount of time given to advertising on private television is impossible to estimate accurately. There is no legal limit, although a 1982 gentlemen's agreement fixed a maximum of 14 percent per hour. However, the threshold is extensively disregarded and in prime time some channels have up to 25 percent of advertising time. The state service, RAI, which now has less than half the total audience, has carried advertising in blocks since 1957 and receives (1983) 36 percent of its revenue from this source. Sponsorship and interruption of programmes are forbidden, rules which do not apply to private television. Italy provides the closest model in Europe to the American system and has, consequently, been regarded as an example of what might happen, if public service frameworks were to be abandoned. While horrific for some, others take comfort from the degree of self-regulation and institutionalization which has occurred and from the survival of RAI on terms not so very different from those which apply to the BBC, in the much more controlled British situation. A legitimation of the status quo as described is to be expected, without major changes in the degree of commercialization, but with more control.

Luxembourg. The radio and television system is purely commercial, the Compagnie Luxembourgeoise de Telediffusion (CLT, but better known as RTL) having an effective monopoly (since 1929) and an importance beyond its size, because of transborder broadcasting. The main company is largely owned by powerful foreign groups, mainly French and Belgian. There is a contract between the Luxembourg state and CLT which specifies some public service obligations, but profit is the main motive. Most television programming is aimed at neighbouring countries, especially Belgium, which has no television advertising of its own. There has been pressure on CLT to share some of its advertising revenue with Belgian broadcasting (revenue now exceeds 1.5 billion Belgian francs). In general, Luxembourg has been and is regarded as a base from which true commercial broadcasting can spread into other countries (especially Belgium and West Germany).

A more complete coverage of Western Europe than has been possible in this survey would probably add four other countries as 'high' in commercialization — Spain, Ireland, Portugal and Greece — on grounds at least of relative importance of advertising revenue.

Group II: countries with 'medium' commercialization

France. From 1968 until 1984, there were three public television channels, receiving some income from advertising (appreciably so in the case of TF1 and A2), mainly concentrated between 6.30 and 8.30 in the evening. Until recently the total permitted advertising air time (18 minutes per day per channel: Syfret, 1983) has remained quite low, but television advertising, nevertheless, accounted for 22 percent of advertising expenditure. The third public channel (FR3) has been regionalized (similar to British Independent TV) and, from 1984, has been able to take advertising on the same basis as the other two public channels. Until now, it seems that demand for advertising opportunity on television has exceeded supply and there are severe restrictions on what products can be advertised. Aside from the question of volume, France does not have a truly commercial system, since it has lacked competition between public and commercial channels. Even so, it has been said that, after the reorganization of 1974, competition for audiences between the three independent channels led to a decline of quality of programming. The main truly commercial element in the French situation is to be found in the so-called 'Radio-Périphérique', especially Europe No. 1, Radio Monte Carlo, Radio TéléLuxembourg and Sud Radio. These very popular radio stations covered large areas of France from outside French territory and were largely bought up by the French government through the agency of SOFIRAD, its commercially operating international media arm. In this way, a significant commercial element has been incorporated into the public system.

West Germany. The German situation has, until recently, been similar to that of France, both structurally and quantitatively as far as the commercialization of television is concerned. Programmes are produced by nine independent and public organizations of the Länder and fed into two channels, ARD national and ARD regional (not unlike the British ITV model). The second national channel (ZDF) originated as an alternative to a truly commercial network (on the British model) which was sought by commercial interests in 1959–61. It is a public corporation, centred on one city (Mainz), drawing 30 percent of its budget from general licence fees and 40 percent from 20 minutes of advertising per day. The ARD national channel receives about 20 percent of its revenue from commercials, on the same basis as ZDF — 20 minutes in blocks of around 5 minutes between 17.30 and 20.00, an arrangement which dates back to 1956. Regulations are mainly in the hands of the separate Länder governments. As with France, there is some competition between (public) channels but no true commercial competition and, as yet, few complaints about neglect of public service aims. There is a limited amount of advertising in Länder (regional) radio channels, though none on WDR. The renewed pressure for more commercialization or privatization since the CDU came to power is taken up below.

The Netherlands. The ground rules, within which a rather moderate amount of television advertising time is available (240 minutes per week) are rather similar to those of France and West Germany. The Broadcasting Law recognizes a number of senders, of which one is a non-profit foundation which sells advertising time on two national television channels, otherwise shared between several independent broadcasting organizations. The income received contributes about 25 percent of the costs of the system as a whole, thus supplementing the revenue from licence fees. This system has been in force since 1969 and has been controversial mainly because of the possible effects on the press. The presence of advertising in itself seems also to have been less a matter of controversy than the disguised forms of commercialism (mainly self-promotional activities and rating-chasing) which have resulted from competition within the 'open' system for allocations of air time. Generally, the entertainment-oriented and more secular senders have gained audiences and more air time and the whole process has been said to lead to a dilution of the original social and cultural purposes of the system. Radio is organized on a similar basis. The extensive cable television network has mainly been developed to improve reception and relay foreign (public) channels for charges which cover only costs. A new element has entered the situation by the admission since 1984 of Sky Channel and other foreign satellite services to several local cable networks (especially in the three largest cities), bringing (non-Dutch) advertising and a programme of light entertainment which is considered to deviate from the principles of the national broadcasting system.

Finland. At the start of the present decade, Finland's degree of commercialization, as measured by the stated benchmarks, was comparable to that of France and West Germany, although the structural arrangements were different and television's share of advertising expediture was rather low (8 percent). Since the beginning of television broadcasting in 1957, advertising has been accepted as an essential component of the system, mainly for financial reasons and has not been an issue of principle. The main public broadcasting organization, licensed by the state, the Finnish Broadcasting Company (YLF), leases channel time on both national channels to a private commercial company (MTV), which sells advertising time in order to pay for its programme output. This produces about 22 percent of the revenue of the Finnish Broadcasting Company. Daily advertising time has been around 25 minutes in breaks between evening programmes. The FBC is mainly licence-supported, but the terms of its own licence allow it to carry advertising. Commercial elements in the Finnish system are somewhat limited, since there is not a lot of competition and content itself, including that of MTV, is quite closely regulated. There are other commercial elements of the Finnish case. Some limited advertising is present in the videotex systems run by newspapers. Private cable television companies (mainly owned by newspapers and private phone companies) transmit some advertisements by way of satellite broadcasting (Sky Channel) and offer other entertainment and information services to subscribers.

Spain. Spanish television probably carries more advertising time than any other country in this 'medium' group (690 minutes per week — Thompson), but it is also contained within the state-owned system (RTVE). This offers two national television channels and (since 1983) an additional regional channel for Catalonia and one for the Basque region. As with other public systems, advertising time is included at intervals between programmes, producing revenue for the whole system. The rest comes from general taxation. There is no sponsorship and the content of advertisements is subject to regulation.

Group III: countries with 'low' commercialization

Denmark. Danmarks Radio has a monopoly of radio and television and neither carries any advertising. This was decided as a matter of principle in 1951. There is little or no commercial exploitation of any of the new media and advertising is forbidden on (experimental) local radio. Cable is not operated for profit, but its relay of foreign programmes is a source of pressure for change and competition with the single national television channel.

Sweden. Advertising is also forbidden here on radio and television. The Swedish Broadcasting Corporation (Sveriges Radio) has a public monopoly, is financed by licence fees, is controlled ultimately by government, by way of representative councils, and aims to achieve a number of public service goals. In the early 1960s, industrial interests pressed for a second channel, socially accountable but commercially financed, on the British model. The Social Democratic government originally rejected advertising on political grounds, but did accept the desirability of competition between public channels under separate direction. The pressure against advertising came also from groups concerned with culture and consumer welfare and from the newspaper press. There is little or no commercialism in Swedish electronic media, although advertising is not excluding from videotex and video is unregulated as yet.

Norway. The Norwegian Broadcasting Organization (NRK) has a monopoly of radio and television and neither carries advertising, being financed by licence and tax. In the prewar period, from 1933, NRK radio did carry advertising, but it was excluded by a decision in 1951, at the initiation of television, and this has been re-affirmed on several occasions since, despite some pressure from trade and industry. In the mid-1960s, the introduction of cable in a few places seemed to be outside the existing law and some commercial programmes were transmitted before it was determined (in 1977) that cable belonged to the broadcasting monopoly of the NRK. Since then, until recently at least, advertising has not been an issue on the agenda of debate. There is still little sign of commercialism, although Sky Channel is now distributed to about 85,000 households in Oslo and five other towns and this carries foreign advertising.

Belgium. The two public broadcasting services, BRT (for Flemish language areas) and RTBF (for Wallonia) carry no advertising on either radio or television channels. However, the Belgian public, because of cabling and overspill, is exposed to commercial broadcasting from Luxembourg and advertising carried by other national systems. The pressure to legitimize advertising, in the national interest, has been considerable.

This overview of the position at the start of the 1980s, in advance of a heralded communication revolution, reveals a fairly clear pattern and certain recurrent themes. Firstly, in all countries, Luxembourg apart, there is a strong public broadcasting agency with a monopoly or large share of control. Commercial activity in broadcasting, where it exists, is everywhere very restricted, except in Italy, and in most countries it is confined to the sale of time on public service channels. The main European tradition has been to extract financial benefit for a very saleable public property, but to limit any effects on programme content or general public service aims. In achieving this, one secondary result may have been to de-demonize advertising, as it appears in the traditional concept of commercialism described earlier.

The forces which have produced that situation are varied but there seems, prima facie, a historical association between limits to commercialism and: northerliness, protestantism, socialism, and possibly, cultural and educational level of development. In some countries more than others, the press has come to be regarded as a 'spiritual' asset for linguistic, cultural, political or regional reasons. A combination of these values has been associated with resistance to commerce in, especially, the Scandinavian countries and the Netherlands. A further factor is linguistic — small language-group countries seem to have been more resistant to commercialism than larger ones (e.g. Britain, Italy, Spain). For the most part, it seems that the question of advertising or not (and which model of advertising) was settled fairly early in television history. In none of the countries has there been a decision in principle to admit advertising since 1967 (Netherlands). Finally, it is noteworthy how attractive the British model has been as a model for proposals or plans elsewhere (e.g. West Germany, Sweden, Spain and more recently in the Netherlands and France), although it remains unique.

The main issues in the debate about commercialism

The climate of opinion concerning commercial involvement in broadcasting in most European countries has, until recently, been unfavourable. In the past, advocates of commercialism have largely been confined to the self-interested, to ideologues of the market place, populists or pure liberals. Now they have been joined by quite a few pragmatists who see no alternative to a degree of commercial exploitation if new media potential is to be fully exploited for a number of different purposes. The new situation has given rise to several specific issues which cannot easily be settled by reference to a set of traditional values and has exposed the existing order to demands for change or clearer justification. The following seem to be the most important on the agenda.

— The 'threat' to public broadcasting, which has until now been largely and widely protected from market forces and expected to use its monopoly position to fulfil social functions, which include giving access to diverse voices and reaching majorities with information, education and culture. Commercialization implies for public broadcasting more than a loss of monopoly status, of audiences and of revenue. Broadcasting as a whole will also be less socially accountable, less committed to the 'public interest'. Matters of this kind are especially salient in countries where the public service tradition has been strong, but where few concessions have yet been made to popular or commercial pressure, such as in Denmark, Norway, Sweden and the Netherlands. An important aspect of the question is whether entirely new media really belong to the scope of existing (old media) monopoly control.

— Choices about the admission of commerce have been faced in the past, but in much more controlled environments. A new component of the situation is that there are more opportunities for commercial provision without permission or accountability and more chance for individual consumers to behave as if in a market for information and culture (as a result of cable, video and satellites). Especially pertinent is the spectre of foreign commercialism, by way of transborder flow, which holds all the most feared components of commercialism as sketched above: weakening of the national culture and the influence of the nation state; uncontrolled advertising; loss of revenue and audiences. One's own national and supervised commercialism looks, by comparison, quite attractive. Central to the issue is the thought that the communication revolution is coming anyway and the best one can do is to try and tame or channel it, for some national advantage. This aspect of the issue is prominent mainly in smaller, more vulnerable 'receiver' countries, but it is also relevant to larger countries, such as France and West Germany, which have some ambition to compete internationally as cultural producers.

— A purely pragmatic version of this issue is not based on fear of commercialism but, conversely, on the wish to profit, for the national economic interest, from this potential growth sector of commerce and industry. The possible benefits include more employment and opportunities for electronics industries at home and abroad. France, Germany and Britain come to mind in this connection, but the issue arises similarly in some smaller economies, such as Sweden, Finland and the Netherlands.

— The possible consequences for the newspaper press attract a good deal of attention. In some countries, it has a special status and protection and seems threatened by changes under way (loss of revenue), while in others the question is whether the press might benefit as a commercial exploiter of new media. Generally, the matter is prominent in countries which have well-developed press subsidy schemes, such as Sweden, Norway or the Netherlands or where, as in Finland, newspapers are already active in the new media sphere.

— Mixed with the issues mentioned are various other positive aspects of commercialization. It can be seen as promoting more supply and more choice, more diversity of expression and freedom, more business enterprise generally. Currently, West Germany and Britain seem to be the places where official thinking at least leans most strongly in this direction. Tied in with the issue of speedy exploitation (e.g. of cable) are questions about technical standards.

As will be apparent, the salience of these points varies a good deal according to national circumstances and the relevant policy traditions of each country. It may seem surprising that this listing of issues makes no mention of the question of what will actually be profitable for investment and has little to say about lifting restrictions on commercial activity (deregulation), aside from the central matter of breaching a public monopoly. These omissions mainly reflect the broadly non-commercial condition of the status quo and the current stage of debate in Europe. This is still mainly concerned with broad matters of principle and with sharing out future spheres of operation. No doubt commercial interests are concerned about matters of profitability and regulation but their first priority is also to settle the matters of principle.

The optional forms for commercial development

Both the expectations from, and fears about, commercialism in electronic media depend on their being able to generate new, or redistribute existing, revenue, so as to pay for expansion and create profit. It is impossible even approximately to estimate total revenue potential and not necessary for the purposes of this discussion. The early 1980s have been characterized by initial high optimism, followed by caution, but without loss of the belief that there is money to be made somewhere in the system for someone. What is useful is to outline the various forms which revenue generation might take, since these alternatives play a part in the policy decision-making. The two main forms of revenue are familiar from existing media: direct subscription and selling of time for advertising. Until now television has had rather little of the former, which is the main source of press income and a fair amount of the latter. There has been very little sponsorship, which has usually been regarded as the most objectionable form of commercialism, although more acceptable for 'high culture' and now showing signs of return to favour.

The (near) absence of subscription-television on any commercial basis is partly the result of technical limitations (lack of networks or effective means of control) and partly of restrictive regulation. There are other distinctions which enter into any plans on the part of would-be investors: between different levels of markets for advertising — local, regional, national, transnational; between those media which fall under an existing broadcasting 'regime' (mainly national television) and new media, for which there may be no legislation; between information and entertainment services; between mass display advertising and targeted specialist advertising; between sponsored and advertising-supported provision; between provision for home-based and for professional/business uses; between international product advertisements and nationally focused advertisements.

The following is an inventory of the main options, with brief comments.

— Publicly owned and operated channels, with slots set aside to carry advertising messages as a means of part-financing. This is a feature of television and radio in several of the countries discussed, including France, West Germany, Italy, Spain and the Netherlands, but not Britain, Belgium, Finland or the other Scandinavian countries. An extension of this option usually provides a relatively easy way of meeting some of the pressures for more expansion financed by private money, without change of principle. However, it may be one of the most directly damaging measures for the press, which gains no benefit and can legitimately object to publicly sponsored competition. Nor does it have great relevance for the development of the new media possibilities.

— Privately owned channels, with slots for advertising in or between programmes, producing all or most revenue. This is most firmly institutionalized in Britain and Luxembourg and, de facto, in Italy. The British model has seemed to offer an attractive way of containing some of the worst features of commercialism, while retaining a profitable business. There have been attempts to copy it in the past and it is still being considered in Spain. In effect, it is a highly sanitized version of the traditional American model. There may now be some doubt as to its suitability for new forms of distribution, especially cable.

— Subscription television — privately provided and financed cable services, for which subscribers pay a regular charge. These may or may not carry advertising messages. Finland offers an example on a small scale as do experiments in Germany. New cable policy in Britain is based on this concept and a variant (without advertising) is providing the basis for expansion of television in the Netherlands. The pay-television version, in which payment is per programme, is feasible and much talked of, but is unlikely to be extensively adopted, partly because of the competition for special programmes and events from continuing public services. The take-up for such subscription services is very dependent on other developments — of DBS television and, of course, laying of cable networks. It may also depend on the competitive response of established public networks.

— Satellite television, direct or via cable, carrying advertising. This was pioneered by Sky Channel, reaching audiences in several countries, including Norway, Finland, the Netherlands, by way of ground cable systems and other services have now appeared. Individual direct reception is not likely to be a reality for some time. The commercial opportunity from satellite television is rather different from that involved in the other developments described. It is destined, almost certainly, to retain a transnational character, with advertising of international brand-names. The once planned GDL Coronet satellite operation, with international finance and a vast potential audience represented, before its abortion, the state of the art and is expected to have a successor in some form. Relative freedom from national regulation is another (commercially attractive) feature of this option. Some national governments are interested in stimulating their own ventures on a commercial basis as a form of self-protection, for instance France (TV5) and West Germany (SAT 1).

— The commercial potential of new, interactive, data-based, services has so far seemed small, whether considered as direct sales to subscribers or vehicles for graphic advertising. The development drive has come mainly from public agencies. However, there may be a potentially large international market for specialist services, which may not be exploited until governments have paid the development costs of systems. There are experiments in France, Britain, the Netherlands and West Germany, which may yield some lessons for commercial potential.

— Teletext has been a successful medium, developed within and by public broadcasting agencies and so far without much commercial exploitation or impact. However, since a very large public is likely to be eventually reachable by this medium, it is likely to have a future as an advertising vehicle, providing revenue for public broadcasting and probably drawing it away from the press.

— The main remaining commercial possibility is video, which is spreading rapidly and is largely unregulated. It is already a not unimportant part of the media industry. There is some potential for carrying advertising along with films, as in the cinema, but the main potential may lie in video magazines or packages of software, often in contexts other than the home, carrying advertising or consumer information of various kinds. So far video has been the cinema-at-home, more or less, but it could become the magazine-on-the-screen.

The USA might seem the obvious place to look for lessons about the commercial possibilities of the new media in Europe, but it may not be so, or not yet at least, mainly because of the enormous baseline differences in the existing degree of commercialization of the electronic media.

Current plans and prospects for commercialization

The status quo described above for the various European countries is now beginning to change and, nearly everywhere, in the direction of more rather than less commercialization, in any of its senses. It is not necessarily the more commercially 'advanced' countries which are in the forefront of further change, although there is some relationship between the historical position and the future prospect. It is convenient to consider what has been happening in a commercial direction and to assess the various driving forces which are at work.

More active commercial policies

The most definite and active movements towards more commercial exploitation, irrespective of the current situation, are probably to be found in Britain, the Netherlands and West Germany, although by 1985 only the former two countries had brought about the necessary legal changes to extend significantly possibilities for one or other form of commercial television. Change in West Germany remains more a matter of expectation than actuality, although there is little doubt that significant change is at hand.

In Britain, the whole political climate was conducive in the early 1980s to almost any kind of deregulation or privatization, both as a matter of principle (for the ruling Conservative government) and as a supposed means to economic and industrial progress. The most relevant instrument of change in connection with mass media has been the establishment by law (Cable and Wireless Act 1984) of a new system of commercial cable networks, each with a local franchise and roughly 100,000 potential subscribers. The operators are expected to pay for the cost of cable installation and to recover the costs either from subscriptions or advertising, or both. While a Cable Authority has been established to enforce certain rules of a public service kind, these will be less strictly enforced than current regulations applied by the IBA to the rest of commercial broadcasting. The rules for advertising are similar, although the possibility of sponsorship and the lack of much own-production capacity on the part of the new cable services will probably have an effect in the direction of more 'indirect' forms of commercialism in programming. The new services will also have to be somewhat aggressive to gain subscribers and it is fairly clear from the example of Sky Channel what this can mean in the way of searching for maximum audiences in competition with established public service channels.

The development of cable in Britain has also stimulated the emergence of a number of new commercial programme providers, in addition to Sky, with a base in Britain, including Music Box, The Entertainment Channel and Screen Sport. More of these are planned, some to be supported by advertising, with an eye on the European as well as the British market, benefiting from cable-to-satellite systems. The BBC and IBA, with other firms and with government support have also been exploring ways of getting into this same market, exploiting the resources of existing large programme archives and production strength. A further sign of the times in Britain has been the appointment by the government of a committee (Peacock) to consider whether and, if so, how the BBC should carry advertising.

In the Netherlands, the principle of public service monopoly, regulated by the Broadcasting Law of 1969, has been breached, and privately financed and controlled television has arrived in the form of subscription channels available by cable, although still on a local basis. The changes have yet to be formalized in a new Media Law. All this has occurred without any great shift in the climate of opinion in favour of commercialism or against the established system, but a combination of factors has led to this significant change. These include: a reluctance to spend any more public money or to raise the licence fee; lobbying by commercial interests; expectations of economic and industrial benefits; availability of an extensive and still under-used cable system; vulnerability to cross-border flow; an insufficiently satisfied demand for television provision, especially in the Dutch language. So far, relatively little expansion of advertising in new media has been realized and a range of strict controls still exists. Nevertheless a new media sector has been opened up with potential long-term consequences for the character of the system and its commercial opportunities.

West Germany has been named in this context as having a system ripe for change in the direction of a more commercial, privately financed, electronic media sector, mainly because of forces similar to those at work in Britain. There has been a more right-wing government as well as a wish to share in the possible economic fruits of the new communication technologies. The changes are likely to come, as elsewhere, by way of additions to the system rather than direct changes in it, thus on the basis of development of cable and satellite. The necessary condition will be the laying down of a more extensive cable system and this is likely to be carried out by way of public investment. The cable 'experiments' in Ludwigshaven, Dortmund, Munich and Berlin are the testing grounds for expected expansion of subscription and pay television and other cable-based services. Large publishing interests, such as Bertelsmann, are involved (as they are in satellite television with RTL) and a range of imported and specially made programmes will be offered. Unlike the Netherlands, advertising will be a component of the new services, although national and regional, rather than local, markets are likely to be involved.

The developments in West Germany seem, as in Britain, to have been more the result of pressure from above (government level), based on ideology and macro-economic motive, rather than from below on the part of would-be consumers. As in Britain, there has been little clear evidence of strong unmet demand for more television provision in general or dissatisfaction with what is offered by the current system. There is clearly still a wider market for certain kinds of programming, but in both Britain and West Germany, the commercial viability of new developments involving cable remains uncertain. This is especially true of Britain where, unlike in Germany, private cable developers have to meet the whole cost of installing cable, the most expensive investment component.

In the Netherlands, there is more reason to suppose an existing demand for a new domestic service and to expect a calculable degree of profitability for at least one or two new channels on cable. The significance of Luxembourg, which should probably also belong in this group, lies in its potential to provide an on-shore base for Europe-wide satellite television, with probable, but unpredictable, repercussions on neighbouring countries. These effects may be either to stimulate commercial development (as in Belgium) or to provide competition for national commercial developments elsewhere, notably in the Netherlands, France and West Germany. It should be noted that the process of legitimation of commercialism within the Italian broadcasting system has begun, with legislative proposals in 1985 which would: limit concentration of ownership; allow national link-ups; set rules for maximum advertising time and proportion of own production; institute a regulatory committee; reassert state control of transmission. This does not mean an increase in commercialism, but it may sharpen competition with RAI.

Medium commercial initiatives

There are several countries which already have an element of commercial financing of television and where further developments are likely to take place according to market-based principles rather than on the basis of public subsidy. This is true at least of France, Spain, Finland and Belgium. In France, deregulation and decentralization rather than privatization have been the keynotes of policy for the Mitterand government, but the over-riding twin goals of economic advance and cultural self-defence have given some encouragement to commercialism and there is a shift in that direction. The legalization of the private radio channels (Radio peripherique) is one sign of this. Other signs are the opening of the new (regionalized) Canal III for regional advertising and the innovation of a new private subscription television channel (Canal Plus) which can accept sponsorship, but not as yet direct advertising. The government is indirectly involved in financing this venture by way of Havas. The plan to introduce herzian private television on a local basis is a further turn in the direction of commercialism, although the degree of commercial opportunity is uncertain, given the strict controls. The state-sponsored plan to cable 1.5 million households is a further stimulus to the advance of commercial television in the not too distant future. National cultural policy, seeking to compete with commercialism, seems to be demonstrated by the initiation of the satellite channel, TV5, in collaboration with Belgian and Swiss public television. Its main functions are to advance the French language and to shield French speakers from Anglo-American satellite penetration. The situation in France has been (mid-1985) significantly changed by the proposals of the government-appointed Bredin Commission to initiate one or two national private television channels from 1986. These would use the TDF1 satellite, thus having a potentially wider European reach and would be expected adequately to represent French or European content.

The French case seems to demonstrate that dislike of economic and cultural subordination is stronger than dislike of commercialism and the same is probably true of West Germany and Belgium, where commercial television is on the verge of being institutionalized. The current (1985) proposed legalization of advertising on television provides for only one channel, whether public or private, carrying advertising, in each of the two language communities. The newspapers have played a decisive role, as the initiators of private television and have, in effect, come to an arrangement with RTL in neighbouring Luxembourg, thus excluding the public service broadcasting organization, RTBF. The Flemish community seems to be following the Wallonian on a similar course.

In Spain, a combination of pressures favours private rather than public financing, although extensive cabling lies some way in the future. The relevant forces are: the wish to modernize; a recoil from state centralism; shortage of public funds. Entry into the EEC also encourages the adoption of the rather liberal guidelines which are being formulated by the EEC for cross-border transmission of advertising. Finland already has a viable mix of commerce and public control, with much involvement by press interests in cable and other new media. Prospective developments include the authorization of one, or even two, private television channels and the extension of local radio carrying advertising. These developments are likely to involve minimum restrictive legislation. As elsewhere, the goals of maintaining national identity and of economic advance take priority over the mainly cultural and political objections to commercialism outlined above. In both France and Spain, it is socialist administrations which are presiding over the extension of the private sector.

Commerce in check

The three Scandinavian countries which have so far held out against any institutionalization of commercial elements in their broadcasting systems remain furthest behind in the prospects for commercial exploitation of new media. These countries are not, however, entirely free from pressures to move in the same direction as the rest of Europe and, in Norway and Denmark at least, it would only take a decision by an already conservative government to take the step in principle which nearly all other states have taken in relation to their public service monopolies. Arguments of an economic and/or culturally defensive kind are much the same as in the situations discussed in France, West Germany and Finland. Denmark is the most exposed of the three to cross-border 'invasion' by television, including advertising from satellite television and from Germany. It is also the country where pressure to have more television in general is probably greatest. The recent decision on the second channel has gone against commercial interests and in favour of public finance, but that in itself may help to open the way for some forms of commercialism in the growing cable network.

In Sweden, the whole question is still under debate and the Broadcasting Treaty, up for renewal in 1986, will be extended unchanged for one or two more years. The issue of commercialism is tied in with the question of the public monopoly and so far it seems likely that, if advertising subscription were to be accepted, it would take place within the existing monopoly framework. An enquiry into the effects of television advertising will have been held in the latter part of 1985. The context of the debate is formed by a now familiar mixture of elements: a reluctance to increase licence fees; a perception of economic threat from foreign competition because of satellite television; a fear of negative effects on the press (although less so than before); liberalizing principles championed by conservative and liberal parties. The Norwegian case is very similar to that of Denmark and Sweden, in that the future of the monopoly is at stake. Whatever degree of liberalization does occur, it is likely to be on a modest scale, probably initially in the form of subscription television based on the ECS II satellite and relayed via cable networks. Finally, the most commercially developed country in Europe (as far as television is concerned), Italy, shows least prospect of new commercial initiatives for now and it cannot be said to be an issue in the policy debate.

Driving forces towards, and resistance to, commercialization

It is not easy to interpret the varied developments in several countries, which have been summarized. There is no simple, single dimension of the kind used originally to order the countries in terms of the status quo, according to which plans for commercial development can be understood. In nearly all countries, some degree of further exploitation of new and existing media, financed by private capital and with some form of profit in mind, is to be expected. It happens that the most expensive and most well-advanced plans of this kind are in Britain, which already stands high in the European league table for commercialism. Italy appears to be temporarily satiated, but further commercial developments in media are virtually certain in West Germany, France, the Netherlands and Belgium, probable in Spain and Finland, possible in Norway and only held back at the moment in Denmark and Sweden (with marginal exceptions).

Diversity of the concept

There are several reasons why it is difficult to present a simple picture of what is happening. One stems from the diversity of what commercialism might, in practice, involve: sometimes more advertising within the public system; sometimes just competition for subscribers and audiences; sometimes a basic change in the monopoly structure, and so forth. Less obvious, perhaps, is the diversity of motive and significance attaching to various kinds of commercialization on the part of both proponents and opponents. For instance, in some countries it has an ideological significance as a spearhead of private enterprise or carrier of liberal values. Elsewhere, it may be advanced as a way of breaking the monopoly, if only in rather minor and symbolic ways, as seems to be the case in

Sweden, Norway, Denmark and, possibly, the Netherlands.

A third motive for commercialization is the protection of national interests — whether cultural or industrial or both. This seems to apply in France and Finland and arguments for 'own country' commerce rather than foreign commerce are also heard in Sweden, Denmark, Norway and Belgium. In the last case, there is pressure to legalize a de facto situation of commercialization and gain some benefit for the press and for domestic advertisers.

Nationally sponsored commercialism can have a variety of origins and forms. Yet another motive (even more widespread) is the reluctance to spend any public money, however raised, to buy the cultural or social advantages of non-commercial communication. Many national situations are characterized by an internal diversity which further complicates the picture. Resistance to commercialism on moral, political or cultural grounds, does, however, seem generally weaker than the various symbolic or practical advantages associated with commercial exploitation.

Centrality of the issue

Commercialization is also of widely varying centrality as an issue in the different national debates and in few countries is it really the critical point on which new media policy turns (not openly at least). It is evidently more central in those countries where it is invested with the greatest symbolic significance as a matter of precedent. The two foremost cases in this respect are Denmark and Norway, where decisions about the extension of a very limited television service have to be taken quickly, where a totally non-commercial monopoly prevails and where there is a threat from abroad. This issue has symbolic significance also in Sweden, where the question of (im)balance between public and private sectors is ever-present, but where no decision about television is imminent.

In West Germany, future developments are tied up with the expansion of the private sector and while this exercises the political opponents of commercialization, further privatization is more or less a fait accompli. Much the same can be said about Britain and the Netherlands (the former without and the latter with, extensive public debate on the matter). In these and other countries where the matter of principle has been settled, attention is turning now to how public broadcasting will cope with the new situation and to how rosy the future will be for commerce. More broadly, the policy debate has shifted (compared with discussions of twenty years ago) from the issue of commercialism as such in its strong and mainly negative meaning, towards discussions of forms of private exploitation and conditions under which it can be allowed.

This shift has been referred to as pragmatism, but it probably has something to do with experience in a number of countries of 'contained' commercialism in broadcasting and, of course, with the weakening of the original basis (regulation of airwaves) on which public monopoly and strict control were established and legitimated. One might add that, given the uncertainty about the future of some of the new possibilities and the high costs (both of which vary a good deal from one country to another), a public policy of allowing private industry to undertake some of the development costs in an experimental phase makes some sense and leaves open the possibility of subsequent public intervention. On the other hand, private investors are not acting out of philanthropy but engaged in staking out claims as well as establishing new principles which will not be easy to reverse. Another factor, which applies rather broadly, is the increasing difficulty of holding a clear frontier between a public and a private media sector, as a matter of both practice and principle.

The actors

A consideration of the stand taken by various actors helps cast some further light on the complexity of what is going on. There is not a great deal of consistency within and between countries in the positions taken up by equivalent actors in the policy debates, in respect of commercialization, if we treat it as a single thing. Perhaps most consistency is to be found amongst the existing public broadcasting bodies who want to protect their present sphere of activity and thus generally favour the status quo. However, these bodies vary a good deal in the strength of their position and even in the degree to which they offer principled opposition to commerce. Some are on the defensive as in Britain, Italy, the Netherlands and Norway and several are interested (without necessary inconsistency) in the chances of opening up new forms of self-financing provision, as in Britain, the Netherlands, Norway and Sweden.

The various business interests which would like to benefit from new media are also fairly consistent, but even in the commercial sphere there are risks and uncertainties and often vested interests in the status quo. These kinds of actor apart, consistency might also be expected from political parties or governments, according to their political colour. This is broadly how it turns out, but there are right or centre parties which are cautious or resistant to more commercial access for social-cultural reasons, as in the Netherlands and in all the Scandinavian countries. On the left of the spectrum, there is even more real diversity, with pressure to accept commercial development in the interests of economic/industrial benefit, despite objections of principle. Sometimes this kind of cross-pressure shows itself in keeping a low profile and leaving the 'dirty work' to right-wing administrations, as in Britain and the Netherlands. In some countries, such as Spain, France and Italy, with socialist governments, commercialization has not been a significant issue of party conflict, as if by unspoken agreement.

The variation in the stands taken by actors is, in turn, a reflection of the strength of other factors at work. One of these is the strength of popular demand for expansion (mainly a function of present level of provision, although Britain seems insatiable). Another is fear of foreign overflow, with cultural or commercial losses (certainly true of Denmark, Belgium, Sweden and the Netherlands). Thirdly, there is the question of national-regional balance. Larger, national, media are more concerned about satellite broadcasting and more commerce on national television. Local media systems are more threatened by cable television, unless (as in Finland) they can share in the rewards.

Summary: cumulative weight of driving or opposing forces

A number of factors have been mentioned as tending either towards or away from further commercialization of electronic media. A very crude indication of their aggregate effect in each country can be given by treating each as having a direction as if working towards or away from commercialism and assigning negative or positive values on this basis. In Table 6 below this is done by assuming all forces to have an equal weight and to be either present or absent. Clearly, this is most unlikely to be the case, but it allows a very approximate comparison to be made of the overall *tendency* in West European countries. One further point to stress: the table is not concerned with the absolute degree of commercialization (which has been summarized above), but with the tendencies to be expected in the latter 1980s, assuming the pattern of forces remains the same. The factors considered are listed below the Table itself.

While for the most part, a given factor has a built-in direction, either for or against commercialization, this is not always so. For instance the press may stand either to lose or to gain from commercialization and its effect will vary accordingly. A similar duality characterizes 'political climate'. Consequently, the value of positive (+) or negative (−) is assigned for each factor to show the direction in a given case. Where the positive and negative working of a given fact or are thought to cancel each other out no entry is made. No distinction is made between this situation and the simple absence of a factor. For this reason also, the Table should be treated as giving a rough summary comparative measure.

TABLE 6
The cumulative effect of factors relevant to more commercialization

Country	Factor (as listed below)									Sum*
	I	II	III	IV	V	VI	VII	VIII	IX	
Britain	(+)	(+)	(+)					(+)	(+)	+5
Italy	(+)	(+)	(+)			(+)			(+)	+5
France	(+)		(+)	(+)					(+)	+4
West Germany		(+)	(+)						(+)	+3
Netherlands		(+)	(+)	(−)			(+)		(+)	+3
Spain	(+)	(+)	(+)					(+)	(+)	+5
Finland	(+)	(+)	(+)			(+)			(+)	+5
Denmark	(−)		(+)	(−)	(+)	(−)	(+)	(+)	(+)	+2
Sweden	(−)		(+)	(−)	(+)	(−)	(−)		(+)	−1
Norway	(−)		(+)	(−)	(+)			(+)	(+)	+2
Belgium	(−)	(+)	(+)		(+)	(+)	(+)		(+)	+5

(+) = Factor present and working on balance *for* commerce
(−) = Factor present and working on balance *against* commerce
* Sum obtained from (+) = +1; (−) = −1

Factors

I	Position at start (acceptance of commerce c.1980)
II	Political climate
III	Industrial policy considerations
IV	Cultural policy considerations
V	Anti-monopoly sentiment
VI	Newspaper press interests
VII	Cable in the ground
VIII	Demand for more television
IX	Commercial actors ready to invest

The sum arrived at in the right-hand column does in fact indicate a distribution not unlike that of the pre-1980 status quo. Most noticeable is the overall balance towards commerce, with only Sweden and Norway lagging behind on this indicator of the future. The concentration of entries on some countries is also an indication of where the issue has been a central one. Otherwise, the Table tends to tell in summary form what has been spelt out in several parts of this book — that the drift towards commercialization of electronic media is mainly accounted for by three things: the availability of investors seeking opportunities; the economic and industrial policy considerations of states; and a favourable political climate. Against these forces the resistance of cultural policy actors has been patchy and commercial opponents of more television commerce (for instance the press) have been weak or divided. Another way of expressing a similar conclusion is by saying that separate national self-interests, represented in government and industry, are working in the same direction, though not always together, to widen the scope of commerce in the control of electronic media.

References

AGB Research Ltd (1983) *New Media Development: TV Advertising*.
Syfret, T. (1983) *Television, Today and Tomorrow*. London: J. Walter Thompson.

Chapter 12

The industrial imperative*

Defining the problem

If we talk about an 'electronic revolution' these days we usually refer to the fact that formerly individually operating technologies are increasingly merging into one large network of technologies which includes computers, communication (e.g. telephone) and broadcasting. In this one integrated network of the future all kinds of audio and/or visual communication messages are transported: private (e.g. telephone), commercial (e.g. computerized business data) and mass media (e.g. television). The effect of this development may already be seen in the introduction of telematics (see Chapter 8 of this book) which makes the dividing line between different types of communication) — individual vs mass — a thing of the past. Key technologies in the era of integrated communication networks will be the computer, the microchip, the optical fibre, communication and direct broadcasting satellites, and related technologies (like satellite boosters).

In order to be able to analyse the impact of the new technologies on the development of mass media it seems to be necessary to introduce a concept to help categorize these developments. In terms of their technological basis as well as their economic activities, a separation between the providers of hardware and software proves to be helpful.

The hardware industry

This sector provides the equipment for all kinds of communication; hardware refers to the material aspect of these technologies. The main companies in this field usually offer a broad range of computers, cables, home electronics, transmitters, etc. We refer to this branch of industry — commonly one of the largest in advanced industrial countries — as the telecommunication industry.[1] Whereas some of their products, like home electronics, always have been sold on competitive markets, other important segments have been traditionally sold to public monopolies like the PTTs and — to a lesser extent — the public broadcasting organizations. As the monopolies of the public broadcasters (see Chapter 9) are in the process of being broken up and the monopoly powers of many PTTs are being reduced or challenged, the whole telecommunication

* Written by Hans J. Kleinsteuber.

market enters a stage of restructuring and uncertainty. As many European governments view the telecommunications market as a key to their industrial future, they follow a type of industrial and technological policy that is scheduled to strengthen this industry in a time of increased competition.

The software industry

The term 'software' refers to the non-material programming element in audiovisual media and includes the producers and distributors of all kinds of television materials: films, serials, videocassettes with entertainment, cultural or information contents. It also includes advertisements, an often neglected part of the software department. Since the time of the world success of the Hollywood film producers in the 1920s, programme software has always been highly mobile and therefore distributed on international markets for a long time. Nevertheless, the introduction of new telecommunication technologies has had a severe effect on the software situation because it enables distributors to offer their programming across national borders; programme overspill greatly endangers the public broadcasting organizations, making commercial television an attractive and profitable alternative to public television.

This chapter will concentrate on the state of, and the changes inside, the hardware telecommunication industry and only touch on the topic of software. It should be noted, that the software industry, though heavily dependent on the transmission technology which the telecommunication industry provides, is largely economically independent from the hardware producers (with exceptions, of course, like Philips and Siemens owning Polygram and Polymedia, large music and record companies). The regulation of media software, as far as it is influenced by state action, is usually referred to as media or cultural policy and as such not an object of industrial policy. The chapter attempts to ask the question of what effect deep-rooted technological changes in the field of telecommunication have upon the telecommunication industry, the industrial policy of European countries and the future of the existing public broadcasting systems. The following paragraphs will be concerned with basics of industrial policy, the European telecommunication industry and its competitors, the national and international actors, including the EEC and OECD, and they offer a (preliminary) conclusion under the heading: coordination or competition in Europe? Europe means, in the context of this discussion, of course Western Europe.

Basics of industrial policy

Industrial and technological policies are always carried out by the state (or international organization) and reflect the notion that the market alone is not always and by nature able to cope with the conflicting problems of economic stability, growth and the positive balance of trade. Industrial policy usually refers to general support of all productive industries as a whole or to specific help to certain industrial branches (like telecommunication industries). Means of industrial policy include: direct subsidies; public purchases of goods; preferential prices; protective measures and customs barriers. Technological policy is less universally oriented, serving the goal of improving the technological quality of a certain industrial branch by the financing of research and development outlays to benefit the improvement of existing technologies or to stimulate new inventions. In European countries, the first type of industrial policy is the more traditional one, in most cases carried out by the economics or finance ministries; technological policy, on the other hand, is usually directed by the ministries for technology or research and by the national PTTs. These two types are coordinated by the national government but are not necessarily congruent. As a matter of convenience, I refer to both types of policies by applying the more general and inclusive term of industrial policy.

A special emphasis on industrial policy may be counted as a sign of economic instability, possibly of a structural or cyclical crisis or of a situation where an established industry is passing through difficult waters, because it has lost export markets or fallen behind in technological achievements. Industrial policy might also serve to build up a national industry to gain independence from costly imports of products and/or know-how.

Industrial policy always takes place in a climate of cooperation and interaction between the respective industry and government. Both sides are trying jointly to reach a goal that cannot be realized independently: industrial policy is by definition always supportive and never offensive to the affected industries (otherwise it might be social policy or economic planning). As industrial policy usually includes transfer of funds, services or other favours from the state to commercial companies it is actually often more rooted in the interests of these companies than in the democratically formulated policies of the government. Furthermore it should be recognized that the present structure of industries already reflects the influence of past industrial policy impacts, especially if a long record of such policy exists.

Industrial policies of Western industrial countries follow three basic principles, usually not in a pure but in a rather mixed way (Kristensen and Stankiewicz, 1982: 11):

1. Defensive policies: the state offers some support to industries exposed to particularly severe pressure, without any specific

technological component. This type of policy is prevalent in the USA where state intervention is traditionally limited to military and space research objectives.

2. Adjustment policies: the proponents of this policy recommend measures which are intended to quickly re-establish what is considered economic equilibrium and foster a competitive climate. Some characteristic means of this policy are support to innovative companies, state financing of research and development activities without imposing a predetermined technological strategy, the liberalizing of regulations or reduction of taxes. A policy of this type may be found in West Germany, in the UK and in Scandinavian countries.
3. Active policies: followers of these policies seek an active role for the state in modernizing industries, creating new high-growth industries to offset the decline of older, low technology industries. Countries in this category devise a specific long-term strategy that is supposed to strengthen a competitive position on world markets, coupled with a continuous protection of the domestic industries. The classical example of active policy seems to be Japan. In Europe France comes closest to this model.

The European telecommunication industry and its competitors

Beginning in the second half of the last century the European telecommunication industry, whose founding fathers were often important inventors (like Siemens and Marconi), for a long time enjoyed a leading position in the world. From its very beginning, it was an object of special government attention and support. Because of its civic importance as a key industry for economic growth and its military significance as a means of linking military units together, much of the research and development money in the past was provided through public sources. The British, for example, had already built an extensive telegraph cable system in the nineteenth century and made it the communication backbone of its world empire, while the Germans made it a point to stay independent from this network by supporting the development of wireless communication to reach their colonies. World War I delivered a boost to the European telecommunication industry and provided the technology and the manufacturing capacities that allowed a rapid introduction of radio in the early 1920s in all major countries.

It is significant for understanding the traditions of European industrial policy that — wherever there was an elaborate telecommunication industry — it could rely on a policy of strong protection within the borders of its country. This statement applies as well to the communications equipment that the national PTT bought, as to the transmission 'hardware', that was purchased by the public broadcasting organizations. The PTTs often acquired their material for a higher price than a competitive market would have allowed, thereby in fact subsidizing the respective 'clientèle' industry. Only the small countries, without a sufficient national industry, preferred to buy their equipment on the world market, enjoying the advantage of the lowest prices available.

Based on the described pattern, the telecommunication industry found large export markets only in countries where there was no relevant telecommunication production: this included mainly countries of the Third World. The markets of Japan and the USA offered up to the 1970s a rather similar picture, with highly protected national markets: Japan with its national telecommunication organization, NTT, and the USA, with the (nearly) monopolistic AT & T that purchased most of its hardware material from its subsidiary, Western Electric.

Besides the protection policy of monopolies like the PTTs and the broadcasting authorities, the establishment of national technical standards was another means of erecting walls against competition. So standards still differ widely in Europe. A familiar example is that of a continental division into two regions of incompatible colour-television systems: SECAM in France and Eastern Europe and PAL in the other parts. Videotex was developed individually and it took years to introduce a European (CEPT) standard, but integration still causes problems. A user of a mobile (car) telephone according to West German specifications cannot use his set in France and vice versa.

There has never been a homogeneous telecommunication industry in Europe. The large countries traditionally have a strong national base for telecommunication production, being able to provide 'their' PTT with all relevant equipment; in this first category fall West Germany, France, the UK and Italy. Two middle-sized countries are the home of multinational telecommunication producers, that manufacture and market most of their products outside their national borders: the Netherlands with Philips (the largest electronics firm of Europe, with only 21 percent of its workforce in the Netherlands) and L M Ericsson of Sweden (again Sweden accounts for only 22 percent of its sales). Another country with a relatively strong base in telecommunications is Finland with the Nokia and Salora companies (see Tables 7 and 8).

There is a second group of countries in Europe that boast a significant telecommunication industry, but it is made up primarily or totally of subsidiaries of foreign multinational companies. A prime example for this industry structure may be found in Spain (ITT, Ericsson, Philips, et al.) and it also applies in Belgium,

TABLE 7
Electronic exports

Country	% Share of total exports of industrial countries, 1979	% Share of OECD exports of telecommunication and sound recording apparatus, 1980
West Germany	16.3	12.8
France	9.5	4.4
Italy	6.8	2.8
UK	8.6	5.5
USA	17.2	11.4
Japan	9.7	40.5

Source: EEC, 1983: 16

Denmark, Norway, Austria, Greece and Portugal. Some of these countries are able to maintain a national position in certain fields, such as Norway in computers or Denmark in hi-fi components, but the tendency is towards concentration and multinational production. For instance, the last independent producer of television sets in Austria recently failed.

TABLE 8
Balance of trade in telecommunication equipment, 1980 (US$ million)

Trade surplus countries	Exports	Imports	Balance
Japan	3,772	209	3,563
Germany	2,222	1,204	1,018
Sweden	993	233	760
United Kingdom	1,240	778	462
France	1,154	781	373
Netherlands	1,269	742	527
Belgium–Luxembourg	725	515	210
Italy	596	593	3
Switzerland	285	250	35
Trade deficit countries	**Exports**	**Imports**	**Balance**
United States	2,655	3,212	−557
Canada	691	760	− 69
Australia	40	246	−206
Austria	100	255	−155
Spain	115	282	−167
Norway	115	199	− 84
Finland	78	136	− 58
Greece	18	122	−104

Source: OECD, 1983: 133

The countries of this second category usually import noticeably more telecommunication equipment than they are able to export. The object of their national industry is to strengthen the telecommunication industry, gain access to latest high technology licences, decrease the dependency on imported technology and become an exporter themselves.

Because of the highly protected market structure of Europe, non-European companies traditionally had very little chance to sell their telecommunication equipment to the PTTs. So the largest telecommunication manufacturer of the world, Western Electric, owned by AT & T and accounting for more than one quarter of world production, was virtually non-existent in European markets. There is one important exception to that rule though: ITT, the second largest telecommunication company of the world, bought up a number of well-established European producers (like SEL in West Germany, STC in the UK) and built up production plants in many other countries like Denmark, Norway and Spain to become the fourth largest electronic firm in Europe (see Table 9).

It is one of the basic characteristics of the telecommunication industry that it is highly concentrated, the main reasons being the buying policy of the telephone monopolies and economies of scale. This applies to all industrialized countries: governments usually purchase between 70 percent (Japan) and 82 percent (FRG) of all communication equipment that is produced for the total country market (EEC, 1983: 74. This does not apply for the USA, where AT & T is private). This situation led to a high degree of concentration in the telecommunication industry, where typically the market share of the four largest firms in domestic sales rank between 85 percent and 90 percent (including Japan and USA; OECD, 1983: 34).

The protected situation of the European telecommunication industry has led to significant developments:

— Compared to the USA, the world market shares are relatively lower (e.g. the largest European telecommunication producer, Siemens, accounts for 6.9 percent of the world market, as compared to Western Electric's 26.8 percent and ITT's 12.4 percent — figures for 1980).
— In some areas of high technology like digital switching equipment, optical fibre, and communication satellites, Europe is several years behind the USA in development and experience.

With the protective walls disappearing in the future, the European telecommunication industry might move in the direction of the computer market, which has never been regulated in Europe. Of the twenty-five largest computer companies operating in

TABLE 9
Major manufacturers of telecommunication equipment: sales, 1980 and 1981 (US$ billion)

Manufacturer	(A) Total sales		(B) Total sales telecommunication equipment		(C) B/A × 100	(D) B/ΣB × 100 total
	1980	1981	1980	1981	1980	1980
Western Electric (USA)	12.032	13.008	12.032	13.008	100%	31%
ITT (USA)	18.529	–	6.041	–	33%	16%
Siemens (West Germany)	17.560	15.292	5.054	4.602	29%	13%
LM Ericsson (Sweden)	2.878	3.200	2.878	3.200	100%	7%
GTE (USA)	9.979	–	2.199	–	22%	6%
Northern Telecom (Canada)	1.758	2.144	1.758	2.144	100%	5%
NEC (Japan)	3.943	4.820	1.448	1.680	37%	4%
Philips (Netherlands)	18.360	16.964	1.285	–	7%	3%
CGE (France)	10.823	–	1.919	–	18%	5%
Thomson Brandt (France)	8.638	–	1.630	–	19%	4%
GEC (United Kingdom)	8.280	8.382	1.325	1.341	16%	3%
Plessey (United Kingdom)	1.968	1.955	0.787	0.850	40%	2%
Italtel (Italy)	0.587	0.616	0.587	0.616	100%	2%
Total	115.335	–	38.944	–	34%	100%

Source: OECD, 1983: 130

Europe, thirteen, more than half, are actually American (EEC, 1983: 211). IBM alone provides Europe with 60 percent of all mainframe computers. Europe shows equal weakness in the field of semiconductor (microchips) production, where the USA alone accounts for 46 percent of world production, Japan for 16 percent and West Germany for only 8 percent, France for 6 percent (EEC, 1983: 211).

Another important development is the loss of Europe's dominant role in the production of home electronics. The Japanese entered this domain of European industry in the 1960s with imitated technology at considerably lower prices. Over the years they improved their quality and were able to take over large parts of the market for hi-fi components, television sets and, especially, videocassette recorders. Confronted with Far-East competition, European companies lost a number of struggles over standards as well, e.g. the Philips norm, Video 2000, against the Japanese VHS that already became the world standard. Besides lower wages, the Japanese success was largely due to a very substantial industrial policy, especially by the famous 'super-ministry' MITI, that harmonizes efforts between the industry and the state.

After European producers had lost large market shares in the home electronics market and had not been able to build up a European computer industry (national and European projects in this respect had failed miserably), a new development outside the Continent endangered the still strong telecommunication industry. 'Deregulation' of 'natural monopolies' like the telephone company, AT & T, became the openly declared policy of the US administration in the late 1970s. The main forces behind the deregulation of the US telecommunication markets, that are regulated by the supervisory authority Federal Communication Commission (FCC), were industrial customers, which felt that they suffered under monopolistic exploitation by AT & T (Schiller, 1982). When it became clear that competition would be part of the telecommunication industry, AT & T agreed to a divestiture procedure in 1982, thereby creating a smaller but much more aggressive AT & T, ready to enter international markets. AT & T has already started joint ventures with Philips, bought shares in Olivetti and cooperated with a number of European companies.

Following the AT & T example, British Telecom and Nippon TT (Japan) lost their public monopoly structure and became private companies. Other PTTs are presently changing their protectionist policy as well, becoming more competitive, beginning to purchase equipment at (lower) world prices and liberalizing the markets for periphery materials. Obviously the European telecommunication industry, as well as the national PTTs, are at a stage of deep restructuring. The industry has to fight mounting competition from abroad and cannot rely on automatic purchases by their PTTs. Reactions are quite diversified: whereas the manufacturers of the traditionally strong countries still prefer the protective approach, smaller countries see a chance to strengthen their national telecommunication base and become less dependent on foreign providers.

The telecommunication industry seeks more cooperation and joint action on the international level but is divided on how to cope with the situation. European coordination and cooperation are definitely increasing (see below) but companies also seek refuge in direct joint actions with US companies and to a lesser extent Japanese companies. A prime example for this strategy is Philips' joint venture with AT & T in the field of digital equipment, where the US company is a world leader in technology and Philips offers its worldwide marketing network.

Governments and international actors

The most important level of industrial policy activity is, of course, the level of national government. In Europe we usually find three main sub-actors, as part of the governmental system: the national PTT, enjoying some kind of monopoly rights; the ministries responsible for industrial or economic affairs; and the ministries for research or technology. Other actors might be found as well like ministries for culture, education or defence, interdepartmental committees or special commissions. In practically all countries with an active industrial policy, reports have been issued on various questions and topics relating to telecommunication development.

We find additional levels of political action in the form of the European Economic Community (EEC), which involves most European countries with a strong telecommunication industry, and of the Organization for Economic Co-operation and Development (OECD), comprising the main competitors of Europe, USA, Japan (and Canada which is strong in telecommunication production, but not a primary challenge to Europe). The EEC and OECD will be dealt with separately.

In European countries with a considerable telecommunication industry, industrial policy ranges between the 'adjustment' and the 'active' types. There are, however, noticeable exceptions to the rule. In Belgium, the telecommunication industry consists mainly of multinational subsidiaries. No coherent policy exists because the industry is heavily integrated into international markets and strategies, the government's objective being to create a fiscal and social climate hospitable to foreign investment. We find a somewhat similar situation in Austria, where multinational companies produce much of the telecommunication equipment needed. As noted above, the last 'independent' Austrian producer of television sets recently went bankrupt because of overwhelming foreign competition. The main intention of the government is to maintain access to advanced technologies via multinational affiliations. The government of Luxembourg is very active in broadcasting policy (i.e. software policy) but, due to the lack of a telecommunication industry, has not defined a corresponding industrial strategy. The policies of these conditions could be defined as the 'defensive' type.

Most other European countries developed their mixture of 'adjustment' and 'active' industrial policies during the 1960s and 1970s, usually referring in an earlier stage to industrial branches like nuclear energy, aerospace, computers and similar 'key technologies'. The importance of telecommunication technologies as the backbone of communication infrastructure was usually 'discovered' only during the second half of the 1970s. As the telecommunication programmes of the European states are very different in their organizational base, their extent and the financing involved, they will not be compared directly. It has to be noted though that their intention was amazingly similar: the creation of a technological basis for what was called an 'information society'. To present a picture of the highly diversified situation in Europe, some examples are given.

The United Kingdom, a net importer of electronics, follows a conservative policy of primarily supporting private industrial initiatives, directly by financing and indirectly by education and promoting awareness. The Alvey Committee devised a Programme for Advanced Technology and proposed more funds in this field. The denationalization of British Telecom (51 percent private) opens the way for competitors (like Mercury/Cable & Wireless to build up a competing fibre optic network for business data links), but allows BT to become a major economic force in other parts of Europe as well. One aspect of this policy is to make the UK, with London, already regarded as the software capital of Europe (satellite programmes and Euro-advertising), the hub for high technology in electronics and telecommunications as well.

The Nora-Minc Report (1980: first published Paris, 1978) had already emphasized the importance of new information technologies and computerization for the industrial as well as the political future of France. Government policy is to cover all sectors of the telecommunication industry by its five-year plan. Two important actors in France are the (recently) nationalized telecommunication companies (Thompson, GCE, and Matra) and the ministry of defence, giving financial support to a large segment of all research and development projects. France is active in all fields of satellite (TDF–1), cable and telematic technologies and has used strong protective measures in the past to protect its national industries, as for instance a blockade of Japanese videocassette recorders by customs authorities.

West Germany, since the late 1950s, has given financial support to private research and development expenditures. A Telecommunications Report (by a commission called KtK) underlined, in 1976, the importance of a continuous extension of the telephone network as well as the experimental introduction of cable television. In 1979, the PTT and the Ministry for Research and Technology decided to hasten the development of fibre optic cables and its large-scale introduction. Other well-financed programmes open the way for videotex and other forms of telematics (programme: Technical Communications 1978–82) and satellites (TV-Sat, Kopernikus). The PTT, claiming to be the largest civil investor in the country and the largest service organization in Europe, holds the leading position in introducing telecommunication technologies.

Italy, with its rather open and somewhat chaotic broadcasting policy, seems to follow a much more consistent hardware policy. A TLC plan (1982–91) is scheduled to help the introduction of large-scale telematic services including homebanking, teleconferencing, telefax and videotex. The government approved a National Space Plan in 1979 that should provide the country with a satellite (Ital-Sat) and auxiliary rocket technology in the late 1980s.

The Netherlands have traditionally been a strong international provider of home electronics (Philips); to strengthen its position in the information industry, Philips cooperates with a number of foreign companies, including AT & T, Siemens and Grundig. A National Commission on Information and other government institutions support industrial projects of cable, electronic publishing and information technologies (*Informatica stimuleringsplan*, 1984).

It has been a long established policy in Sweden to assist industry through a highly developed infrastructure. A report (*Svensk Informationsteknologi*) recommended further support for the information industry and a microelectronics programme for five years is under way. A focal point of industrial policy is the development of the Tele-X satellite that is primarily financed by Sweden (82 percent) with the cooperation of Norway (15 percent) and Finland (3 percent).

The structure of industrial policy in Europe is widely accepted within the political spectrum of each respective country, but is also viewed with scepticism. Often, the necessity of an industrial policy is not called into question, but the actual performance is criticized. Whereas in France all political parties favour an active involvement of the state, telecommunication policy in the UK is sharply polarized: the Conservatives favour a 'leave-it-to-the-market' strategy, but Labour demands more traditional PTT type of policy. In Italy, we find no opposition to a strong industrial policy, but the Christian Democrats stress private initiative quite contrary to the Left demands for special support for the nationalized industries. In West Germany, the parties of the political left are clearly divided over questions of industrial policy. The Social Democrats favour an aggressive modernization policy, the Greens fundamentally oppose the development of technologies that they consider unnecessary and dangerous to human communication and employment. In many countries the public broadcasters remain critical since they expect an immense rise of commercial competition through new telecommunication networks which, they fear, might finally lead to their destruction.

The European level

It was the OECD (Organization for Economic Co-operation and Development) that first made telecommunications a policy topic for Europe. Beginning in 1969, it started to emphasize the danger of 'gaps in technology', meaning that the USA had achieved technological breakthroughs — especially with satellites and computers — and that Japan was closely following with an aggressive modernization strategy. Both were challenging the traditional export markets of the European telecommunication industry. OECD propagated as a defence the 'informatization' of the European society and later the introduction of telematics in Europe (OECD, 1974) to overcome its technological backwardness. It further supported with its arguments the lessening of national controls over procurement policies and the liberalization of telecommunication markets — such as recommending a change in the structure of the European telecommunication industry closer to the structure and scope of the US model. 'At the domestic level, increased competition in equipment markets is seen as an important pre-requisite for technical advance, particularly as regards new services' (OECD, 1983: 13). Finally OECD argued that European integration could be fostered by the integration of new information technologies. The idea was that, in a technically already unified territory, it would become increasingly difficult to follow national self-interests: technology could create a truly united Europe.

The EEC recognizes the backwardness of the European telecommunication industry, as described, but offers solutions markedly different from OECD. Whereas OECD tends to argue in favour of the strongest companies in world markets, which in most cases are multinationals from the USA or Japan, the EEC is much more concerned with the strengthening of EEC-based companies. The EEC especially emphasizes the point that European companies are smaller in size and that 'there are very few truly pan-European firms in the industry, the leading examples being subsidiaries of the US firm ITT, Philips of the Netherlands and to a lesser extent L M Ericsson of Sweden' (Commission of the EEC, 1983: 13). Research and development expenditures of European companies are low and often lead to a duplication of work in different countries. An EEC report of 1983 argues that EEC members 'consistently perform below the level achieved by Japan' (Commission of the EEC, 1983: 17). In 1979–80 EEC companies accounted for only 37 percent of all OECD exports, compared with Japan alone for over 40 percent in the telecommunication and sound recording sectors. The more successful exporters in world markets (1980) are West Germany with 12.8 percent of all OECD exports, the Netherlands 5.6 percent, UK 5.5 percent, France 4.4 percent, Sweden 3.7 percent and Italy 2.8 percent. The relative success of smaller countries like the Netherlands and Sweden should be noted.

The EEC proposes to increase concerted efforts for its member countries to overcome the lag in telecommunications development. This includes joint efforts in research and development, cooperation in production and marketing, joint ventures and the standardization of telecommunication norms. In 1984 the Commission of the EEC presented a report (*Green Paper*) to the public, entitled *Television without Frontiers*, that strongly argued in favour of a common market for broadcasting, based on harmonized legislation in the member states (see above, pp. 29–30). The idea seems to be that a community-wide distribution of programme software could help create a European unity of information and opinions. Also the Commission pointed out (in a discussion paper) the hardware effects of this policy, claiming that the 'creation of a common market for broadcasting and cross-frontier distribution of broadcasting services will help push through the new information and communication techniques needed in terms of the economy as a whole' (*Financial Times*, 2 February 1984).

The most ambitious programme of EEC is ESPRIT (European Strategic Programme for Research and Development in Information Technology); it features close cooperation between the community and twelve of the largest telecommunication companies for the years 1984 to 1994 and includes spending US$ 1.25 billion for joint industry–government research projects. The main goal of this programme is to become to a large extent independent of information technology imports from the USA and Japan (see pp. 30–31 above). Already in 1978 the EEC had decided to initiate a five-year experimental programme 'Forecasting and Assessment in the field of Science and Technology' (FAST) that was latter extended to become FAST II. One of the main emphases of the project is on the 'information society' including the aim of throwing light on possible and desirable options for research and development and the studying of possible sources for alternative developments (Bannon 1982). In 1985, countries of the EEC discussed the establishment of a joint research agency (based on a EUREKA proposal by France) that should help to counteract a new push of military 'Star Wars' research in the USA.

During the last few years, the large European telecommunication manufacturers have also increased their joint efforts in research and development standardization, production and marketing (some examples were given above). One of the most pressing problems of Europe's telecommunication industry is that of standards: often the policy of 'sheltered industries' led to the introduction of national standards that are competing on the European market and divide the continent with differing hardware norms. The most striking example is the division of Europe into two colour-television systems, based on the French SECAM and the West Germany PAL specifications. It is intended to use a unified colour-television standard on future European broadcasting satellites (D–2–MAC). The introduction of videotex, based on national PTT research orders, led to a diversity of standards (Prestel, ANTIOPE, BTX), that are now being harmonized by CEPT. In still other fields European companies proved to be competitive in the quality of technology, but unable to succeed on world markets because of competing standards, used by larger companies: this applies to the video standards as mentioned above.

After earlier attempts for cooperation failed totally (Unidata project), six European leading minicomputer manufacturers have decided to develop a common software operating system (Bull, Olivetti, ICL, Siemens, Nixdorf, Philips) that is to compete with IBM software systems. Such a common standard is considered a prerequisite for the survival of the European computer industry through 1990 and beyond. The standard is not universal, as Ericsson stays out and will keep its computers compatible with IBM material. As was pointed out before, the main threat to European cooperation is the tendency of individual companies to seek special partnerships with US-based manufacturers (like Philips and A T & T in digital telephone equipment) and to a lesser extent with

Japanese firms (like Siemens and Fujitsu in large computers).

Another disadvantage of European telecommunication development is the wasteful duplication of research and development and production of similar technologies in many countries, usually based on national industrial policy priorities. The introduction of optical fibres in Europe may serve as an example. All countries with a relevant telecommunication industry are developing and testing the technology with considerable public support. In the UK, British Telecom plays the leading role, in France the Direction Générale des Telecommunications (DGT) is promoting the application of fibre optic cables; in West Germany the Post and the Research and Technology Ministry support the BIGFON projects and, in Italy the service providers, SIP and ASST, work with the collaboration of cable producers. In the Netherlands, Philips and in Sweden, Ericsson, both the leading telecommunication companies in their respective countries, are active in this field. Even the Danish government supports the production of optical fibres in that country. OECD (1983, 124) describes the European scenery in the growth industry of optical fibres as rather diversified, with sometimes strong government intervention (France, Germany), sometimes more private initiative (Netherlands, Sweden). These countries try to build a national base for better export opportunities and as such are making joint European cooperation impossible. It is precisely by way of this pattern of European industrial policy, that the large-scale production of optical fibre is obstructed and success on world markets becomes questionable. In addition, the effect of this policy upon the national broadcasting structure might be highly damaging, because it eases the import of foreign programmes. The high emphasis on industrial policy leads to the introduction of technologies, not so much on the basis of public demand and necessity, as on the basis of an assumed international marketing success.

Conclusions: coordination or competition?

European governments traditionally follow the 'adjustment' or 'active' type of industrial policy in the field of telecommunication. Governments attempt to provide their national industries with the strength to survive and compete well on world markets. Among the many instruments of industrial policy we find the direct financing of research and development in telecommunication technologies and the indirect subsidies via the procurement practices of the PTTs, and often the public broadcasting organizations.

Industrial policy in Europe is still basically national policy. As a similar policy is pursued in many European countries, there is a clear danger of duplicated research and development expenditures, wasted public subsidies, over investment and small-scale national production. The EEC, as well as the telecommunication companies, is well aware of this problem and has become increasingly active in joint efforts, that include public and private planning, research, marketing and production. But we also find strong countertendencies in European companies, that prefer individual cooperation with US- or Japan-based firms, because they seek access to high technology know-how.

We find a strong pressure in Europe to liberalize markets for hardware equipment, forcing the PTTs to buy outside their sheltered industries (or the PTTs themselves become private as in the UK). The tendency towards deregulation and privatization started in the USA in the late 1970s and the introduction of these principles will open the European markets for stronger competition from the USA and Japan. As the non-European companies are, for the most part, larger and technologically more advanced they might further threaten the future of the European telecommunication industries.

The policy of liberation and privatization of hardware production correlates with the opening of software markets and the commercialization of broadcasting providers. Even though in most cases the interested companies are not identical (hardware and software producers being economically separated), they clearly need and support each other to foster the introduction and exploitation of new media technologies.

The conventional public broadcasting organizations of Europe are the main losers of the concerted industrial and governmental efforts to introduce new media technologies, offering many more channels of transmission, that the public providers are unable to fill with their programme software. Industrial policy strategies of national governments as well as the EEC — based on concepts of an 'information society' — tend either to ignore this impact upon public broadcasters, or — especially among more conservative governments — to welcome this side effect to strengthen commercial elements in broadcasting. Understandably, the analysed industrial policy is not universally accepted in Europe but meets some opposition, mainly on the political left.

The industrial policy approach in telecommunication development favours electronic and audiovisual ways of communication over less technical ones: e.g. computer storage and databanks over books and libraries; or multichannel television over cinemas and theatres. In the continuous competition between different modes of communication, it creates a clear bias towards centralized, non-material, and mass media structures. The introduction of the many newly developed telecommunication technologies — highly subsidized by the taxpayer and not necessarily based on public demand — might enjoy the support of profiting industries, but will further reduce the amount of direct and human communication in favour of indirect and machine-type communication.

Note

1. This term is not always used consistently in publications, because of differing definitions in offical sources like EEC and OECD.

References

Bannon, Liam et al (1982) *Information Technology: Impact on the Way of Life* Dublin: Tycooly International Publishing.

Commission of the EEC (1983) *The EEC Telecommunications Industry: Concentration, Competition and Competitiveness*. Brussels.

Commission of the EEC (1984) *Television without Frontiers (The Green Paper)*. Brussels.

Goldsmith, Maurice (ed.) (1978) *Strategies for Europe: Proposals for Science and Technology Policies*. Oxford: Pergamon Press.

Goodmann, R.A. (1984) 'A comparison of industrial policies in five nations: Brazil, France, Germany, Israel and the Netherlands', in R.A. Goodmann and J. Pavon (eds.), *Planning for National Technology Policy*. New York: Praeger.

Hills, J. (1984) *Industrial Policy and Information Policy*. London: Croom Helm.

Hollins, Timothy (1984) *Beyond Broadcasting: Into the Cable Age*. London: Broadcasting Research Unit.

Kristensen, Pear Hill and Rikard Stankiewicz (eds.) (1982) *Technology Policy and Industrial Development in Sweden*. Malmö: Research Policy Institute.

Nora, S. and A. Minc (1980) *The Computerization of Society*. Cambridge (Mass.): MIT Press (first published Paris, 1978).

OECD (1974) *Informatic Studies: Computers and Telecommunications*. Paris.

OECD (1980) *Technological Change and Economic Policy*. Paris.

OECD (1983) *Telecommunications: Pressures and Policies of Change*. Paris.

Schiller, Dan (1982) *Telematics and Government*. Norwood (N.J.).

Soete, Luc and Giovanni Dosi (1984) *Technology and Employment in the Electronics Industry*. London: Frances Pinter.

Van Houten, H.J. (ed.) (1983) *The Competitive Strength of the Information and Communication Industry in Europe*. The Hague: Nijhoff.

Chapter 13

A new media order in Europe — actuality or illusion?*

The aim of this chapter is to comment further on some of the answers that have emerged in response to questions posed at the outset of this study, questions which have been dealt with in relation to each of the main new media and the main issues for policy. We have found a number of things: that there is, throughout Europe, a new and expanding field of media policy in response to the threat or promise of new communication technology; that there is also a very similar pattern of significant actors at national level; that the issues and nature of the debate are very similar across Europe; that there is some movement towards a European-level policy, although no policy as yet; that economic, industrial and market considerations predominate over cultural and social concerns, thus threatening public broadcasting institutions; that countries can be differentially ranked according to their relative position on a dimension of cultural vs industrial concern and one of public vs private initiative. These are some of the main general matters for commentary, with an eye, especially, to the global communication situation and the reality or otherwise of the heralded 'communication revolution'.

New media — myth or reality?

A strong impression derived from looking closely at what has been happening in Europe in respect of new media and from comparing national experiences is that, while there are real challenges facing the existing electronic media order, after a thirty-year period of near-stability, the perceptions of the challenge and the responses to it are still very much clouded and confused by myths, dreams, ideologies and uncertainties. It is not that the specific actors involved are not usually clear and hard-headed about what they want to gain or defend in their own interest, but there is much unclarity about what is really on offer or what is to be feared. Several factors contribute to this state of obscurity, quite apart from the permanent unpredictability of the future. One is the mystique associated with high technology for most of those — mainly officials, politicians or business-people — involved in policy debate and formulation. Another is the tendency of business in search of

* Written by Denis McQuail, Karen Siune and Jeremy Tunstall.

investment to exaggeration and excessive optimism. A third is the very similar tendency of governments as they clutch at any future chance of economic salvation. Novelty, technology and quantity have become almost overriding criteria of higher level policy-making and their pursuit becomes hard to resist lower down.

There is no doubt that technological advance in the twin fields of computers and satellites has undermined the technical foundations of the established electronic media order, the first offering, amongst other things, a reversal or major modification of the current relationship of inequality between receiver and sender of communication, the second an end to scarcity of distribution channels and national frontiers in broadcast transmission. Since the existing order is based on strict management of centralized, one-way, communication within national frontiers, it cannot, seemingly, survive unchanged in liberal societies committed to economic and technological change.

The general situation is a historically recurrent one, with new technologies in search of new uses, vested interests trying to protect themselves and new actors trying to gain access. This historical familiarity does not make the situation any easier to cope with and there are no specific lessons from history about the outcome. In any case, the resulting situation seems to be characterized by a curious mixture of mindless optimism, half-baked theory about society and small-minded self-interest which does not promise much for rational, far-sighted policy-making. Even where the latter is aspired to at the national level or on particular issues (and examples can be found), the effect is likely to be circumscribed by the loss of full national control and the inherent economic and technological uncertainties.

Certain contours of the situation are, nevertheless, becoming clearer for those more interested in the reality than the myths. One message to be derived from an inspection of what is actually happening is that there are separate paths in terms of scale and pace of change for the genuinely new media — especially telematics — and for the new ways of distributing old media content — especially popular forms of television by way of cable and satellite. Under the existing broadcasting order in Europe, there has been, with inter-country variations, a relative starvation of the latter, so that there does seem to be a considerable unmet demand simply for more television, something which adds to the excitement of the whole issue for politicians and business as well as for the public. As a driving force for change, this potential demand is somewhat undependable and there must be a limit to what it holds out by way of economic and industrial benefit. There is likely to be a rearrangement, as well as an increase, of existing p distribution and a good deal more import and exp remain in terms of available consumer time and mone revenue or other sources of funds, and software capacity. The main immediate benefits are likely to satellite and cable sectors; yet it seems that military or imperatives had already taken care of initial satellite developments and cable had been laid in several countries independently of any wish to provide more television. There is no very good reason to suppose (as it seems to have been in Britain) that demand for entertainment will be a very effective stimulus to communication modernization.

On the other hand, in the sector where there is more long-term economic potential — that of broad-band cable and interactive systems — supply appears well ahead of demand and rapid change is going to require some as yet undiscovered motor. In general, it is commercial interests who are associated with the path of 'more television' (by satellite and cable) and governments with interactive media development. Both want each other to help them in their respective goals, a circumstance which produced uneasy, perhaps temporary, forms of cooperation, which is a relatively new feature of the situation in Europe. One consequence, however, seems to have been a mutual but unspoken, agreement not to expose each other's myths and a general absence of inquiry into the real needs which exist in society and which new media might help to meet. The 'secondary' goals of profit or economic development have largely displaced ideas of what public communication systems are really for. Even if this last matter is open to many different formulations, the attempt to grapple with it has, in the past, helped to organize public discussion and political decision-making in a meaningful way and it could still contribute a much needed measure to discipline and sense to current sloganizing about new media.

The transition from cultural to industrial policy goals

It has been remarked several time in the course of this book that policy-making has come, almost everywhere, under stronger influence from considerations of 'industrial' rather than 'cultural' policy, even if the issues, for most European politicians involved, are still framed more in cultural than in industrial terms. This is not surprising, given the fact that the electronic media order which we have (mainly public broadcasting) is largely a social-cultural invention, a framework of law and convention within which the broadcast technologies are used to meet a mixture of believed social needs and consumer demands for information and culture, while the

.ıallenge' is mainly economic and technological in character. Hence the terms of debate are set by what exists, as something to be replaced, changed or retained. Yet it is worth noting that relatively little action is taken (leaving words aside) to reap social and cultural benefit from the new media, an effort which strongly characterized the original development of radio and television. It is not only that national economic situations have come to dominate all spheres of government, which could be just a temporary historical accident, it is also that a new 'logic' has developed, a way of thinking and argument, which helps to incorporate cultural and information services and communication more generally into economic and industrial thinking. Thus, in countries which have had broadcast services strongly based on cultural considerations (in the widest sense), such as France or West Germany, cultural arguments (e.g. about encouraging production in the national language and resisting cultural 'invasion') are now deployed because of their relevance to economic competition rather than for their own sake. What were once seen as purely cultural assets are being re-examined for their potential value in world markets. This state of affairs is unlikely to be quickly, if ever, reversed and it has tended to make many of the cultural arguments which were politically and ideologically compelling in the past, seem out of touch or irrelevant.

The situation will require a considerable effort on the part of cultural actors to rethink their position, not only by exposing the flaws and unsupported assumptions in the new economic 'logic', but by developing new concepts of appropriate cultural objectives for media policy and by revising ideas about how these might be reached. It is not enough to complain that quality is being sacrificed to quantity, which does seem to be the case, but to say more clearly what quality means, especially in relation to a legitimate public interest in how public communication systems perform in relation to the society as a whole. The cultural issues will not go away and there will persist an ultimately political demand to match media system provision to what societies decide they want. This is not necessarily an argument against the expansion of supply and distribution facilities over which policy is now presiding. There is a risk that cultural actors in the policy process of Europe may weaken their own position if they automatically oppose change and rely on earlier forms of strict regulation and maintenance of the status quo automatically to achieve their objectives. This risk is quite widely recognized and one consequence is, in fact, a somewhat unexpected giving of ground in some countries, especially on the part of the political left. There need be no total inconsistency between the cultural and the economic logics, as the proponents of the latter have evidently discovered. It is also useful to recall (see Chapter 12) that industrial policy does not necessarily mean commercialization or privatization. There are alternative means of implementing such policies, one being through encouragement of market forces, another on the basis of public direction of media and via the PTTs. In Europe, only Britain seems so far to have gone far along the former course, while others prefer the latter or adopt mixed strategies in powerful combination, as in France and West Germany.

Deregulation European-style

Although the word 'deregulation' is widely used, sometimes interchangeably with terms like 'privatization' and 'liberalization', it is arguably an inappropriate term for the European media situation. The American style of regulation was generally a system of rules and regulatory agencies operating outside the commercial media system in order to set various requirements and conditions in what was believed to be the public interest. While there are examples of this kind of regulation in Europe, notably in the case of cable operations, the dominant form of regulation is still practised by the broadcast media themselves at the behest of parliaments and often following national or regional 'media laws'. Nevertheless, regulation is inextricably mixed with the operating policies of the electronic media. Regulation in Europe has, consequently, a more positive connotation than in the United States, in the sense of being more prescriptive and purposeful than proscriptive. What is happening in Europe is certainly a measure of privatization, in that a private media sector is being newly established or extended, especially in relation to cable systems and radio. But this effectively involves an extension of regulation to set standards, control operating conditions and 'police' the boundaries between the public and private sectors. Examples of new regulation include the British Cable Authority or the new Media Law in the Netherlands, or the laws being prepared by the German Länder. At the end of the current phase of policy-making and new media development, there is likely to be a good deal more regulation than before, even though there will be more media and more freedom of operation in several respects. As yet there has been no privatization of any existing broadcasting authority, although their scope of operation may be restricted (or even widened) and some of the rules may be relaxed to enable them to operate more competitively. They may even become more 'commercial' in one or more of the senses discussed in Chapter 11.

As we have seen, the existing broadcasting monopolies provide the starting point and the frame for virtually all policy-making which has to do with radio and television. However vulnerable they are and over-dependent on coalitions of political forces mainly composed of parties of the left and centre and on social cultural elites (they do also have some attraction for conservative social forces), they are everywhere rather firmly established as employers and cultural producers and entrenched in law, custom and public expectation (even appreciation). It is significant that so far they seem to have survived the first stage of policy revision in Europe even in countries, such as Britain and West Germany, most in pursuit of the hoped-for economic advantages of private enterprise. Nevertheless, they are in danger of stagnating or being whittled away and they are at risk from sources other than politically opposed forces, especially: the disappearance of the scarcity of channels argument which legitimated monopoly; decentralization tendencies fostered by new media and sought by some states; the increased internationalization of supply and reception of content; deregulation generally in the telecommunication sector.

One cannot yet foresee how these various forces will operate and take effect, but so far European countries have generally proved rather cautious about innovating new organizational forms for television. They have mainly chosen against public sector growth, but also against 'denationalization' and in favour of additional services provided locally or regionally in a fragmented way. In other words nothing really new is being institutionalized on any large scale, while several distinctly non-institutionalized forms of provision are being tacitly allowed to appear, as the market dictates, notably by way of international satellite-to-cable systems and via the whole video distribution system.

One general tendency to be observed which seems not to be a very conscious act of policy, is a gradual separation between control of hardware (means of distribution) and control of software (content). The original broadcasting model linked the two inextricably in most European countries, placing both in the hands of a public monopoly. This was in contrast to the fairly universal model of telecommunications, according to which states, directly or indirectly, controlled the hardware and offered them as common carriers. It differed also from the American broadcasting model, in which independent local stations mainly distributed content originating elsewhere, although retaining legal responsibility for it. In Europe, PTT control of cable in several countries has helped to extend the common carrier principle, in that other organizations were responsible for content and videotex is almost everywhere strictly along common carrier lines. The proliferation of local cable networks is more akin to the American model, but in general we can observe a shift away from the unified control typical of the past towards several different variants which have not yet acquired any single dominant form. While no generalization is adequate for Europe as a whole, the pattern seems to be towards a relaxation of monopoly control on software production (mainly television programmes) and a re-affirmation of the right of the state to control distribution, although a control exercised in a more relaxed fashion and motivated mainly by industrial policy considerations rather than for political control or cultural reasons.

Actors in the policy process

There have been few surprises in what has been learnt about the behaviour of different categories of actors in the media policy scene in Europe. This has been dominated by governments and national politicians operating according to logics which fit their traditional goals and their ideological standpoints. Notable, perhaps, is the relative failure of parties of the left and allied trade unions to take a strong or consistent line against 'commercialization', wherever this might mean more economic opportunity or work. This has been most evident in the case of France, but Spain is following on a similar path and Italy might be considered in the same light. This seeming inconsistency is not, however, purely a 'Mediterranean' phenomenon. It is not very easy to understand, given the widespread assumption that private ownership of media is generally more helpful to the right and that public broadcasting has been relatively beneficial to social democrat or liberal interests (if only by guaranteeing fair access). Generally, social and cultural elites have been weaker than in the past and there have been some significant additions to the spectrum of interests closely involved. Amongst the latter are, especially, the large publishers and multinational media conglomerates with interests in operating cable systems and providing services by satellites, often internationally.

There are other international actors (of a non-technical kind) which appear to be playing a more active role than in the past, as was apparent from Chapter 3, largely in response to a need for supranational coordination and regulation. Most significant is probably the EEC itself, which is beginning to overcome its preoccupation with agriculture. Its current initiatives, notably the RACE project, are, nevertheless very much attributable to pressure from large firms concerned with European competitiveness in the field of information technology. The EEC has not shown much tendency to give direction in matters of media structures or content, but its treatment of the advertising question in its 1984 *Green Paper* brings it very definitely, if not very intentionally, into this terrain. The demand from some European politicians for unifying communication structures could strengthen this tendency. Activity in relation to information technology networks may also eventually link up with these other matters. Thus, separate initiatives in respect of market harmonization, political Europeanization and technological development may converge powerfully.

By comparison with the EEC, the EBU has seemed to decline somewhat in significance as an actor, reflecting the tendency of large countries and large broadcasting organizations to seek short-term self-interest rather than longer-term cooperation and also the dominance of political-economic motives over cultural and professional concerns. This last consideration helps to explain the increasing influence of the EEC as a framework for cross-national initiatives. A discussion of actors would not be complete without reference to the role of national PTTs and their regional organization, CEPT. For much the same reasons of an increasing industrial logic and technological imperatives, the PTTs have generally acquired much more salience either as instruments of national policy or even as independent actors in semi-commercial undertakings (as, for instance, in Spain).

A European policy?

While it has been possible to generalize about trends in European policy according to one or the other tendency and as to the direction and pace of development, it has already been observed that at the level of Europe there is no coherent policy. There are shared problems and common approaches, here and there steps towards bilateral or multilateral agreement (especially in relation to satellites), but, as seen in the mid-1980s, the European policy scene is characterized by a dual fragmentation — at national level and at European level. Some countries have made more conscious efforts at national coherence than others — for instance France and the Netherlands and others have at least been fairly consistent in the underlying spirit of their policy, as in Britain, or in maintaining the status quo, as in Sweden. But the idea that plans should be made with a view to the prospects for all main mass media and with international development in mind has nowhere been realized. In any case, countries have responded in varying ways and with varying time-scales, some having no tradition of media policy-making and some no inclination to cooperate with other countries in the media sphere.

The pursuit of national self-interest remains the predominant tendency on the part of politicians and governments of small as well as large countries and neither large broadcasting organizations nor media businesses are likely to be any more altruistic. An illustration of non-altruism is provided by the very lukewarm support for the pan-European television service sponsored by the EBU or the tendency of the BBC and ITV in Britain to seek maximum advantage from their large accumulated programme archive. Both failed to cooperate effectively with each other and with other firms in the British satellite television venture which the government wanted to encourage.

It is probably too early to expect much change in bodies which are essentially national in their remit and, within nations, in a competitive or defensive situation. However, to raise questions about the possible emergence of a coherent European approach to media policy is to be reminded of the many divisions and discontinuities in Europe, despite many steps towards cooperation and harmonization which have been taken since the Second World War. It is also important to record that European coherence is not universally regarded as good in itself or national self-interest and autonomy as bad. Many vocal participants in the policy debate want to hold back transnational media concentration and to strengthen national control as well as promote some internal decentralization (localization). Europeanization carried out in the name of political or economic goals can work against many established cultural and political interests. Even if cultural policy is possible at the level of the European region (e.g. by way of the Council of Europe), the fear is widespread that Europeanization will mainly mean either more commercialization in the form of European multimedia transnationals or greater American penetration by way of satellite television services. It is mainly smaller countries which have most to fear from these developments. They probably have less to gain from Europe-level industrial policy and more to lose in terms of loss of national control over their own cultural environment.

Concern with Europe is also held by some to divert attention from possibly more important long-term aspects of international communication, notably those which have to do with East-West contact and North-South communication. The combination of an industrial emphasis with a European focus is inimical to a wider view of world communication, even if Europeanization is not in itself inconsistent with improvements in other areas. There is evidently a need and a place for consideration of policies and structural arrangements appropriate to several different levels of communication: global; world-regional; national; and local. However, at present there is no way of balancing the different interests associated with each level and most power is concentrated still at the level of national governments. Policy is thus also concentrated at this level.

Europe vs the United States

For some, although not it seems for many, of the most vocal participants in national media policy-making in Europe, a major goal and preoccupation is the competitive position of Europe in relation to international challenges, especially from Japan and the United States. Given the predominance of industrial policy considerations which has been observed, it might have been expected that policy for media would have been more openly concerned with this issue and that a more coherent response would have emerged. There are two main aspects to the issue: one, the division of spoils in the computer, aerospace and communication technology industries, another the relative share of US and European programme content in the world's expanding mass communication channels. On the first matter, aside from the relatively recent EEC projects, it seems that Europe is not acting together and has no coherent plan to compete, especially in the face of accelerated competition from a deregulated American communication industry. There are some European success stories, for instance in satellites and in the establishment of London as the combined financial-data telecommunication capital of Western Europe and thus with some world standing. On the matter of television production, Europe does have some definite advantages, despite the assumed dominance of American content in world television to date.

In both respects, Europe suffers from several weaknesses, which have already been mentioned. It is not yet a unified market for telecommunications or other industries, thus limiting the scope for European firms. Yet if it were to become unified it might only be more accessible for Japanese or American competition in both hardware and software, unless other changes were also made. The fragmentation of Europe at supranational level and the proliferation of international bodies are also of little benefit. Beyond that, Europe may be said to suffer from the grip of its several national PTTs, with their traditions of negative universalism and also from anti-trust legislation which prevents even quite modest European mergers.

But the biggest weakness of Europe is that all communication areas are dominated by national government and policy, particularly in terms of their capital investment and acquisition of hardware from sheltered 'traditional' electronics suppliers. This leads to hardware purchasing in small batches within each national military, within national radio and television, within telecommunications and in government computer purchases and rules. European electronics purchasing is thus split up into literally dozens of sheltered markets, each of which does its own research and development. Europe's electronics research and development is bigger than Japan's and nearly as big as that of the USA, but it is enormously duplicated and wasteful. The obvious need, if Europe is to survive in information technology and telecommunication hardware is for Germany, France and Britain to cooperate in much less token ways than in the past. To date each had cooperated in modest European projects, but has mainly pursued its national ambitions.

In respect of software — especially broadcast programming — Europe has considerable strengths by virtue of its many national television channels, with much more production than any other world region. The problem is how to extend the reach of the multichannel offerings of the producing countries beyond national frontiers and in addition to current unintended cross-border overspill. There is clearly a considerable potential for several international channels, made up of existing material suitably packaged, if language problems can be acceptably overcome by subtitling or dubbing. So far the will seems weak to share even in modest ventures such as the Europe project of the EBU. One possible effect of the European equivalent of deregulation is that a successful commercial initiative will be taken in this direction, along the lines of Robert Murdoch's Sky Channel, but with a firmer base in continental Europe. Luxembourg has still probably the best chance of initiating multichannel satellite television broadcasting within Europe, but there are now several contenders. An act of striking competitiveness or of unaccustomed cooperation might be sufficient to trigger a move which could capitalize on Europe's cultural strength. The concept of Europe as a 'media power' matching the United States is not entirely fanciful, but it will take some powerful economic incentive to achieve this 'cultural victory'.

End note

Not surprisingly, this book has to end on a note of multiple uncertainty, partly because it describes a process which has not long been under way, partly because several vital components are missing from any adequate guide to even the short-term future. It should have become clear from what has gone before that neither Europe as a whole nor the separate nations within it are actually planning the media future in the sense of drawing a blueprint and seeking to construct something according to design. At best they are reacting and adapting to change in a rational way and ordering some bits of the future. No national plan, and there is no European one, will actually settle some crucial questions. One of these concerns the degree of demand for powerful DBS satellites beaming television to individual households. A related uncertainty hangs over the rate of installation and capacity of cable, even in countries, such as Britain and France, which have definite plans for expansion. There is also a general uncertainty about the relation between cable and satellite, whether they are alternatives or best used in combination. Tied in with all this is the uncertainty over the level of demand for videotex and related interactive services, in fact over the reality of the whole telematics 'revolution', which has been heralded. Acts of policy will influence the answers to these questions, but there are too many other possible influences to allow even intelligent guesses. In the light of this, the hesitancy, procrastination and inconsistency of European policy-making may not seem too unrealistic or as irrational as suggested at the start of this chapter. But one should also not underestimate the importance of myth as a stimulus to action and a bridge to some new reality.

Index